Conceiving Normalcy

Rhetoric, Culture, and Social Critique

Series Editor
John Louis Lucaites

Editorial Board
Richard Bauman
Carole Blair
Dilip Gaonkar
Robert Hariman
Steven Mailloux
Raymie E. McKerrow
Toby Miller
Austin Sarat
Janet Staiger
Barbie Zelizer

Conceiving Normalcy

Rhetoric, Law, and the Double Binds of Infertility

ELIZABETH C. BRITT

THE UNIVERSITY OF ALABAMA PRESS
Tuscaloosa

The University of Alabama Press
Tuscaloosa, Alabama 35487-0380
uapress.ua.edu

Copyright © 2001 by the University of Alabama Press
All rights reserved.

Hardcover edition published 2001.
Paperback edition published 2014.
eBook edition published 2014.

Inquiries about reproducing material from this work should be addressed to
the University of Alabama Press.

Typeface: Perpetua

Manufactured in the United States of America
Cover design: Robin McDonald

∞

The paper on which this book is printed meets the minimum requirements of American National Standard for Information Science–Permanence of Paper for Printed Library Materials, ANSI Z39.48-1984.

Paperback ISBN: 978-0-8173-5790-0
eBook ISBN: 978-0-8173-8789-1

A previous edition of this book has been catalogued by the Library of Congress as follows:
Library of Congress Cataloging-in-Publication Data
Britt, Elizabeth C. (Elizabeth Carol), 1964–
Conceiving normalcy rhetoric, law, and the double binds of infertility / Elizabeth C. Britt.
p. ; cm. — (Rhetoric, culture, and social critique)
Includes bibliographical references and index.
ISBN 0-8173-1098-3 (alk. paper)
1. Human reproductive technology—Social aspects. 2. Infertility—Social aspects. 3. Insurance, Health—Law and legislation—Massachusetts. 4. Human reproductive technology—Law and legislation—Massachusetts.
[DNLM: 1. Infertility—therapy—Massachusetts. 2. Reproduction Techniques—legislation & jurisprudence—Massachusetts. 3. Health Services Accessibility—legislation & jurisprudence—Massachusetts. 4. Insurance, Health—legislation & jurisprudence—Massachusetts. 5. Socioeconomic Factors—Massachusetts. WP 33 AM4 B862c 2001]
I. Title. II. Series
RG133.5 .B756 2001
362.1'98178'009744—dc21
2001000388

British Library Cataloguing-in-Publication Data available

The effects of performatives, understood as discursive productions, do not conclude at the terminus of a given statement or utterance, the passing of legislation, the announcement of a birth. The reach of their signifiability cannot be controlled by the one who utters or writes, since such productions are not owned by the one who utters them. They continue to signify in spite of their authors, and sometimes against their authors' most precious intentions.

—Judith Butler, *Bodies That Matter*

Contents

Acknowledgments
ix

Introduction: Pursuing Normalcy
1

1. Defining Infertility
17

2. Insuring (In)Fertility
49

3. Success and Failure
70

4. Order and Discontinuity
95

5. Control and Constraint
119

Epilogue: The Cultural Work of the Double Bind
142

Appendix A: Text of the Massachusetts Infertility Insurance Mandate
151

Appendix B: Legislative Information
153

Appendix C: Research Methods
159

Appendix D: Interview Participants
169

Notes
177

Glossary
181

Works Cited
187

Index
199

Acknowledgments

Many people have helped to create this book in its various incarnations over the past few years. Although I accept the ultimate responsibility for the contents, including its gaps and shortcomings, I would like to acknowledge the many individuals who have contributed.

This book would not have been possible without the generosity of the people (who must remain nameless) who invited me into their homes and workplaces to talk about their experiences of infertility. I owe an enormous debt of gratitude to twenty-eight women and one man for sharing very personal stories with a complete stranger. Attorney Susan Crockin directed me to the Massachusetts statute analyzed in these pages; I thank her, Peg Beck, and Martha Griffin for their time and for providing me with documents and contacts that were instrumental to the study. Edward L. Burke, Sherwood Guernsey, and the Women's Bar Association of Massachusetts granted permission to quote from their correspondence. Dozens of other professionals who work with the infertile also contributed time and expertise.

Portions of the introduction, Chapter 1, and Chapter 2 originally appeared in modified form in "Medical Insurance as Bio-Power: Law and the Normalization of (In)Fertility," in *Body Talk: Rhetoric, Technology, Reproduction,* edited by Mary M. Lay, Laura J. Gurak, Clare Gravon, and Cynthia Myntti, copyright © 2000 by the Board of Regents of the University of Wisconsin System. Used by permission. Portions of Chapter 2 were reprinted, with modification, from Elizabeth C. Britt, "Constructing Authority: Medical and Moral Discourses in Legislating Insurance Coverage for Infertility," *Studies in Law, Politics, and Society* 17 (1997), 121–145, with permission from Elsevier Science.

The dissertation project on which this book is based took the shape that it did largely because my committee was willing to help me craft an interdisciplinary project. I thank Roxanne Mountford, my chairperson, for inspiration, countless hours of conversation, and guidance; Kim Fortun, for helping me to think more like an anthropologist (although I cannot blame her for my lingering failures in this regard); Jim Zappen, for helping me to reorganize the project around normalization; Karen LeFevre, for asking difficult questions; and June Deery, for stepping in at the last moment. This project was funded partially by a grant (Gr. 5873) from the Wenner-Gren Foundational for Anthropological Research and by a fellowship at Rensselaer Polytechnic Institute sponsored by Jean and Robert Wagner in memory of their daughter, Joanne. Jen Bacon, Elizabeth Shea, and the late Stan Organ transcribed dozens of hours of taped interviews with insight and good humor. Thanks to my graduate school colleagues at Rensselaer (especially Nancy Bayer, Elaine Graham, Laura Gurak, Kevin Hunt, Sue Mings, John Monberg, and Liz Wright) for support and friendship. Special thanks go to Ellen Cushman for insights, Terese Guinsatao Monberg for companionship in the gym and for intellectual stimulation (sometimes provided at the same time), and Bernadette Longo for long hours of conversation about Foucault and Lyotard as well as for advice about the pragmatics of dissertating and publishing.

A number of other people have contributed ideas, support, and inspiration, including Michelle Ballif, Amanda Barker, Elizabeth Bartholet, Hugh Baxter, John Caher, Todd Cherkasky, Ralph Cintron, Greg Clark, Celeste Condit, Diane Davis, Stacey Dogan, Bill Endres, David Engel, Mike Fortun, Bob Jerry, Patricia Irwin Johnston, Mary Lay, George Marcus, Judy Norsigian, Helena Ragoné, Joan Ruttenberg, Austin Sarat, John Sloop, Steve Wasby, and Peggy Weisenberger. Thanks to the members of the New England Insurance and Society reading group, especially Tom Baker and Deborah Stone, for helpful feedback. Kris Ratcliffe gave advice about publishing, reviewed the proposal for this project, and made substantive comments. Several of my colleagues at Northeastern, including Mary Loeffelholz, Stuart Peterfreund, Guy Rotella, and Susan Wall, offered support and constructive criticism. Kathleen Kelly supplied publishing advice and wonderful meals, and former Northeastern colleague Barbara Rodriguez offered wise counsel and friendship. I thank Marina

Leslie for substantive comments, emotional support, culinary diversions, and mentoring that should be rewarded with a medal. Finally, Elizabeth Shea reinvigorated my scholarship with thoughtful criticism and many hours of lively dialogue (intellectual and otherwise).

Thanks to Curtis Clark and Suzette Griffith at The University of Alabama Press for their thoroughly professional oversight of this project and to Mindy Wilson for her prompt help in answering questions. The two anonymous reviewers selected by the press contributed enormously to the final shape of my argument, and series editor John L. Lucaites helped me refine it further. This book is much more theoretically grounded and more mature because of their comments.

My deep gratitude for lifelong encouragement and support go to my mother, Carolyn P. Hammond; my father and stepmother, Earl and Judy Britt; my brothers, Mark and Cliff; and my maternal grandmother and late maternal grandfather, Edna and Paul Pugh.

Finally, I thank my husband, Jeff Strobel, for unending patience, support, and humor and for distracting me when I needed it most. I dedicate this book to him.

Conceiving Normalcy

Introduction:
Pursuing Normalcy

Why do people pursue parenthood? To many, the answer is so obvious that the question seems unnecessary: to want a child is a natural, normal desire. Before the age of biomedicine, Americans who wanted children and were unable to have them relied on folk remedies, found other ways to incorporate children into their lives, or resigned themselves to what was often considered God's will. In contemporary America, the involuntarily childless are expected to follow a different path by seeking advice from a physician for a condition that has been both medicalized and brought into the public spotlight.

While there is no consensus that reproductive technology is a natural or normal way to have children, medical treatment for infertility is increasingly understood as an acceptable way to exercise what many see as the right to reproduce. By the turn of the millennium, the federal government had created National Infertility Awareness Week, had commissioned several reports on the condition, and had pending legislation that would require insurance companies to pay for its treatment. The passage by thirteen states of laws requiring some form of insurance coverage for infertility indicated increased public willingness to accept reproductive technologies as part of the mainstream.

Massachusetts enacted the broadest of these laws in 1987. Defining infertility as a medical condition, the statute provides almost unlimited access to medical treatment for infertility, including advanced reproductive technologies such as in vitro fertilization, to individuals with both private medical insurance and a medical diagnosis of infertility. Like the other twelve state laws and the initiatives at the federal level, the Massachusetts statute was introduced and lobbied for by RESOLVE, a support and advocacy group headquartered in Massachusetts that was originally founded as an outgrowth of an adoption organization. To the RESOLVE advocates, infertility is a medical condition that demands medical treatment; advocating for infertile individuals means educating the general public and government officials about the true nature of the condition, supporting the advance of reproductive technologies, and lobbying for increased access to medical treatment.

Within this narrative, the medicalization of involuntary childlessness reflects the condition's true nature. The function of law, in this story, is to remove barriers to the reproductive technologies that provide the best hope of restoring the body's natural order. For RESOLVE advocates and others, mandatory insurance coverage provides a solution to the problem of infertility by removing the economic barriers that keep the infertile from realizing their natural desires.

In this book, I argue that instead of solving the problem of infertility, mandatory insurance coverage helps further define its contours.[1] In my account, based on eighteen months of ethnographic research, law does more than provide access to reproductive technologies: the Massachusetts statute itself functions as a technology. Construing technologies as "formalizations, i.e., as frozen moments, of the fluid social interactions constituting them" as well as "instruments for enforcing meanings" (Haraway, *Simians* 164), I examine how the statute operates in what philosopher Michel Foucault calls an era of biopower—an epoch concerned with the efficient management of life. I argue that the Massachusetts mandate functions as a technology of normalization, helping to identify the normal and abnormal (here the fertile and the infertile) and to create procedures by which the abnormal can be subjected to reform.

Functioning as a technology of normalization, mandatory insurance coverage for infertility is most successful when it sustains, rather than resolves, the tension between the normal and the abnormal. This tension is achieved in part by the rhetorical mechanism of the double bind, a contradictory pair of demands that compels the individual to act and simultaneously makes action problematic. As long as those undergoing medical treatment for infertility feel caught in double binds—in this case, between success and failure, order and discontinuity, and control and constraint— the work of normalization continues.

Understood in this way, infertility has implications for everyone, not just for those unable to have desired children. Through the processes of normalization, *fertile* and *infertile* become cultural categories that frame our understanding not only of families, parenting, and gender roles but also of disease, disability, and what members of social collectives owe to each other in relieving private burdens. This book, then, is about how we define infertility, families, and parents. It is also, more broadly, about the dominance of medical approaches to contemporary social problems, the power of definition to frame experience, and the role of law in everyday imaginaries.

Stratified Reproduction

The Massachusetts statute, entitled *An Act Providing a Medical Definition of Infertility,* requires most insurers[2] to cover medical treatments of infertility to the same extent that they cover other procedures related to pregnancy. At least to some degree, mandatory insurance coverage for infertility contributes to what anthropologists Faye Ginsburg and Rayna Rapp call "stratified" reproduction (*Conceiving* 3). Sociologists Leslie King and Madonna Harrington Meyer report that insurance benefits for working- and middle-class women increasingly include infertility but exclude contraceptives, while benefits for the poor include contraceptives but exclude infertility, resulting in a "de facto fertility policy that discourages births among poor women and encourages births among working- and middle-class women" (26).

In the case of the Massachusetts mandate, the stratification occurs according to class, race, and sexual orientation although not (as is the case with other state mandates) according to marital status. (See Appendix A for the text of the Massachusetts statute and Appendix B for information on all the state legislation at the time of this book's printing.) Infertility affects nonwhite women in greater numbers than white women, and women with less education more frequently than those with more.[3] The Massachusetts mandate does not exclude nonwhite, working-class, or less educated women. When it is considered in context, however, the mandate appears to be geared more for the white and middle class, who made up the bulk of the membership of the Massachusetts chapter of RESOLVE when the mandate was introduced.[4]

While the mandate gives people in a broader socioeconomic spectrum access to medical treatment for infertility, it serves only those with employer-provided health insurance, excluding many of the working and nonworking poor and including more whites than nonwhites.[5] In addition, the logistics of the medical treatment provided by the mandate tend to privilege people with flexible work schedules and easier access to infertility clinics, most of which are located in the heart of Boston or in the affluent western and northern suburbs. Finally, the focus on treatment rather than prevention can be understood as privileging those with faith in medical technology and a trust in the medical system. The history of medical experimentation within poor and minority communities, as well as the history of white interest in black fertility during slavery, may make members of these groups less trusting of medicine and its practitioners (see Collins; A. Davis; Nsiah-Jefferson).

The mandate also privileges those with "medical" rather than "social" infertility. Rather than specifically excluding single women and men and those in same-sex relationships (as do mandates in some other states), the Massachusetts mandate provides insurance coverage only when the underlying cause of the infertility is a physiological condition. In other words, those who are unable to conceive a child because they are single or are not partnered with someone of the opposite sex are not eligible for full coverage. While members of this group who have a medical diagnosis of infertility fall partly within the scope of the mandate, at least part of their infertility is defined as social and is not covered. A single woman, for example, may be unable to conceive both because she has blocked fallopian tubes and because she lacks sperm from a male partner. In her case, her insurer would be required to pay for any procedures that attempt to correct or bypass her blocked fallopian tubes but would not be required to pay for the procurement, storage, and preparation of sperm. The same procedures would be covered for a partnered heterosexual woman whose male partner lacked sperm or had low sperm count.

In these ways, the mandate stratifies reproduction by economically and symbolically encouraging some groups to reproduce and not others. The mandate is also part of the tradition of practicing infertility treatment on women rather than on men regardless of whether the underlying physiological cause of the infertility is located in a male partner. As historians of infertility (Marsh and Ronner; May) and feminist critics of reproductive technologies (see especially Corea, *Mother,* "Brothel"; Rothman, *Recreating;* Rowland, "Woman"; Spallone and Steinberg) have noted, medical treatment for infertility is much more likely to be practiced on women than on men even though the cause of infertility is just as likely to be located solely with the man or with both partners as it is with the woman alone (Carson, Casson, and Schuman 4). While I do not agree with some critics that all reproductive technologies are an effort by a patriarchal medical establishment either to control reproduction completely (for example, see Corea, "Brothel") or to eliminate the need for women altogether (see, for example, Rowland, "Woman"), I do read the phenomenon of practicing infertility treatment mostly on women as indicative of a historical pattern in medicine of pathologizing women's bodies and blaming women both for their own illnesses and for social problems (see especially Martin). While the issues of inequitable distribution of resources and how women, as a group, are faring in the age of assisted reproduction are important questions, they serve as a backdrop rather than as a central focus for this book.

"A Blessing and a Curse"

If white, middle-class, heterosexual women are those primarily served by the mandate, what is the "problem" of infertility for them, and what kind of answer does the mandate provide? I reject the assumption, which draws on the Enlightenment faith in answers provided by science, that infertility is simply a physiological problem. Instead, I have adopted the stance of interpretive anthropologists working to understand health and illness. Medical anthropologist Byron Good explains that, in this tradition, "*disease is not an entity but an explanatory model.* . . . Complex human phenomena are framed as 'disease,' and by this means become the objects of medical practices" (53, emphasis in the original). In this tradition, categories of disease are understood as imposed by the human imagination, with all its cultural assumptions, rather than as existing a priori. By adopting this stance, I do not deny the underlying physiological causes of the inability to conceive children. Instead, I maintain that we cannot understand the biological in and of itself. I maintain that, like all medical conditions, infertility can be understood only within, and as a part of, particular cultural contexts.

The label "infertility" obscures the sociocultural context of involuntary childlessness by defining the condition within a biomedical framework. While the condition of being unable to have a biological child is often discussed as having social or cultural implications, it is nonetheless understood primarily as a medical condition with medical solutions. This medicalization of involuntary childlessness glosses over the complex cultural contexts within which the condition occurs and assumes its significance. In this sense, "infertility" may be understood as a metonym for the experience of involuntary childlessness. Kenneth Burke understands metonymy as a figure that reduces complexity by conveying "some incorporeal or intangible state in terms of the corporeal or tangible" (506). The metonymic reduction of "involuntary childlessness" to "infertility" gives the condition a physical location in the body, where it can be investigated and treated. The reduction also temporalizes the experience so that social, economic, psychological, and cultural "factors" are understood as *implications* that *result from* or *come after* the physical condition, not as conditions that are complicit in its construction.

By describing the cultural context within which infertility takes on meaning for white, middle-class women, that is, those whose interests are most closely intertwined with the Massachusetts mandate, I argue that we cannot understand these women's desire for a biological child—and their pursuit of pregnancy—apart from a more overarching desire for normalcy. For them, the normalcy represented by pregnancy is constituted not just by a biological drive but by a constellation of desires. Borrowing from Ralph Cintron, I see each of these desires as "instantiations of a definitive ideological position that [is] not merely the perversion of an individual psyche but, indeed, a distinctive *topos* in a larger cultural imaginary" (155, emphasis in the original). Middle-class white women in America to some degree share the expectation that life will proceed fairly predictably, that they have some measure of control over their destinies, and that hard work will be rewarded with success. These commonplaces, the shared definitions of a normal life, are disrupted by infertility.

If infertility is not simply a physiological problem, then its treatment, and the provision of support for that treatment, is not just a physiological solution. Understanding the function of the mandate thus means asking what cultural work the mandate performs. Advocates maintain that it helps to alleviate the problem of infertility by providing economic support for medical treatment for the condition. I argue instead that the Massachusetts mandate operates as a technology of normalization—that is, it helps to identify the abnormal (the infertile) and to create procedures by which the abnormal can be reformed.

As a technology of normalization, however, the Massachusetts mandate does not alleviate the problem of infertility as much as it helps to create and sustain the categories of *fertile* and *infertile*. By authorizing a medical model for infertility, in other words, the mandate normalizes both fertility and infertility: it both places the infertile within the realm of standard medical practice (thereby helping the infertile feel less isolated and more "normal") and authorizes a system by which the infertile are differentiated from the fertile (hence reinforcing their "abnormal" status). Furthermore, the tension created by the mandate's function as a technology of normalization and by women's desire for normalcy is manifested in double binds —simultaneous and contradictory experiences of control and constraint, success and failure, and order and discontinuity. In short, for many middle-class white women, the experience of the mandate, which normalizes both fertility and infertility, is, as one woman remarks, "both a blessing and a curse."

I believe that these double binds are not unfortunate consequences of infertility treatment. Instead, I understand the double bind as a rhetorical mechanism through which normalization does its work. For middle-class white women, the double bind helps to create and sustain the tension between fertility and infertility, which is essential if the process of normalization is to continue. However, the cultural work of the discourses of infertility affects not only those who find themselves unable to have children. These discourses inform and reflect how all of us understand disease, disability, and the social safety net. Although this book focuses on the manifestation of the double bind in the everyday discourses of the infertile, I suspect that it may be a widespread phenomenon in an age of biopower.

Normalization: A Brief Introduction

It is tempting to look back on the history of childlessness and ask such questions as "Did childless colonial Americans feel abnormal?" Nevertheless, there is evidence that normality itself is a relatively recent concept that we cannot universalize. We have come to regard comparing ourselves to a norm as natural, as something that humans must always have done. From attributes ranging from our intelligence to our height and weight, we are measured and compared to average values. These values influence our daily routines, our educational opportunities, our work compensation, and our medical care. Lennard J. Davis, however, notes that words associated with "the norm," as it is regarded today, did not come into use in Western languages until between 1840 and 1860 (24), during the Industrial Revolution.[6] Prior to that period, the Western human imagination conceived of the "ideal," which differed markedly from the "normal." The "ideal" represented perfection that could be attained only by the divine and therefore lay beyond human reach (24–25).

The norm, a standard to which humans *were* expected to conform, emerged with the advent of industrialization. During industrialization, human productivity became a central concern (L. Davis; Foucault, *Discipline*); ranking and comparing individuals to increase the usefulness of a population was vital. A population's usefulness could be maximized by making the individual body a productive component of social systems, and the process of normalization was a vital part of this endeavor. Attention was focused "on the body as a machine: its disciplining, the optimization of its capabilities, the extortion of its forces, the parallel increase of its usefulness and its docility, its integration into systems of efficient and economic controls" (Foucault, *Sexuality* 139). On the most obvious level, factories needed workers who produced at optimum efficiency. This way of conceptualizing the usefulness of human bodies permeated not only factories but also a variety of other institutions, including hospitals, schools, the military, and prisons (Foucault, *Discipline*). Normalization was not limited to the human body, of course. Industrialization created a need for models according to which products could be manufactured; normalization, as the "language of the engineer," provided the standards by which practitioners of disparate industrial processes could agree on models toward which they would all aim (Ewald 149).

The discipline of statistics, emerging during the "probabilistic revolution" of the nineteenth century (Ewald 142), both developed the modern notion of the norm and established the link between the individual body and social systems. From astronomy, statisticians borrowed the idea of averaging errors (a procedure used to locate a star), which they then applied to humans in order to construct averages of physical and moral attributes (L. Davis 26). Human attributes were measured and plotted just like the data derived from observation of the stars. An entire population could be described using a graphical representation (what has come to be known as the bell curve, or the "normal distribution") that depicted norms (those toward the center of the bell curve) and deviations (those at the extreme ends). The ability to describe human characteristics in scientific terms was a boon to social engineers and commentators of divergent political stripes; it provided scientific justification both for the "middle way of life" (L. Davis 27) of the bourgeoisie and for a standard that Marx could use to ground his critiques of the distribution of wealth (L. Davis 29). By "recasting it in the neutral language of science" (Dreyfus and Rabinow 196), a political problem could thus be transformed into a technical problem with an attainable technical solution.

With modernization and industrialization, the norm became one of the means by which bodies could be disciplined, that is, made more docile, more able to be "subjected, used, transformed and improved" (Foucault, *Discipline* 136). In a disciplinary system—such as modern medicine, education, or corrections, for example—bodies are individually and minutely observed, their activities measured, and their measurements compared and averaged. Those individuals falling outside desirable values are subjected to reform. The result is a process that is both individualizing (in that it describes particular characteristics in minute detail) and homogenizing (in that it is part of a general collective of information used to create categories and distributions of populations, and in that it is used to help the individual conform to the norm) (Foucault, *Discipline* 184).

The techniques of normalization are essential to the process of discipline because they help organize, classify, and control anomalies. Although these techniques initially appear designed to eliminate anomalies, they are actually designed at the same time that the anomalies are themselves "discovered." In other words, the techniques of normalization do not so much identify and correct the abnormal as they create and perpetuate the distinction between the normal and the abnormal. The normal and the abnormal, therefore, exist not as discrete entities to be observed but as "functions" that "stimulate modification" (Canguilhem 77).

The categories *fertile* and *infertile* operate in this way. Textbook definitions of infertility, and the definition adopted by the Massachusetts mandate, place the boundary between normal and abnormal fertility at one year. The criteria for infertility, however, are neither clear-cut nor the result of consensus. The World Health Organization, for example, places the boundary at two years (Wagner and Stephenson 3), while the U.S. Office of Technology Assessment reports that only 16 percent to 21 percent of couples who are infertile according to the twelve-month definition will remain infertile during their entire lifetimes (U.S. Congress 35).

In practice, the ability to procreate—a continuum rather than a set of binaries—operates throughout populations as well as within an individual's lifetime. Normalcy in the area of fertility does not mean that all couples will conceive every time they try. For a practitioner of reproductive medicine, "normal fertility" means that a couple (based on an average age of twenty-five) has a 20 percent chance of conceiving in any given month (Tan, Jacobs, and Seibel 30). The goal of intervention, for a practitioner, is to give an individual or couple the normal chances of conception. In addition, some individuals within a population will never be able to conceive. In other words, it is normal for a certain number of people within a population to be unable to conceive; a 1975 report by the World Health Organization suggests that the normal infertility rate for populations is 5 percent (Heitman 91). The categories *fertile* and *infertile* therefore do not correspond to conditions that have been discovered by reproductive specialists. Instead, the categories are created (by deciding how much time passes before the "average" person can be expected to become pregnant) so that interventions can be made.

The reality that some people will never conceive a desired child helps to sustain the distinction between the fertile and the infertile. Foucault notes that this is a key feature of normalization: in order for the process to continue, rehabilitation must sometimes fail. Although the experiences of the infertile and prisoners are not the same, a comparison of the function of normalization for both populations is instructive. Writing of the failure of the prison to reform hardened criminals, a goal claimed by prison advocates, Foucault notes that the high rate of recidivism leads to the conclusion that prisons do not really work. Rather than judge prisons by this stated criterion, Foucault argues that we should seek to identify what their failure accomplishes. He writes: "One would be forced to suppose that the prison, and no doubt punishment in general, is not intended to eliminate offenses, but rather to distinguish them, to distribute them, to use them; that it is not so much that they render docile those who are liable to transgress the law, but that they tend to assimilate the transgression of the laws in a general tactics of subjection" (*Discipline* 272). In other words, "penitentiaries, and perhaps all normalizing power, succeed when they are only partially successful" (Dreyfus and Rabinow 195). In the case of infertility, medical treatment succeeds as a normalizing process only when it does not eliminate the category of infertility altogether.

As a rhetorical process, normalization operates through persuasion and negotiation. A norm is an argument about what is desirable (for example, you "should" go to church, or you "ought" to be within an ideal weight for your height), a feature often hidden by the norm's roots in statistics. By employing the language of mathematics, statistics has claimed the objectivity ascribed to that language. Yet like mathematics itself, the norm can be regarded as an argument about which qualities or characteristics should be measured, about which units of measurement should be used, about the dividing line between the normal and the deviant, and, in a more general sense, about the importance of ranking and comparing individuals in a population and about ascribing significance to an occurrence of an event (rather than, say, its meaning to an individual).

In addition, normalization can achieve its purposes only through negotiation and agreement about language (Ewald 150). Seeking to eliminate ambiguity in measurement, normalization attempts to settle on common definitions, terminology, and categorizations. Industrialization requires that this language be common not only within a specific discipline (for example, reproductive endocrinology) but across disciplines and institutions (for example, the law and the insurance industry) and within the field of consumers (for example, infertility patients). The end goal is both to reach agreement about measurement standards and the expression of those standards and to "teach this language to all those who are involved in one way or another in the system of economic exchange" (Ewald 151).

The Double Bind as a Rhetorical Mechanism of Normalization

Normalization, then, is characterized not by the correction of anomalies so that all individuals conform to a norm but by the distribution of individuals according to their similarities and differences, what might be characterized as "the play of oppositions between the normal and the abnormal or pathological" (Ewald 140). I maintain that one of the ways by which normalization does this work is through the double bind.

In the classic text on double bind theory, a 1956 article on the etiology and treatment of schizophrenia, Gregory Bateson and his colleagues argue that schizophrenia can result when a child is exposed to communicative patterns in which the child is faced both with contradictory injunctions (usually from the mother) and with an inability to escape.[7] Contradictory injunctions often take an ironic form. The parent might, for example, verbally prohibit the child from a certain behavior while simultaneously nonverbally demanding such behavior. Faced with this double bind situation, the child feels the necessity of understanding the contradictory messages and of acting appropriately but cannot engage in metadiscourse about the contradictions. After repeated exposure to double binds, the child comes to miscategorize acts of communication, including utterances from others and utterances and thoughts from her or himself. Central to their analysis are the ways in which the schizophrenic is hypothesized to confuse the literal and the figurative by finding hidden meaning in every utterance or by taking all communication literally.

The double bind is not simply a contradiction or an instance in which an individual feels "damned if she does or damned if she doesn't." Instead, the contradiction exists at multiple levels. Jay Haley provides an example: "When faced with two conflicting levels of message, [the individual] cannot choose one without the other. If I say to someone, 'I will be angry if you obey me and I will be angry if you disobey me,' he [sic] can choose one or the other. However, if I say to someone, 'I want you to disobey me,' . . . He cannot choose the least bad of two possibilities. His bind is this: if he obeys, he is disobeying, and if he disobeys, he is obeying" (71). Coupled with the contradictory messages is a desire to respond to them, which contributes to the sense that the individual is bound. Faced with what might be called an ironic imperative, the individual feels both the need to move and the disturbing effect of moving. As with all ironic constructions, the messages are integrally interrelated and comment upon each other, so that neither "can be treated as either precisely right or precisely wrong" (K. Burke 512).

Although the theory of the double bind as a source of schizophrenia has been replaced by biomedical models, the concept of the double bind provides a helpful framework for understanding the relationship between language and materiality. While early research on the double bind focused on interpersonal communication, usually within the family, more recent efforts have examined larger discursive forces as they contribute to its operation.

Kim Fortun, for example, writing of her experience as an activist and researcher in Bhopal after the Union Carbide gas leak, details the crosscutting demands of acting as a translator of human tragedy. At one level, Fortun felt the double bind of directing her advocacy of gas victims both to the India Supreme Court (which would be moved by "calculated logic") and to journalists (who were more convinced by testimonial). But she also felt doubly bound on another level: "I had to learn languages of law and bureaucracy, while learning how badly these languages represent everyday life. I had to learn to speak in terms of environmentalism, while learning how badly environmentalism represents the Third World poor. I had to learn the many truths of theoretical critiques of representation, on the ground—while producing one representation of Bhopal after another" (210).

Similarly, Michael Fortun has explored the double binds inherent in his dual position as intellectual and activist. Writing that his work for the Institute for Science and Interdisciplinary Studies is "dedicated to both science in the classical sense *and* its post-classical critique, to democratic politics *and* intellectual inquiry" (174, emphasis in the original), Fortun situates himself not as an individual within an interpersonal relationship but as an individual within a framework of intersecting global discourses.

Although the subject matters of these studies differ from my own—I am not saying that the experiences of gas victims or their advocates are the same as those of the infertile and their advocates—the way that these studies conceptualize the double bind is useful. Like Kim Fortun and Michael Fortun, I see the double bind as a way to understand both how discourses create spaces within which individuals act and how individuals act within these spaces. I attempt to illustrate how some middle-class white women are caught in contradictory logics imposed not by individuals but by competing normative frameworks. I argue, for example, that a desire to reestablish continuity compels some women to submit to the "limbo" of medical treatment, that a desire to regain reproductive control leads some women into treatments that make them feel constrained, and that some women continue to seek success despite repeated failure.

It is the expression of the double bind in the form of irony that contributes to normalization. If irony is understood as being "about contradictions that do not resolve into larger wholes, even dialectically, about the tension of holding incompatible things together because both or all are necessary and true" (Haraway, *Simians* 149), the double bind can be seen as emphasizing for these women the categories of normal and abnormal, order and discontinuity, control and constraint, success and failure. As long as the woman feels the force of the pull of each demand, the double bind—and the tension necessary for normalization to continue—is sustained.

A Preview

This book is based on observation, archival research, and interviews with the infertile and those who serve them. The first chapter, "Defining Infertility," argues that the medicalization of infertility is the product of a particular cultural time and space, not the inevitable result of the advancement of scientific knowledge. The chapter, which provides a historical look at involuntary childlessness in America, starts with the colonial period and moves into the present day. I show that the inability to have desired biological children is neither new nor experienced uniformly. In addition, the chapter describes current medical practice in infertility treatment, how the experience is understood by some of the people in this study, and how RESOLVE has attempted to address the problem of infertility through education, support, and advocacy.

Chapter 2, "Insuring (In)Fertility," examines insurance coverage for infertility as a mechanism of biopower. The first part of the chapter focuses on debates within the courts about the nature of infertility, examining three fundamental legal questions: whether infertility is a disease, whether treatment for it should be considered necessary, and whether particular treatments can be excluded because they are experimental. I argue that these debates indicate law's modern interest in the efficient management of life and that definition is central to law's modern role as normative. The second part of the chapter analyzes RESOLVE's rhetorical strategies in its advocacy for the mandate and tells how a combination of medical and moral discourses naturalized the experience of infertility and made treatment for it seem necessary. I argue that this advocacy served more to stabilize and authorize definitions of infertility than to open up the issue for public debate and scrutiny.

Chapters 3–5 analyze three commonplaces that partially constitute the experience of infertility and its medical treatment for the women in this study. I present these commonplaces—the expectations that success will be rewarded, that life proceeds predictably, and that individuals can more or less control their fate—as binaries that create tensions which bind the infertile. The boundaries of the binaries—success and failure, order and discontinuity, and control and constraint—are not as firm as this organizational scheme might suggest. Rather than being discrete categories, the sets of binaries might best be regarded as overlapping layers helping to create a sense of normality and abnormality. In addition, while I present these commonplaces as those shared by the white, middle-class women in this study, they may also be shared by members of other groups. Chapter 3, "Success and Failure," argues that some middle-class white women are drawn to medical treatment for infertility, despite its capacity for ultimate failure, because they understand the drive for success as an obligation. In Chapter 4, "Order and Discontinuity," I argue that medical treatment presents the infertile with an opportunity to repair the sense that their lives have been disrupted while at the same time creating a limbo from which it is difficult to extricate themselves. Chapter 5, "Control and Constraint," argues that some middle-class white women, seeking to regain control over their lives in the midst of a disruptive event, enter into a regime that they experience as constraining.

The Epilogue is a meditation on the cultural work of the double bind. I speculate on the ability to resist the double binds sustaining normalizing processes; I argue that such resistance should aim at vigilant, local, and partial intervention, especially in the institutional discourses that give power to normalizing forces.

The book has four appendixes. Appendix A contains the text of the Massachusetts infertility mandate, while Appendix B compares the Massachusetts legislation with similar statutes in other states. Appendix C explains my research methods, and Appendix D provides biographical information about the twenty-three participants quoted in the book. Finally, a glossary defines medical terms used in the book that are likely to be new to readers unfamiliar with infertility and its treatment.

I

Defining Infertility

Socrates: . . . Well then, my dearest, what the subject is, about which we are to take counsel, has been said and defined, and now let us continue, keeping our attention fixed upon that definition.
—Plato, *Phaedrus*

The Massachusetts mandate defines infertility as "the condition of a presumably healthy individual who is unable to conceive or produce conception during a period of one year." For members of RESOLVE, the advocacy organization for the infertile, defining infertility as a medical condition was fundamental to their goal of mandatory insurance coverage. It would not be adequate for a statute to specify a range of procedures that insurers were required to cover, as new techniques are constantly being developed and would require new legislation. Pinpointing the nature of infertility as a medical problem with medical solutions would compel insurers to cover all procedures as soon as they ceased to be considered experimental.

The advocates in RESOLVE also had other reasons for wanting to define infertility as a medical condition. Doing so, they hoped, would help reduce blame (usually directed toward women) and the associated stigma and would identify the condition as a serious one deserving serious professional attention. Locating the problem of infertility within the realm of medical science was therefore more than a strategic move designed to help pass the proposed legislation; it was also an opportunity to educate the public on the "real" nature of infertility.

This move, situated within the Platonic ontological tradition, sought to arrive at a fundamental truth (in this case, about infertility) that could serve as a foundation for further discussion (in this case, about the remedies that the law should provide). Once legislators understood what infertility *is,* the advocates reasoned, they would be more inclined to agree on how the problem should be treated. This philosophy guides RESOLVE's activities in a larger sense. With a stated mission of education, support, and advocacy, RESOLVE's goals are to help individuals to make decisions while changing perceptions of the situations and needs of this group.

Reaching consensus on terminology and definitions in this way is essential for technical normalization, which requires a common language by which all participants in the process can communicate (Ewald 151). Among physicians, common definitions and terminology allow for standards of observation, measurement, and intervention. They allow patients to be able to compare diagnoses and treatment regimens and to observe themselves, and they allow insurers to categorize claims consistently. Common definitions and terminologies also allow groups of individuals to communicate with other groups—physicians with patients, patients with insurers, insurers with physicians. They permit the routinization of practices and the creation of subsequent assumptions about standards of care. A woman diagnosed in the late 1990s with anovulation, for example, might have expected to be prescribed a drug to induce ovulation, a practice considered to be a contemporary standard in infertility care.

Privileging certain definitions requires ignoring or subordinating others. This chapter presupposes that a definition, as a social construction, is less about the true nature of the definition's object than it is about the context of its production. In other words, how a culture defines infertility says as much about that culture as it does about the condition itself. The Nāyars of South India, for example, believe that infertility is a disruption in a divine energy that women possess in greater amounts than men. In this matrilineal society, both the infertile woman and her matrilineal kin are held responsible for her inability to conceive, and both take part in rituals designed to appease family fertility gods (Neff).

Among the Egyptian poor, infertility is sometimes attributed to "pollution" of a reproductively vulnerable woman (those who have been recently circumcised or married or who have recently given birth or had a miscarriage) by a liminal person, usually a woman. Women determined to have been polluted undergo rituals involving the sharing of bodily fluids, which are thought to reverse the pollution and thus the infertility (Inhorn

487). In America, middle- and upper-class women, who regard infertility as a medical problem, believe that they have a right to take medical risks to remedy infertility (Becker and Nachtigall, "Born").

In this chapter I provide a brief history of involuntary childlessness in America. I use the term "involuntary childlessness" to distinguish it from the condition as it has been medicalized (that is, "infertility"). I then outline the medical model of infertility treatment in contemporary America, showing through stories how the model is experienced by those defined as infertile. I end the chapter with a discussion of the role of RESOLVE in advocating for the infertile.

A Brief History of Involuntary Childlessness in America

The deeply ingrained ideology of the family has proven difficult to denaturalize because its demands and rhythms seem intimately connected with biology (Thorne 10). Like other social institutions, however, the American family that is today seen as natural (that is, a heterosexual married couple, with children, residing in an individualized space, and connected by love or mutual concern) is the product of a particular space and time.

To take one example, the anthropologist Bronislaw Malinowski advanced the theory that the family unit is universal, a theory that Collier, Rosaldo, and Yanagisako have refuted by describing cultures in which no language exists for defining parents and children, in which living arrangements are not organized around biological kinship, and in which no "loving sentiments" (35) are expected to bind those who are biologically related. They argue that the contemporary family unit is not a given but "rooted in a set of processes that link our intimate experiences and bonds to public politics" (41). In particular, the form of the modern industrialized state has helped to create the family unit as an intimate space (marked in the American family by the ideology of nurturance) in opposition to the public sphere (marked by the ideology of competition).

Two recent book-length histories of infertility and childlessness in America illustrate how ideas about the value of children in the family and the meanings of childlessness have shifted over the centuries. *The Empty Cradle: Infertility in America from Colonial Times to the Present,* by Margaret Marsh and Wanda Ronner, and *Barren in the Promised Land: Childless Americans and the Pursuit of Happiness,* by Elaine Tyler May, both dispel the popular notion that the inability to have children is a recent phenomenon and show that the experience has not remained constant. These histories suggest that the experience of childlessness cannot be separated from its historical, cultural, economic, and political contexts and that its medicalization, rather than being the inevitable outcome of scientific progress, is but one way of framing reproductive choices. A complete summary falls beyond the scope of this chapter or this book, but the following section highlights some of the key features of these accounts.

Both accounts argue that the meaning of childlessness in America has changed with the structure of the family. As the family unit became more privatized and focused on the marital couple, the value of biological children born to that couple increased. In colonial America, the family unit was the flexible and changing household, which might include children and stepchildren as well as related and unrelated dependents. The ideal household included many children, as they were needed to sustain the demands of a largely rural life. May notes that the average colonial woman had eight live births (and even more pregnancies, as they often ended in stillbirth or miscarriage) and lost at least one child in infancy (25). Households might gain even more children through remarriage, by taking in children of relatives after the death of one or both parents or by taking in apprentices to learn a trade.

Those who could not conceive probably attributed the fact to God's will and accordingly addressed the problem through prayer. While neither May nor Marsh and Ronner denies that colonists who were unable to have children felt loss, they agree that the nature of communal life made it relatively easy—and sometimes expected—to participate in the raising of other people's children. Like those with biological children, those without children participated in rearing and disciplining the offspring of other members of the community, took in the orphans of relatives, received children as apprentices, and "adopted" children of living relatives without the biological parents' completely giving them up (Marsh and Ronner 17).

Beginning near the end of the eighteenth century, when the family came more and more to be defined as nuclear and separate from the community, the absence of biological children was felt more acutely. As Manifest Destiny compelled the people of the new republic to expand westward, "men were the builders of the nation, women the vessels of propagation, and children the hope of the future" (May 37). As this expansion occurred, the household ceased to be the center of the economy. Men, going out to the commercial centers, created an apparent distinction between the "public" world of business and government and the "private" world of the home.

The new ideology of domesticity positioned women—especially middle-class, white, nonimmigrant women—as contributing to the new republic through their roles as guardians of the home and moral educators of their children. Children, no longer valued primarily for their labor in the middle-class household, became objects of attention and devotion as their parents strove to mold them into good citizens. Among the immigrant poor, children both were needed to contribute to income and sometimes became a financial burden. Parents determined to be "unworthy" (especially those who were immigrants or poor) were encouraged to give up their children so that others could raise them "properly" (May 42). As children's value as individuals increased, as Victorian ideas about sex encouraged restraint, and as slavery (and white interest in black fertility) ended, overall fertility rates dropped (especially among the white urban middle class) from an average of seven children per couple in 1800 to three or four children in 1900 (May 44, 57).

Several factors—the increased privatization of the family, the contradictory messages of Manifest Destiny both to populate the republic and to nurture each of its new citizens individually, the limitation of women's roles accompanying the ideology of domesticity, and the introduction of adoption laws beginning at midcentury—contributed to the discomfort felt by nineteenth-century Americans, especially women, who were unable to have children. While significant numbers of Americans chose to remain both single and childless (May 48), and while evidence suggests a good number of nonlegalized adoptions (Marsh and Ronner 104), married couples who wanted children but could not have them enjoyed fewer social options for bringing children into their lives.

At the same time, medical activity designed to alleviate childlessness increased in the nineteenth century. While in the colonial period the inability to reproduce was seen as reflecting God's will, infertility during the nineteenth century came to be seen more and more as a disease. As the century wore on, women continued to rely on prayer and self-help (for example, by taking herbs and tonics, changing diet or exercise, or applying compresses) but increasingly sought out physicians.

Middle-class white women—who were increasingly resorting to abortion and contraception as they made greater forays into the world beyond the home—were widely understood to be weaker and in poorer health than their mothers and grandmothers, a "fact" that boded ill for their ability to have as many children as, or more children than, their immigrant sisters (Marsh and Ronner 31). In the first half of the century, physicians, uncredentialed healers, and social commentators alike often advised women to improve their general health through devotion to the private sphere, for the sake of their own reproductive capacities as well as for the sake of the nation. In the last decades of the nineteenth century, however, new medical instruments—including the speculum—made it possible for physicians both to observe and to alter women's reproductive systems to address what was now being called "sterility" (Marsh and Ronner 42). Surgeons made cervical incisions and repositioned the uterus in order to correct malformations. Ovariotomy—removal of the ovaries—became a standard gynecological procedure for addressing a range of conditions, not only reproductive problems. Surgeons, believing that a woman's entire physical, mental, and emotional health depended on her reproductive system, removed women's ovaries in order to cure supposed disorders such as hysteria and nymphomania; thousands of women underwent such unnecessary procedures before the turn of the century (Marsh and Ronner 83). By the end of the century, however, at least some gynecologists began to question whether sterility was related to women's willingness to assume traditional roles. These physicians focused their attention instead on the reproductive organs themselves, especially the ovaries and the fallopian tubes. More conservative doctors advocated less invasive surgeries that left the reproductive organs essentially intact but that removed pelvic adhesions or ovarian cysts or that opened the fallopian tubes (Marsh and Ronner 96).

At the same time, investigations into the possible role of gonorrhea, which was thought to be curable but would not in fact be so until penicillin was introduced in the 1940s, revealed that husbands were bringing home the disease after having sex with prostitutes. While the husbands might be asymptomatic, the disease often rendered their wives sterile. These investigations brought with them an attention to the related issue of male sterility. Physicians were discovering that the husbands of "sterile" wives often had no sperm, a diagnosis that was attributed to causes ranging from disease to masturbation. While some men followed advice to undergo surgery, take tonics, or exercise, physicians assumed that some cases could not be cured. The practice of inseminating a woman with the sperm of a donor occurred but with unknown frequency (Marsh and Ronner 94).

In the early twentieth century, surgery continued to be a preferred method of treating sterility, although with little success, but the emerging science of reproductive endocrinology eventually changed the approach in ways that are still evident today. The discovery of estrogen in the 1920s, which led to both the birth control pill and contemporary hormonal therapies, created a role for scientists and pharmacologists in the newly emerging discipline. Marsh and Ronner characterize the 1920s through the 1940s as a time of rapid changes as a collective of physicians, scientists, pharmaceutical companies, and others, well funded by research institutes, sought to understand the nature of female reproduction and to create synthetic hormones (Marsh and Ronner 139). Physicians, eager to put the new scientific knowledge into practice even without firm evidence about either the efficacy or the possible dangers of hormones, argued that the increase in voluntary childlessness (which according to some historians reflected economic pressures from the Great Depression more than an inherent desire not to have children) made it all the more important to help those who did want to have children (Marsh and Ronner 143).

While treatment in the first part of the century was generally limited to urban centers and was not seen as hopeful, the introduction of hormonal therapies and nonsurgical means of diagnosing and treating blocked fallopian tubes (including the hysterosalpingogram) led to new confidence and a surge of information in the popular press. Nevertheless, success rates remained very low. By the late 1930s, the inability to have children had come to be understood as a condition that resulted from problems associated with both the man and the woman, a condition that demanded treatment through a series of diagnostic tests and planned interventions. The ideal diagnostic regimen included tests to determine the shape, quantity, and motility of sperm as well as the condition of the fallopian tubes. Some physicians began asking their female patients to take their temperatures daily and to record them on charts as a way to determine when ovulation was occurring. In short, physicians were coming to believe not that one *partner* was absolutely "sterile" but that the *couple* was "infertile" (Marsh and Ronner 152).

The development of medical technologies addressing infertility did not occur in a vacuum. Along with the medicalization of involuntary childlessness, the eugenics movement became increasingly visible in the early part of the twentieth century. Marked in 1903 by Theodore Roosevelt's warnings of "race suicide," the movement exhorted the white middle class to fulfill its duties to the "race." Ignorant of the evidence that suggested that childlessness among African American women was growing at a faster rate than among white women, eugenicists expressed alarm that the birthrate of immigrant and nonwhite women as a group exceeded that of whites (May 75). White middle-class couples who chose not to have children or not to have enough children were denounced as selfish; those who could not conceive felt both the public burden and the private. Abortion or the use of birth control by the white middle class was widely seen as immoral and as contributing to later infertility.

Accompanying the encouragement of reproduction by whites were governmental policies that led to compulsory sterilization of many in the underclass: the poor, the "feebleminded," the promiscuous, black Americans, new immigrants, and the physically disabled (May). Often, advocates of birth control (including feminists) were also eugenicists who saw contraception as a way to make sure that immigrants, the poor, and nonwhites had smaller families than the white middle class. The Rockefeller Foundation, which funded much of the research into women's reproduction that led to treatments for infertility, was primarily interested in developing birth control for the poor (Marsh and Ronner 149). At the same time, however, specialists were also providing infertility treatment to the poor. Records suggest that the Free Hospital for Women in Brookline, Massachusetts, provided the same treatments for low-income and poor patients as for those with means (Marsh and Ronner 158–159).

Marsh and Ronner have associated the early to mid twentieth century with a "culture of matrimony" (123) that limited women's marital and childbearing options. While in earlier centuries unmarried or married women without children could play respected roles, both groups of women were now considered abnormal (123). Educators, the popular press, and social commentators argued that women could be completely fulfilled only if they married and had children. Even those women who had fought most vocally for women's rights believed that a woman's highest calling was motherhood (May 69).

A growing number of childless couples sought adoption as a way to complete a family. In the eighteenth or nineteenth centuries, a family might have preferred to take on an older child who could contribute to the family by working. Now, however, childless couples began to seek infants whom they could rear as their own. Private and agency adoptions were available, though both often entailed high legal fees; a black market also existed (Marsh and Ronner 169). Although children had no market value outside the home, they were increasing in value as a commodity because they symbolized a happy and complete family life (Marsh and Ronner 113).

The years after World War II reversed the trend of declining birthrates. The baby boom, fueled by postwar prosperity and by a rhetoric that linked domesticity with anticommunism (May 133), cut across boundaries of race, ethnicity, and class. The suburban ideal of the nuclear family became a goal for personal fulfillment and for the prosperity of the country; at the center of that ideal stood the child. Motherhood was portrayed in the popular culture as sexy; women who did not aspire to be what Betty Friedan called the "happy housewife heroine" were understood to be denying their central femininity. Fatherhood was seen as a marker of adulthood and good citizenship (May 135–136). Government programs sought to keep birthrates on the rise through subsidized housing and other incentives (May 137–138). Couples had children at an earlier age, sooner after marriage, and wanted larger families (Marsh and Ronner 186). May argues that infertility first became an important issue in the media during the postwar years, when family life was celebrated in the popular imagination and became the object of an increased consumerism (Marsh and Ronner 140). While the media sometimes proclaimed that infertility was on the rise, rates were probably close to their levels in 1870 (Marsh and Ronner 187). Nevertheless, those who were voluntarily or involuntarily childless felt an increased pressure to procreate. Those who wanted children could turn to medical treatment or to adoption, a process whose focus was changing from serving children without parents to serving childless couples. May notes that by the midforties, infertility had become the only acceptable reason for wanting to adopt a child; adoption was not only seen as a solution to the conditions of unwed motherhood and infertility but was also widely believed to "bring out a woman's 'maternal instinct' which could stimulate fertility" (May 176).

During the two decades after the war, the numbers of people (mostly women) who sought medical treatment for infertility increased markedly. Even though treatment was only marginally more successful in these years than it had been in the past, some physicians as well as some members of the popular media were optimistic in their claims for treating infertility (Marsh and Ronner 187). Physicians during this period understood infertility as being caused by problems with ovulation, the fallopian tubes, the cervix, and the sperm. A significant number of specialists held to the idea that as much as 75 percent of female infertility resulted from psychological disorders (Marsh and Ronner 196).

While surgery was a less popular option for treating infertility than it had been before the development of reproductive endocrinology, gynecologists did still perform diagnostic laparotomies and tubal surgeries, procedures that in very few cases led to pregnancy. Problems with sperm were both difficult to assess (men were still reluctant to subject themselves to examination) and difficult to treat. There was little agreement among practitioners about what constituted normal sperm and how abnormalities should be corrected. Men might be told to change their diet, exercise and rest more, reduce stress, and wear boxer shorts to reduce the testicular temperature; they might also be given one of the new hormonal therapies or operated on for a varicocele. Artificial insemination, in which the husband's sperm was subjected to various techniques before placement in the wife, was used more and more frequently to address problems with the man's sperm or the woman's cervix. Insemination by donor sperm was being increasingly accepted in cases where the husband had no sperm (Marsh and Ronner 198–202).

The biggest change in medical treatment for infertility, however, came in the midsixties, when the development of two hormonal drugs (Pergonal and clomiphene citrate, widely known as Clomid) made it possible to control ovulation, although physicians were not entirely sure how they worked. Increases in success rates of infertility treatment may be partly attributable to this new technology as well as to the fact that more and more women were seeking medical treatment earlier and earlier, sometimes after only a few months of trying to becoming pregnant. Because these women could possibly have become pregnant without medical intervention, treatment for infertility may have had little to do with some of the pregnancies that followed among women in this group (Marsh and Ronner 207).

While the first successful fertilization of a human egg with a human sperm outside the body occurred in 1944, the first live birth from in vitro fertilization (or IVF) would not occur until 1978. The intervening period saw the birthrate rise until the midsixties, decline in the seventies, and rise again (but never to the postwar highs) in the eighties (Marsh and Ronner 211). The decline in the sixties and seventies has been attributed to several cultural factors, including the youth revolution of the day, which questioned the institution of the family, the meaning of sex, and the global impact of overpopulation; and the growing women's movement, which questioned traditional gender roles. And while voluntary childlessness after 1960 did not reach prewar levels, the "childfree" movement became increasingly visible during the 1970s. May argues that this movement—fueled in part by an economic downturn as well as by the progressive political philosophies of feminism, environmentalism, and gay and lesbian rights—was not so much a rejection of the culture of domesticity as a reconfiguration of it.

Unconvinced that children were the route to personal happiness (and sometimes persuaded of the opposite), many of the voluntarily childless were nevertheless seeking personal fulfillment in intimate relationships. Unlike the baby boomers, however, they saw these ideal relationships as unencumbered by children. The new pronatalism that emerged in the 1980s, May argues, reconfigured intimate relationships once again. While in the baby boom years the most important intimate relationships were formed through a mother and father with children, and in the 1970s childless couples sought intimacy with each other, the 1980s' ideal intimate bond was that between a parent and a child. Social commentators and the media, ignoring data suggesting that women who were less educated and less financially secure were more likely than others to be unable to conceive, began to warn that professional women who delayed childbearing were causing an "infertility epidemic." The new pronatalism encompassed both conservatives who warned of a decline in Western values and liberals who sought relief from traditional parental rolls. In the 1980s, motherhood increased, both in the population and in the popular media, among single white and African American women as well as among gay and lesbian couples. Donor insemination, previously limited to married couples, was now more available to individuals and same-sex couples, as was adoption (May 213–217).

Physicians in the 1970s increasingly used Clomid and Pergonal to regulate ovulation. In spite of questions about the safety of the drugs—especially coming on the heels of the 1971 disclosure that diethylstilbestrol (DES), a drug often prescribed in the 1950s and 1960s to prevent miscarriage, caused cancer and abnormalities in the reproductive organs of children whose mother took the drug during pregnancy—they were seen as the only hope for women who ovulated irregularly or not at all. Artificial insemination, including insemination with donor sperm, remained the primary method of bypassing male infertility. IVF, however, was just around the corner and would change the mainstream approaches to infertility (Marsh and Ronner 221–222).

Rather than seeking primarily to cure underlying conditions that caused infertility, IVF and related techniques bypassed an assortment of conditions to produce the desired result: pregnancy. While the 1944 successful experiment in IVF dropped from the public eye, a successful 1969 British experiment renewed the possibility of live births using this method. There followed intense negative media coverage, a statement in 1971 by the American Medical Association seeking to prevent further research, and public sentiment against any kind of embryo experimentation around the time of the *Roe v. Wade* decision. While ethicists in America debated the morality of the procedure, scientists in Britain continued experimentation. The first documented successful birth from IVF occurred in Great Britain in 1978 to a woman whose blocked fallopian tubes had been removed. The birth of Louise Brown, who appeared to be a completely normal baby, convinced many members of the scientific community and the public that IVF offered hope to the infertile, especially those with blocked fallopian tubes.[1] The first American clinic offering IVF opened two years later in Virginia. By the time the first American child conceived through this method had been born at the clinic, fifteen other live births had been reported worldwide. Throughout the 1980s and 1990s, IVF clinics opened throughout the country (Ronner and Marsh 229–242).

The Regimen of Contemporary Medical Treatment for Infertility

Medical treatment for infertility in contemporary America is undoubtedly varied and is constantly changing. The kind of treatment a person receives for the inability to conceive likely depends on multiple factors, including (among others) geography; the knowledge and training of physicians; patient knowledge, wishes, and tenacity; race; ability to pay; marital status; sexual orientation; class; and age. In the following discussion I therefore do not presume that all people who consult physicians about the inability to conceive receive the same treatment or that medical professionals all agree on diagnoses and appropriate treatments. Nor do I intend the discussion to be comprehensive, a review of all possible diagnoses and treatments. Instead, I mean to highlight some common features of medical treatment for infertility in America at the turn of the millennium, drawing on literature from medical professionals, RESOLVE, and the experiences of the women who participated in this study.

The discussion that follows relies on statistical evidence, which some readers may find ironic, given that this book critiques, implicitly and explicitly, the role of statistics in normalization. By using this kind of knowledge for my argument, I am borrowing from Donna Haraway, who finds statistics useful as a "speculum . . . for opening up otherwise invisible, singular experience to reconfigure public, widely lived reality" (*Modest Witness* 199). To employ statistics in this way is not to deny its contribution to the so-called objectivity of science but to use this objectivity for cultural critique.

Diagnosis and Treatment

Infertility is thought to be attributable to problems with the man in 30 to 40 percent of cases, to problems with the woman in 40 percent, and to problems with both in 15 percent; no cause can be found in 5 to 10 percent of cases (Carson, Casson, and Schuman 4). The investigation and treatment of infertility are often not distinct temporal phases. While initial testing may indicate an abnormality with one partner, infertility is often caused by a number of problems involving one or both partners. In the contemporary context, creating a pregnancy is therefore not so much about correcting an abnormality that is preventing pregnancy as it is about creating conditions under which pregnancy is likely. In addition, interventions themselves can be diagnostic as well as therapeutic. Physicians, for example, can use the technique of IVF both in an attempt to create fertilization and to see whether it is occurring at all.

Textbook definitions of infertility, and the definition adopted by the Massachusetts mandate, place the boundary between normal and abnormal fertility at one year. The World Health Organization, however, places this boundary at two years, and the disparity suggests that the criteria for infertility are neither clear-cut nor the result of consensus (Wagner and Stephenson 3). Some critics argue that both definitions allow people to be misdiagnosed and unnecessarily treated; they cite data from the U.S. Office of Technology Assessment that only 16–21 percent of couples who are infertile by the twelve-month definition will remain infertile throughout their lives (Wagner and Stephenson 3). Still, most of the women in this study began to suspect a problem with fertility sometime before one year of unprotected intercourse had passed or before twelve attempts at insemination had occurred. Some of these women had a general awareness of infertility or knew someone who had had difficulty getting pregnant; others said that a history of irregular periods (or other conditions, such as endometriosis) had led them to believe that they might not conceive easily.

Single women and women in same-sex relationships, on the other hand, can self-diagnose themselves as "socially infertile" as soon as they decide to have a child. This diagnosis is the result not of failed attempts at conception but of a decision-making process that takes into account the money available for insemination and for second-parent adoption (for those with partners), the strength of the couple's relationship or of external support structures, and the social and cultural context in which the child would be born. Single women and women in same-sex relationships can of course also be diagnosed with medical infertility after a certain number of unsuccessful attempts at artificial insemination or after discovering an irregular cycle or other condition that would make it difficult to conceive.

A family physician or gynecologist is often the first professional a woman seeks out when she suspects impaired fertility.[2] Using the twelve-month definition, some physicians might advise patients to keep trying for a full year (and might perhaps suggest that the woman begin charting her menstrual cycle in order to have intercourse at the optimal time), or they might advise preliminary tests. If the woman is over thirty-five, or if either partner's medical history indicates a problem that might prevent pregnancy, the physician might recommend preliminary tests before a year has passed.

For heterosexual couples, preliminary testing involves both the man and the woman. While male infertility was routinely neglected in the United States until at least the 1960s (May 158–159), sperm analysis and an examination of the penis and testicles are now routinely completed early in an infertility workup. Clinicians consider the number of sperm and whether or not the sperm are moving (motility) and examine the shape of the sperm heads (morphology), as these factors appear to influence whether a sperm is capable of fertilizing an egg. Clinicians may also evaluate other characteristics of the semen sample, such as the volume, whether the sample contains any sperm antibodies, and whether the sperm can penetrate a hamster egg. The definition of what constitutes a normal sample differs even among the experts; a commonly accepted definition is that a normal sample contains at least 20 million sperm per milliliter of semen, that at least 50 percent of the sperm are moving, and that at least 30 percent of the sperm are shaped normally (Tan, Jacobs, and Seibel 66). Abnormalities are attributed to a variety of factors, including infections (sometimes caused by sexually transmitted diseases), varicoceles, obstructions, undescended testicles, impotence, hormonal imbalances, environmental toxins, or injury. Men with abnormal sperm might be advised to make lifestyle changes such as lowering the temperature of the testicles by wearing boxer shorts, not taking hot baths, and avoiding smoking, drinking, and drugs. Men may also undergo surgery to correct anatomical abnormalities or take prescribed hormones.

The focus of contemporary infertility treatment, however, is on creating a pregnancy, whether or not the underlying physiological problem is corrected. For this reason, and because many cases of infertility are the result of multiple factors, many problems with male infertility are not corrected but "treated" through assisted reproduction. Consequently, most of the procedures in assisted reproduction are focused on the body of the woman even if the cause of the infertility is found to reside in the man.

Women also undergo a medical history, physical examination of the reproductive organs, and diagnostic tests. About 25 percent of infertility in women is thought to be caused by problems with ovulation, 35 percent by problems with the fallopian tubes, 35 percent by abnormalities in the abdomen (such as endometriosis), 5 percent by growths in the uterus, and a fraction by problems with cervical mucus (Carson, Casson, and Schuman 5–7). Women who have had sexually transmitted diseases may develop pelvic inflammatory disease (PID), which can block the fallopian tubes; those who were exposed to DES in utero may develop abnormally shaped reproductive organs (as well as cancer). Infertility in women is also attributed to hormonal imbalances, scarring from previous surgery, abnormal weight, smoking or the use of alcohol or drugs, and environmental toxins. Treatment can include hormones, surgery, and assisted reproduction.

To determine whether the woman is ovulating, the physician may order laboratory hormone tests, ask the woman to use an over-the-counter ovulation predictor kit, or ask the woman to chart her menstrual cycle. When charting her menstrual cycle, a woman takes her temperature at the same time each morning on a basal body thermometer, which measures in tenths of degrees. She then records each measurement on a chart. During ovulation, the temperature rises slightly. It falls again at the onset of menstruation. Charting her menstrual cycle gives the woman an indication of when (and whether) she is ovulating so that she can time intercourse or artificial insemination. She can also bring the charts to her physician to help diagnose ovulatory problems.

The charting of the menstrual cycle is a technology of normalization. The data that the woman collects and records will be compared to data on the menstrual cycle of the "average" woman; a physician uses the comparisons to help determine a course of treatment. Through this technique, the woman becomes an object of knowledge, something that can be described and about which arguments, in the form of hypotheses or diagnoses, can be made (for example, "The patient has an inadequate luteal phase"). Like other technologies of normalization, the knowledge created about the woman is both individualizing and homogenizing. She is known as a discrete entity and as a member (and data point) in a certain population.

The collecting and recording of menstrual data is one striking example of the role of writing in normalization. Charting the menstrual cycle "situates [individuals] in a network of writing; it engages them in a whole mass of documents that capture and fix them" (Foucault, *Discipline* 189). A cycle is no longer just a bodily experience that is known viscerally. Instead, the menstrual cycle takes visual shape with each temperature reading a woman records. The data points become a way of knowing the menstrual cycle as a graph of highs and lows that can be compared in an objectified way to that of the average woman.

A woman who charts her own menstrual cycle is participating in self-observation and providing information to health care providers who will subject her to further disciplinary processes. It is important to remember that when she participates in the process of normalization, she becomes a subject as well as an object of knowledge. For women using artificial insemination by donor (often single heterosexual women and lesbians with no indications of reproductive impairments), charting (or using ovulation predictor kits) is part of the standard practice of becoming pregnant. For single heterosexual women and lesbians in particular, charting can be part of the routine of babymaking, much as frequent intercourse is for heterosexual couples when they first attempt to conceive. Because sperm is expensive, women using artificial insemination by donor need to inseminate when there is the greatest likelihood of conception.

The physician may also order other tests to determine whether the woman has a hormone imbalance; these tests include blood tests and an endometrial biopsy, in which a sample of the lining of the uterus is examined at a certain point in the menstrual cycle. To see if the woman's cervical mucus allows penetration by sperm, the physician may also conduct a postcoital test, in which the mucus is examined a few hours after a couple has intercourse.

Depending on the results of these initial tests, as well as other factors such as the age of the woman, the physician may advocate that the couple (or the woman, if she is single or in a same-sex relationship) time intercourse (or insemination) using charting or ovulation predictor kits. If the woman does not appear to be ovulating or seems to be ovulating irregularly, the physician may prescribe clomiphene citrate, or Clomid, which is taken orally, or gonadotropins, which are taken by injection, to regulate the menstrual cycle. If the woman is older or if tests indicate possible other problems, the physician might order still more tests. A hysterosalpingogram, in which dye is inserted through the cervix into the uterus and fallopian tubes, is used to determine whether the uterus is shaped normally and whether the fallopian tubes are open. In laparoscopy, which is performed under general anesthesia, the surgeon uses a telescopic instrument (called a laparoscope) inserted into the abdomen through a small incision at the navel to examine the reproductive organs. Using the laparoscope, the physician can see and correct abnormalities that might be interfering with fertility, including pelvic adhesions, tubal blockages, and ovarian cysts.

If the results of all these tests fall within a normal range, a woman or couple may be diagnosed with unexplained infertility. For these patients, the physician may advocate a gradually more invasive treatment plan, depending on the woman's age. The plan may start with artificial insemination, in which sperm is inserted into the vagina, or intrauterine insemination (IUI), in which prepared sperm is inserted past the cervix directly into the uterus. These types of insemination may or may not be accompanied by hormonal treatment. After several attempts at insemination (sometimes varying the amount and type of hormonal stimulation), the physician may advise the couple to move to a more aggressive therapy, such as IVF or one of its cousins, such as gamete intrafallopian transfer (GIFT), in which the egg and sperm are placed in the fallopian tubes, where they may fertilize and then move onto the uterus for implantation; or zygote intrafallopian transfer (ZIFT), in which fertilized eggs that have not yet divided are placed in the fallopian tubes. In these procedures, a woman takes hormones to stimulate production of eggs. Eggs are then surgically retrieved and mixed with sperm.

Because IVF allows the clinician to tell whether fertilization is occurring, this procedure can serve a diagnostic function as well. After several days, embryos can be transferred to the woman's uterus, where they may or may not implant. The number of embryos transferred depends on the clinic, the physician, the patient, and the presence of insurance coverage.

One physician in the Boston area argues that patients without insurance coverage are more likely to have a very high number of embryos transferred, often resulting in multiple births, which can be dangerous for both the woman and the fetuses. Some women opt to have what is known as "selective reduction" surgery to remove one or more of the implanted embryos.

The same treatment plan may be followed for women or couples with other diagnoses. In some cases, early testing may indicate that the physician should begin with an advanced technique. If a male partner has a low sperm count, for example, a physician may recommend intracytoplasmic sperm injection (ICSI), in which a single sperm is injected into an egg, or insemination using donor sperm. For a woman with completely blocked fallopian tubes, intrauterine insemination is unlikely to produce a pregnancy; she may instead be advised to try a procedure that bypasses the fallopian tubes, such as IVF. A woman diagnosed with premature ovarian failure (also called early menopause) might be advised to consider using an egg from a donor, which can then be fertilized using any of the techniques mentioned previously. Women who cannot carry children might look into gestational surrogacy, in which a surrogate carries the embryo of a couple to term, or traditional surrogacy, in which the surrogate's own egg is fertilized with the sperm of the male partner.

Because the site of most treatments for infertility is the woman's body, women bear most of the risks, including increased risk of diseases associated with pregnancy (such as anemia, diabetes, bleeding, and high blood pressure) and of cesarean section, even with single pregnancies (Maman et al.; Schenker and Ezra). Some studies have reported links between the use of fertility drugs and ovarian cancer (Rossing et al.; Whittemore et al.), while others have reported no increased risk (Potashnick et al.). Perhaps the greatest known hazard to women and their fetuses is the risk of multiple births; in 1997, about 9 percent of all cycles of IVF, ZIFT, and GIFT (a little less than a third of the pregnancies) resulted in multiple births (U.S. Centers for Disease Control 18). Women who carry pregnancies of more than two fetuses have a higher likelihood of complications during pregnancy, and their fetuses are more likely to be born prematurely or to have developmental abnormalities (Collins and Bleyl; Lipitz et al.). While some researchers and practitioners advocate minimizing these risks by transferring fewer embryos (Hershlag; Milki, Fisch, and Behr), there is no consensus on this approach.

Insurance coverage is thought to influence the number of embryos that physicians (and patients) are willing to transfer during IVF and related procedures; patients with little or no coverage may only have one try. To minimize this risk and others, some practitioners advocate improving informed consent procedures so that women are more aware of the possible dangers. Once a medical approach has been initiated, however, American women may be willing to see these risks as acceptable (Becker and Nachtigall, "Born").

Experiencing Infertility

The experience of Susan and Paul, as well as others in this study, illustrates both the process of diagnosis and treatment and one way of understanding this experience. Paul had been married before and had had children, conceived without assistance, with his former wife. Susan recalls first thinking that she might have a fertility problem:

> For the first five, maybe six months, I was just like any other woman who is trying to get pregnant, disappointed when you get your period but not devastated. . . . It never even occurred to me that there was something wrong. I was 34 at the time, and after about six or seven months, maybe eight months, . . . we said, well, maybe there's something wrong, maybe we should talk to somebody, and still thinking, . . . we know sometimes it takes a little while when you're older.

A noted fertility specialist informed Susan and Paul in an early phone consultation that they were still within a normal time frame but that initial testing could do no harm. Sperm tests were normal, a hysterosalpingogram confirmed that Susan's fallopian tubes were clear, an endometrial biopsy showed a healthy uterine lining, blood tests fell within normal limits, a postcoital test proved inconclusive, and a diagnostic laparoscopy showed healthy organs. Susan and Paul were diagnosed with unexplained infertility.

Throughout the diagnostic procedures, Susan had a gut-level feeling that there was nothing wrong with her. She recalls stonewalling against some of the procedures, afraid of the pain or angry that she had to undergo tests only to prove what she felt she knew all along. Still, when the couple were diagnosed with unexplained infertility, Susan kept hoping to find something wrong so that they could fix it. She says:

> At the lab they kept saying that I was normal. But I started saying, I want them to find something wrong so they can fix it, 'cause I've heard so many stories, "Well I had a blocked tube, but they opened it up and then I got pregnant," "Oh I did have endometriosis, but they gave me such and such and I got pregnant." . . . If they can't find anything wrong they can't fix it, so it was just really a catch-22. Unexplained infertility is really, really hard.

Susan's frustration grew out of the sense that if her reproductive system were working normally, then she would conceive. Because she was not conceiving, she believed that there must be some identifiable cause that, once located, could be corrected through modern medicine. Like Susan, many other women expressed belief in a technologically inspired view of the human body as a machine (Greil 53) with interdependent, fallible parts (Whiteford and Gonzalez 29). According to this worldview, "you take your body, like your car, into the shop for periodic checkups and for repair when it is not operating optimally" (Stein 81). Several other women in this study used mechanical metaphors to describe their bodies, referring to their reproductive systems as "plumbing." Using this metaphor, they perceived their bodies as systems that could be evaluated, diagnosed, and repaired. Sarah, for instance, felt that she was an ideal candidate for in vitro fertilization because "it was a very clear-cut situation where the plumbing wasn't working."

Susan's new physician, an infertility specialist, recommended a conservative course of treatment: intrauterine insemination. Although some people with unexplained infertility will become pregnant on their own, a physician at a Boston-area infertility clinic uses assisted reproduction to bring members of this population back into the range of the normal. In other words, with treatment, those in the unexplained category have the same chances of conception, per cycle, as the general population (about

25–30 percent). For those with unexplained infertility, he says, IUI is the least invasive procedure that will bring results, so he prefers to try six medicated IUI attempts (varying the medication with each one) before moving to more invasive procedures such as in vitro fertilization. Susan's physician took a similar approach, although he did not vary the medication. Although Susan and Paul asked that a more aggressive approach, such as IVF, be taken immediately, their physician was reluctant, saying that it made no sense to start with a more invasive and expensive procedure when Susan might get pregnant through IUI.

By the time Susan was ready for her first IUI treatment, two years had passed since she and Paul had started trying to have a child. She was excited and optimistic, saying "this is what we had been waiting for." Although their sex life had disintegrated over the course of the infertility testing, the IUI procedure gave her and Paul a chance to try to fit this experience within the realm of "normal" procreation. As he held her hand during the insemination, she remembers thinking, "okay, we're making our baby." During the time of the first IUI attempt, their sex life also became rejuvenated as they began to separate lovemaking from babymaking. At that point, she says, their sex life returned to some semblance of normalcy, only to deteriorate once more as the IUI failures took their toll. Within a few months, the couple had undergone three IUI cycles, none of which had worked.

Susan's case illustrates how the norm is operationalized in current infertility practice. As recently as the 1970s, doctors spent more time attempting to find and fix the particular anomaly that was causing the infertility. A woman might undergo repeated surgeries to open blocked fallopian tubes (an abnormal condition), for example, so that she could then become pregnant normally. In contemporary treatment, the goal of practitioners is to bring a couple's chances of conception back within normal range, regardless of whether the underlying anomaly is corrected. In vitro fertilization, for example, was developed to bypass—not correct —blocked fallopian tubes so that the end goal of pregnancy could be achieved. IVF and related procedures are now used for many conditions besides blocked fallopian tubes, including male factor infertility. That is, a woman may undergo IVF as a method of treating the condition of low sperm count or poor sperm quality in her partner.

After three IUIs and no pregnancy, Susan and Paul were more adamant about wanting to move on to IVF so that they could see whether the egg and sperm were fertilizing. Their physician, who wanted to continue with intrauterine inseminations on a higher dose of medication, finally agreed, and Susan became pregnant on the first IVF cycle. After several weeks, however, an ultrasound showed that the fetus was not viable. After a few weeks' rest, Susan tried two more cycles, each one cancelled after the initial ovary stimulation because not enough egg follicles had been produced. Blood tests showed that her ovaries were probably slowing down, and her doctors were not optimistic about her ability to become pregnant without using a donor egg. For Susan, this knowledge that she had begun the "normal" transition into menopause made her feel old beyond her years. She says:

> While it's not technically premature ovarian failure, it's the kind of thing that [for] women my age, that's happening all the time, but if they're not having infertility problems, they don't know it, and it's just that slow decline towards menopause. It could take ten years, and women who've had their children, or don't want children, or aren't considering, it's irrelevant. You don't feel this at all. And now that I know that this is happening to my body, I feel a hell of a lot older than 37. I'm going to be 38 next month, but I feel 48, I feel 58 some days.

While Susan understood that the processes her body was undergoing were to be expected in women her age, she still felt betrayed. Although her body was behaving normally, Susan felt that it was giving up on her before she had had the chance to have children. That is, because she was approaching menopause earlier than she had expected, Susan found it harder to fulfill accepted "life course norms" (Greil 133). In this instance, the idea that she was normal did not comfort her because it conflicted with her unfulfilled desire of pregnancy.

Until she became pregnant, Susan and Paul told only a few people about their infertility experience. She says: "We've kind of been in the closet about this whole thing, because we always figured we'd be pregnant the next month. We're not going to tell anybody but a couple of our closest friends, mostly for my support. So we didn't tell my family what we'd been going through because we figured . . . we may never have to tell them. Once you have the baby, what's the point?" Their reasoning, that Susan might be pregnant within the next month, is part of the compelling nature of infertility treatment.

Many physicians approach medical treatment from a statistical modeling framework. In this framework, events become significant because of the frequency of their occurrence, and effects are more important than causes (Ewald 144). While physicians do seek to understand underlying causes of infertility, the more important concern for them is whether the treatment will bring about a pregnancy. For each couple, then, the physician asks, "What is the likelihood that this treatment will work?" Hoping for better results, the physician might adjust parameters for the next cycle on the basis of results from the previous one, but no approach is guaranteed to work. Many cycles bring about some diagnostic knowledge, however, that tells the couple something about their chances of conceiving using a particular method. This knowledge, along with the knowledge that couples do conceive through these methods (Sandelowski, "Compelled"), often catches patients up in a cycle of hope and disappointment. The renewal of hope each month can both keep couples in treatment and often (as in the case of Susan and Paul) convince them that if they wait just a little longer, no one else need know.

Like Susan, many of the other women in this study told few people about their infertility. For Diane, telling people about treatment was an invasion of the privacy between husband and wife. She had learned a lot about infertility by listening to a woman at work talk about her treatment, but she did not view such disclosure as appropriate. While Diane thought her mother might suspect (because she knew Diane loved children), only Diane's physician and her insurance agent knew for certain. Single women and women in same-sex relationships may have different reasons for limiting disclosure to close friends. Aware that families, co-workers, and acquaintances might view single or lesbian motherhood as abnormal, these women might tell only those they know would be accepting.

Because infertility is an invisible stigma (that is, it is not obvious to strangers and acquaintances), the infertile can have "mixed contact" (Goffman 12) with fertile individuals without these "normals" ever knowing of their private pain. Medically infertile women in this study talked of the difficulty of encountering, every day, reminders of their condition. They noted the discomfort of being treated by pregnant health care workers and of noticing pregnant women and babies everywhere. Jean W. Carter, coauthor of a book on deciding to be "no longer infertile," knew that she had to come to terms with her infertility if she were going to continue in her occupation as an obstetrician, where pregnant women were her patients. Some of the women in this study avoided supermarket aisles where they would encounter baby products or sections of shopping malls where baby clothing would be displayed in store windows. News of the pregnancy of a friend or family member, or an invitation to a baby shower, was almost always a source of pain, envy, and anger.

Compounding the pain is that the infertile often feel as if the seriousness of their condition is trivialized. "Normals" who know about the infertility may make jokes about the couple not knowing how to have sex or about the fun the couple must be having trying to conceive a child. Well-intentioned people may give advice about what doctors to see or what procedures to try. A few, offering what RESOLVE characterizes as folk wisdom, may advise the couple to get a pet, take a vacation, or adopt first. Some may not know what to say, while others might suggest that infertility is a blessing in disguise or not as bad as other problems.

While some normals might see infertility as a problem, not as many compare it to life-threatening illnesses, a comparison frequently made by the infertile. Susan, for example, says: "If we had cancer or high blood pressure or any other one of a million things or conditions, not even diseases, . . . nobody would even look at you. But because you're talking about something that is supposedly is so optional, [they say,] 'Oh well, so what, so you don't have to have a baby, so what, just adopt.'" Susan responds, "It's not that simple." Adopting, as both infertility and adoption experts contend, is not the cure for infertility.

The reaction of many infertile women, as with other stigmatized individuals, is to avoid contact with painful reminders. Writers of articles in the RESOLVE newsletters frequently advise the infertile to avoid events or topics of conversation that they know would be painful. An infertile woman should not feel guilty, they say, when she does not attend a baby shower for her best friend or sister-in-law, if such an event would cause her great anguish. By avoiding contact with normals, or at least those whose fertility is obvious, the woman might be trying to dodge prodding questions or insensitive remarks. For the most part, however, "fertile people promote the stigmatization of the infertile not so much by deliberately discriminating as by promoting a definition of normality that excludes the infertile" (Greil 133). These definitions of normality are especially painful for some women, who may experience infertility as the cause of "spoiled identity" (Greil 53) and as a disruption in an expected life course (Becker, "Metaphors"). That is, women are more likely than men to link parenthood both with a sense of self and with a sense of future. The inability to become pregnant prevents an infertile woman from fulfilling one part of her identity and from moving through her life as she had expected.

Those who avoid contact with fertile others can find themselves isolated, however. Susan and Paul did not seek any support until they began considering adoption. She says:

> This was the first time in three years that we ever connected with anybody else who's going through what we're going through . . . I look back and I think, oh my god, how could three years have gone by? We've been doing this all by ourselves, no wonder we're basket cases. Maybe that was a mistake. But again, it was that whole mentality: well, we'll be pregnant next month, we don't have to get involved in anything, this isn't really a serious life-long problem, this is going to be over.

While a feeling of isolation leads some to seek the company of similarly stigmatized people in self-help organizations such as RESOLVE, others delay this move or never make it at all. Some, like Susan and Paul, sense that the experience is likely to end soon and that seeking support will therefore be unnecessary. In this study, a little over half of the single and married women belonged to RESOLVE; almost all of the women in same-sex relationships belonged to some formal or informal support group.

When I interviewed Susan, she and Paul were trying to decide whether to stop treatment, live without children, or adopt. Like many prospective adoptive parents, Susan was anxious about the process. Along with fears of the expense (which can exceed $10,000) and of not being able to adopt a healthy white infant (supplies are short), Susan did not know whether she and Paul would look enough like normal parents to be chosen by a birth mother. She reasons: "You may never be chosen by a birth mother. They might say, oh god, you're as old as my parents, I'm 16, I don't want you. On the other hand, they might say, oh, I was raised by my grandmother, older people are good. You just never know if you're going to get chosen." She was similarly worried when she considered international adoption. The age limits for adopting children from other countries vary, but Susan was afraid that her husband, at forty-five, would be seen as too old.

Susan also feared that adopting a child from another country would mark her family as different. A child who does not look markedly different from the adoptive parents will not draw the attention, or often invasive questions, of strangers and acquaintances. For Susan, having a child of a different nationality would be tantamount to telling the world about her infertility—an invasion of her privacy. Even though she liked the idea of adopting a girl from China, she was bothered by how strangers might react.[3]

During our interview, she recalled the story of a woman with a daughter from China. When the girl was with only one of her parents, people sometimes asked whether the other parent was Asian. But when the child was with both parents, Susan said, "It's right there in your face, all the time, it's right there for the world to see." Having a child of the same race, therefore, was part of looking normal and having more control over information about her reproductive life. She says: "I want to be as damn normal as I can be at this point. I think I would prefer to have a child of the same race, because then I was in control of who knew, when they knew, and how they knew, not because I want to hide it, but because I want more control in my life, and I want to present it to the child in a certain way."

At a much deeper level, too, Susan did not know whether adoption would work for her, simply because it didn't seem normal. She says: "I just want to be normal again. I don't think I'll ever be normal again, because adopting or childfree are not considered normal. Only biological children are considered normal." Here Susan demonstrates an acute awareness of how kinship is hierarchically ordered in contemporary America. Whereas in colonial America, "fluid and flexible arrangements" made the raising of children "more communal, less private, and less biologically or legally defined" (May 31), contemporary American family life is centered on an ideal household in which two parents live with their own offspring in a private dwelling. The preference for parenting biologically related children runs deep, and the bias against adoption forms part of everyday culture. The adoptive relationship is widely seen as inferior and as the last resort when other options fail (Bartholet, *Family*, "Why"). Not surprisingly, the preference for biologically related children voiced during this study extends to the single women and to women in same-sex relationships. While some considered adoption as well as artificial insemination, the pull of a genetic link was strong. Ellen, single and undergoing artificial insemination, intensely wanted a "little me," a desire she called "almost like a male ego thing." Although Anne did not believe that she experienced the ticking of the "biological clock," she did experience a strong urge to carry a child; at the time of our interview, she and her partner were considering a second child, which her partner wanted to carry.

Other women in same-sex relationships offered very practical reasons for wanting biological children. Lauren and her partner felt that a biologically related child would stand a better chance of being accepted by their families. Another couple, Janice and Theresa, each secured their biological (and therefore legal) ties to their son through an unusual procedure: Theresa's egg was fertilized with donor sperm and was transferred to Janice, who gave birth. This procedure also satisfied Theresa's desire for someone who looked like her (she had been adopted and wanted to be biologically connected to her own child) while helping to alleviate Janice's menstrual disorder.

Failure to remove the stigma of involuntary childlessness can take at least two forms. In the first instance, an individual or couple may be in the percentage of the population who will never conceive. When Susan's physician described the statistical probabilities for pregnancy, she never imagined she would be in the percentage of those whom even the most advanced medical intervention could not help. She says: "Nobody told us how bad it would be if we failed. And nobody told us how wonderful it was to be successful by a different option, earlier, and we didn't realize that we could have walked away." Her trust in the "medical miracle," she says, prevented her and Paul from exploring other options sooner, when she might have had more mental, psychological, and physical reserves. Coming from a "medical family," they believed that medicine would have the answer.

The stigma of infertility can also remain after an individual or couple has resolved the current desire for a child. After giving birth to a child or adopting one, parents may struggle not to be too protective or too lenient with their "miracle" children. They may want to expand their families further, and they may face both subtle and overt pressure from those who believe that an only child grows up to be spoiled and selfish. Sarah, having had one child without assistance and then twins through IVF, was grateful not to have to answer questions about having more children. With three children, she felt safe in answering that she did not want to have more. Susan and Paul, eleven months after our first interview, were beginning to deal with this issue. They had adopted an infant girl, a procedure that was much easier and less traumatic than Susan had imagined. She was now wondering whether they might want to someday have a sibling for their daughter. Despite their good experience with adoption, Susan thought that another adoption would be impossible because of the financial expense of the first. The adoption, what Susan calls a "yuppie adoption" because they "got what [they] paid for," cost them over $30,000. Their only option, she said, would be to go back to medical treatment, this time using an egg from a donor.

RESOLVE: Support and Advocacy for the Infertile

RESOLVE, Inc., a national support and advocacy group for the infertile, was formed in 1974 as an outgrowth of the Open Door Society of Massachusetts, an adoption advocacy organization. Its founder, Barbara Eck Menning, was a nurse who had experienced infertility and who had subsequently adopted children. In her work with the Open Door Society, Menning came to believe that many of the infertile people who eventually adopted children needed to resolve "the problems of infertility" before pursuing adoption (Simons 106). RESOLVE's charter was to provide for the needs of the infertile couple through support services.

Because of the limited medical interventions available in the 1970s, early RESOLVE members did not so much learn about new methods of treatment as attempt to come to terms with their inability to have children. While the organization supported adoption, it took the position early on that the inability to have a child biologically must be dealt with before any other "resolutions" could be considered. This primary emphasis on the medical aspects of infertility would become magnified in later years as the infertility industry grew. With many women undergoing whatever treatments were available, RESOLVE's publications began regular discussions of new medical treatments. Elizabeth Bartholet, an adoption advocate opposed to the proliferation of reproductive technologies, later argued that RESOLVE's focus on medical treatment contributed to the view of adoption as "the choice of last resort" (Bartholet, *Family* 216).

Described as a charismatic "role model of someone who had survived and resolved the issue [of infertility]" (Simons 110), Menning had the goal of reaching the isolated and stigmatized members of the infertility community and of building the case for infertility as a medical condition deserving serious attention. As the reputation of Menning and RESOLVE spread beyond New England, individuals in the rest of the country began expressing interest in affiliating with the organization (Simons 118). In 1976 the first local chapter formed in Minnesota, and fifty-seven other local chapters had followed by November 1994. In 1983 the Massachusetts chapter (RESOLVE of the Bay State) was formed to give local services to those for whom the national organization, located in the state, had originally provided.

With the formation of local chapters, the national office could become more active in education and advocacy (Simons 122). Newsletters urged the infertile to come out of the closet by telling a friend or by coming to a meeting. This organizational function is typical, in Goffman's terms, of those for stigmatized individuals; in addition to other goals, such organizations seek to change the perception of the stigmatized through speeches before groups of "normals" (24) and through publications that identify "enemies," record "atrocities" and success stories, and relate ways of overcoming the stigma (25). Enemies of the infertile are those who try to sensationalize infertility (such as the popular press), those who are perceived as trying to limit the options of those with infertility (such as those who would make surrogacy illegal), or those who see medical treatment for infertility as optional. Contributors who tell of atrocities relate stories of insensitive remarks (such as "you must be having fun trying to have a baby," often delivered with a knowing wink or nudge, or "you must not be doing it right") or of humiliation (such as having to tell a boss about treatment).

Even early on, while the organization had issued formal statements of neutrality on political issues affecting infertility (such as proposed legislation to ban independent adoptions or to allow physicians to perform in vitro fertilization), members testified at hearings, and statements appeared in the national newsletter urging members to talk to their representatives (Simons 122–123). By the time RESOLVE had adopted advocacy as a national goal in 1983, the local chapters were looking to the national office for policy statements on issues affecting the infertile, such as surrogacy, insurance coverage for medical treatment for infertility, and adoption (Simons 127–128).

In addition, members increasingly felt the need to advocate for better medical treatments for infertility. As a nurse, Martha Griffin, the first president of RESOLVE of the Bay State, believed that medical treatment for the condition lagged behind other medical specialties. Aside from being on the receiving end of procedures that Griffin calls "primitive," women she knew were being told that their infertility was psychosomatic. Women, she explains, were told that they were working too hard at getting pregnant (or that they were not working hard enough), that they needed to take a vacation or change the wallpaper, or that they needed to get a pet. Sometimes a physician offering a diagnosis to a woman would explain the condition in a way that blamed her. In Griffin's own case, a noted infertility specialist diagnosed her endometriosis without even examining her, saying that endometriosis was a "career woman's disease."

Griffin believed that these ideas about infertility carried over into health insurance coverage. Women in her infertility support group reported inconsistent coverage, with variations occurring among medical providers and insurance companies as well as from one procedure to another. Women were finding that a procedure or a prescription might be covered one month but not the next. According to Griffin, most insurers would automatically deny a procedure coded as treatment for infertility; they often scrutinized and denied coverage for treatments that were coded for related conditions (such as endometriosis), and they accused women and their physicians of attempting to beat the system. RESOLVE invited representatives from insurance companies to meet with them, hoping that such a meeting would rally support for coverage. Instead, insurers reiterated their position: infertility treatment was optional. Unable to solve the problem informally, both the national organization and the newly formed Massachusetts chapter made mandatory insurance coverage their primary goal by 1985 (Simons 141).

2

Insuring (In)Fertility

> Insurance is not imagined simply as an institution or system within the state for which the state must provide an order or organizing principle; rather, the state can now be conceived of in terms of the actuarial view of society. Insurance is no longer a simple subordinate function of the state but an essential part of the state's organization that affects its very nature—the state itself becomes a vast system of social insurance.
> —François Ewald, "Norms, Risks, and the Law"

Accompanying media reports in the mid-1980s that infertility was on the rise—a claim that was countered by historians of infertility (Marsh and Ronner 1)—was what Susan Faludi calls a media campaign about the dangers of the "birth dearth." The chief spokesperson for this campaign was the demographer and syndicated columnist Ben J. Wattenberg, whose 1987 book *The Birth Dearth* cautions that declining Western birthrates will mark the end of the dominance of Western economics, democracy, and culture.

In what the author himself calls an alarmist tract, Wattenberg argues that while the poor in Western countries continue to have children at or above replacement levels, the middle class (of all races) has fallen behind, with an adverse effect on the overall birthrate and the ratio of well-educated, well-prepared workers. This pattern is repeated on a global scale: while the wealthier Western countries have declining birthrates, the Soviet Union and the "Third World" (which also has declining birthrates but a much greater population base) continue to add proportionately more people to the world's population. Eventually, he says, the "free, modern, industrial world" (6) will shrink to such a tiny fragment of the globe that everyone will suffer enormous consequences. The advances of capitalism will be lost, the impetus toward democracy will disappear, and the rest of the world will cease to aspire to Western values and culture.

The causes of this decline, Wattenberg argues, are fourfold: socioeconomic factors (such as urbanization; rising education for women; rising income; and more women in the workforce, which he describes as the most important cause); increased access to legal abortion and better contraception; lifestyle factors (such as delayed marriage, delayed birth of a first child, divorce, decreased fecundity, an increased incidence of never-married women, and homosexuality); and changes in values (for instance, women's liberation and environmentalism).

Wattenberg argues that it is in the best interests of Western civilization, and, consequently, the rest of the world, for the citizens of these countries to have more children. He blames the middle class for not reproducing enough; the poor, he claims, are already doing their share. While the author declares himself opposed to reproductive coercion (such as the Chinese one-child policy and what was then Romania's criminalization of abortion), he does argue that the governments of Western countries should adopt pronatalistic policies to "encourage" Western middle-class women to have more children and to urge "less developed" countries reduce their birthrates. Of paramount importance in these new policies would be educating the young Western middle class to understand the global implications of their personal decisions. Wattenberg advocates building on neofeminist demands for better day care, job sharing, flex time, and other incentives for women to work and to have one or two children while doing so. He also advocates encouraging some women, through tax breaks and other monetary incentives, to stay at home in order to have three or more children. Although he does not favor outlawing abortion, Wattenberg argues for making adoption more attractive, for encouraging research on infertility, and for requiring insurance to cover medical treatment for infertility.

The demographically based argument of *The Birth Dearth,* which appeared the year that the Massachusetts mandate was passed, represents what Foucault calls biopower, or the "numerous and diverse techniques for achieving the subjugation of bodies and the control of populations" (*Sexuality* 140). Biopower is a mechanism of the modern state, in which populations are seen as central to the success or failure of governments, countries, or species. It is marked by two features: first, a shift in focus from the person of the sovereign to the individual bodies that make up the population, and, second, a shift from the power of threatening death to the power of managing life. The modern state rationalizes actions or policies by referring not to the desires or rights of the head of state but to those of the people, both individually and collectively. In this sense, biopower operates simultaneously on the "individual body" and the "species body" (*Sexuality* 139). For Wattenberg, the link between individual and species is clear: the future of Western civilization lies in the hands (or, more specifically, the reproductive organs) of the middle-class woman.

The rise of biopower is accompanied by a change in the nature of the law. Foucault argues that since the classical period, power has become increasingly productive rather than prohibitive. That is, power is now less concerned with taking life and more concerned with making life more efficient, more productive, and more useful.[1] The power of law comes less from traditional locations (such as the head of state or the courtroom), although such locations still exist with considerable influence. Instead, the power of law comes from "a continuum of apparatuses (medical, administrative, and so on) whose functions are for the most part regulatory" (*Sexuality* 144). These regulatory apparatuses work not only by providing mechanisms for completing the work of governing but also by helping to construct the imaginaries of the populations that they govern. In this sense, "law's power rests not only in the technologies of coercion and control that are invoked through it, but in the cultural frameworks for action that are created by regulatory policy" (Reichman 234).

The present chapter examines insurance coverage for infertility, especially in the case of the Massachusetts example, as a regulatory mechanism of biopower. The primary questions debated in the courts—which center on the nature of infertility—illustrate the importance of definition in law's modern role as normative. In this role, law is focused less on overt displays of power over death (although it still retains this power) and more on evaluating ways to make life more productive and efficient through protection of what come to be defined as basic needs. For RESOLVE of the Bay State, the law functioned as a space within which to advocate for the basic need of fertility. Public hearings were a suitable place for validating the experience of the infertile. The public hearings, however, functioned less as a place where the general public could debate the plight of the infertile and decide how this plight should be addressed and more as a venue for stabilizing and authorizing definitions and solutions that RESOLVE advocated. For the advocates, law was a resource both to be called upon to enforce rights and to be controlled in one's best interests. In the end, medical and moral discourses circulating during the advocacy period made the biological family seem natural and made medical treatment for infertility seem necessary, transforming insurance coverage for the treatment into what appeared to be a natural right.

The Legal Treatment of Infertility as Disease and Disability

In its modern role as normative, law does not relinquish its right to take life but shifts its focus to the management of life. Central to this modern role is law's power "to qualify, measure, appraise, and hierarchize, rather than display itself in its murderous splendor" (Foucault, *Sexuality* 144). The legal debates over insurance coverage for infertility illustrate the importance of definition to this normative role. Before the passage of the Americans with Disabilities Act (ADA) in 1990, courts faced with the issue of insurance coverage for infertility generally addressed three fundamental questions: whether infertility is an illness or disease, whether treatment for infertility is medically necessary, and whether some treatments for infertility (especially IVF) can be excluded from coverage because they are experimental. Whether infertility can be defined as an illness or disease is the most basic question. If infertility is not defined as such, then treatment is generally not considered medically necessary, and even procedures not considered experimental may be excluded. Therefore, the nature of infertility must be determined before it is decided whether and to what extent insurance should cover it.

The case of *Egert v. Connecticut General Life Insurance Company* (1990) illustrates two different approaches to the question of whether infertility is an illness. One approach, defining infertility on the basis of some intrinsic quality of the condition, was adopted both by the insurer in this case and by the lower court. In this case, Christine Kraft-Egert—who had only one fallopian tube, which was blocked—brought action against her insurance company, Connecticut General, for refusing to cover IVF. Connecticut

General maintained that while it would cover treatments that attempted to enable patients to conceive naturally (that is, surgery), it would not cover procedures that bypassed but did not treat the underlying problem (such as IVF).

The lower court agreed that Kraft-Egert's blocked fallopian tubes, not her failure to attain pregnancy, were the illness. As a result, her insurance company could reasonably reject treatment that did not address the "actual" illness of blocked fallopian tubes. The court of appeals that reviewed the case adopted a second approach. Rather than trying to determine whether some intrinsic quality of infertility makes it a disease, this court only considered whether infertility fit the definition of illness within the meaning of the insurance plan. In this case, while the insurer purported not to consider infertility an illness, its own plan referred to the "illness of infertility" and the "diagnosis of infertility" (1037), evidence to the appeals court that the insurance company did in fact consider infertility an illness. Because of these inconsistencies, the court overturned the decision.

The court of appeals in *Egert* thus avoided having to decide whether infertility was or was not an illness in a larger sense, but it did rely on the definition in use by the insurance company. The court made a similar determination on the question of medical necessity. Kraft-Egert's insurer had maintained that IVF was not a necessary treatment for her infertility because it bypassed her underlying illness (damaged fallopian tubes) rather than curing it. The court pointed out, however, that the insurer explicitly covered another treatment that did not cure the underlying condition: counseling for infertility. Stating that "after several sessions with a trained counselor, it is unlikely that Kraft-Egert's fallopian tubes will somehow repair themselves and allow her to conceive naturally in the future" (1038), the court found that Connecticut General had acted "arbitrarily and capriciously" in denying coverage for IVF. The court relied on this inconsistency for support of a ruling in favor of the patient.

Like the lower court in *Egert*, other courts have attempted to pin down the nature of the illness in infertility. In *Kinzie v. Physician's Liability Insurance Co.* (1987), the Court of Appeals of Oklahoma reasoned that IVF was different from procedures for other illnesses that "were performed to the insured's body in order to physically alleviate or correct a serious illness, disease or affliction" (1142). Unlike these other procedures, IVF did not correct Karin Kinzie's infertility because it did not address the underlying condition (fallopian tube adhesions), even though the Kinzies did conceive a child. Here the court defined her illness as the underlying physiological impairment. Using this definition, the court of appeals argued that IVF was not necessary "to cure or preserve Mrs. Kinzie's health" and "that it was not medically necessary to a woman's health to give birth to a child" (1141). The court reasoned that the "conception of a child, although certainly important to married couples who have a problem conceiving, was not 'medically necessary' to the physical health of the insured" (1142).

Similarly, a small claims magistrate dismissed the case of Thomas and Jill Witcraft, who sought reimbursement for procedures that allowed them to have a child (*Witcraft v. Sundstrand Health and Disability Group Benefit Plan* [1988]). Thomas Witcraft had low sperm count and low motility, and Jill Witcraft had irregular ovulation. They sought to have artificial insemination covered, but their insurer, who refused, argued that the procedure was not being performed because of an illness. A small claims magistrate dismissed the case, saying that "*although improper function of ovaries or testicles may be an illness,* the condition of being not pregnant is not an illness. Therefore, any procedure i.e. artificial insemination used to change that condition is not compensable under the terms of the plan" (788, emphasis added in the opinion of the Iowa Supreme Court).

For the small claims magistrate, infertility is the underlying physiological impairment, not the inability to have a desired child. A district court and the Iowa Supreme Court disagreed; both argued that the Witcrafts each had impairments that prevented their reproductive organs from functioning normally, that is, from achieving conception. Thus, even though the underlying conditions of low sperm count, low sperm motility, and irregular ovulation were not corrected, the "function" of the reproductive organs was effectively restored to normal by creating a pregnancy. Quoting from the district court, the Iowa Supreme Court argued: "The defendant urges, and the magistrate agreed, that the condition of not being pregnant is not an 'illness.' The court on review finds the natural function of the reproductive organs is to procreate. . . . The mere fact that the treatment may occur outside the body of one or the other or in the subsequent course of insemination is not material because it is the natural function of the organs, reproduction, which is in fact treated" (788–789).

The idea that the natural function of the reproductive organs is to allow procreation is also present in *Regnier v. Industrial Commission of Arizona* (1985). The plaintiff, Stephen Regnier, who worked as a test driver for Ford, suffered an accident at work that rendered him paraplegic and unable to have an erection or to ejaculate. He asked for medical treatment (an implant in himself and artificial insemination for his wife) to enable him to father children. An administrative law judge concluded (and a higher court agreed) that because treatment would not improve the patient's condition (his paralysis), the employer did not have to pay for this procedure. The Arizona Court of Appeals rejected this reasoning, arguing that "the fact that the procedures will not render claimant ambulatory or no longer a quadriplegic is irrelevant. Just as claimant's previous bladder surgery improved or restored a functional loss caused by the industrial injury, the procedures at issue here may *restore* claimant's ability to father children" (336, emphasis added). Because the procedure, if successful, would provide a substitute for the "body function" lost in the accident, this procedure was considered medically necessary.

In this analysis, the court assumed that a normally functioning Stephen Regnier would be able to father children, even though he had an undescended testicle from birth (a condition that often causes men to have very low sperm counts). The assumption here is that everyone should be able to have children, because the average person is able to have children. The "average" person, however, is "a fictional entity," a creation of a normalizing society (Ewald 145). The presence of norms means that some individuals, by definition, must fall outside the norm in order for the scale of normalcy (the bell curve) to exist at all. In other words, the inability of one person to reproduce is not abnormal on the scale of entire populations; the World Health Organization, in fact, maintains that "a five percent rate of infertility might be a *human* norm" (Heitman 91, emphasis added).

In at least two cases, courts have considered whether voluntary sterilization should be defined as a disease. In *Marsh v. Reserve Life Ins. Co.* (1987), Larry and Beverly Marsh argued that their insurance company should pay for the reversal of her voluntary tubal ligation, because her "inability to have children was a sickness which was not manifested until she desired to conceive" (1314). The Second Circuit Court of Appeal of Louisiana disagreed because both the sterilization and its reversal were "voluntary" and held that "the inability to have children after the voluntary sterilization is not a 'sickness' " (1315). In *Reuss v. Time Ins. Co.* (1986), the Court of Appeals of Georgia rejected a patient's claim for reversal of a vasectomy. In this case, the insurer had covered the vasectomy, even though it was considered voluntary, but refused to cover the reversal, also voluntary. The court agreed that sterilization and its reversal, in this instance, were "voluntary and unrelated to any disease, illness, or injury" (625). Like the insurer, the court distinguished between the vasectomy and its reversal, even though neither was considered treatment for a disease. Although a vasectomy could be considered usual and customary, the court argued, a reversal is not a "usual and customary" part of the vasectomy procedure.

The Americans with Disabilities Act, passed in 1990, is to some extent changing the nature of the arguments about infertility within the law. Designed to prevent discrimination against those with disabilities in many areas of life (such as employment, housing, and health services), the ADA defines a disability as an "impairment that *substantially limits* one or more of the *major life activities*" (42 U.S.C. § 12102(2), emphasis added). For an individual hoping to compel coverage for treatment of infertility, a legal argument based on the ADA would not need to focus on whether infertility is a disease and whether treatment for it is medically necessary. Instead, the legal questions are whether reproduction is a major life activity and whether infertility is a substantial limitation of that activity.

The question of whether reproduction is a major life activity has been asked in both federal courts and in the Supreme Court. In *Pacourek v. Inland Steel Co.* (1996), a woman diagnosed with infertility and undergoing treatment that caused her to miss work sued her employer for discrimination after her employer fired her. A federal district court ruled in her favor, arguing that infertility is a disability within the meaning of the ADA because reproduction is a major life activity and infertility limits that activity.

Other courts have seen the issue differently, however. In *Zatarain v. WDSU-Television, Inc.* (1995), a television station had refused to renew the contract of a news anchor who requested a reduced work schedule to accommodate her infertility treatment. The anchor sued for discrimination under the ADA, but the federal court ruled that reproduction is *not* a major life activity because it does not occur with everyday frequency. Hence, the court argued, infertility could not be considered a disability. Finally, in a case directly involving insurance coverage for infertility (*Krauel v. Iowa Methodist Medical Center* [1996]), Mary Jo Krauel sued her employer for refusing to cover treatment for infertility, arguing that its refusal violated the ADA. Krauel's position was that her infertility impaired both reproduction and "caring for others," which she argued were major life activities. A federal appellate court ruled that neither reproduction nor caring for others could be considered major life activities because neither affected her "ability to care for herself, perform manual tasks, walk, see, hear, speak, breathe, learn, and work" (677).

The U.S. Supreme Court came to a different conclusion, although not in the context of infertility, in *Bradgon v. Abbott* (1998), a case involving a woman whose dentist refused to treat her because she was HIV-positive. She sued the dentist for discrimination under the ADA, arguing that her HIV status limited the major life activity of reproduction. The Supreme Court agreed, arguing that "reproduction and the sexual dynamics surrounding it are central to the life process itself" (2199).

Other questions about the applicability of the ADA to infertility are still being debated. These questions include the extent to which the ADA covers health insurance and whether the ADA allows certain exclusions to treatment (see Gilbert; Millsap; Morgan; Rydel; Tischler). In addition, the impact of two 1999 decisions by the U.S. Supreme Court remains to be seen (*Murphy v. United Parcel Service, Inc.* [1999]; *Sutton et al. v. United Air Lines, Inc.* [1999]). These decisions found that the definition of a disability must take into consideration whether the condition is correctable. It is likely that courts will now need to ask whether infertility treatment actually "corrects" the condition that it is intended to address.

All these cases draw on the stasis of a definition to help characterize the nature of individual rights and the place of law and other institutions in guaranteeing those rights. While definition has been and continues to be used to determine what can be taken away from individuals in the interest of the state (as, for example, in the question of whether a given act can be defined as murder), definition in the modern state also works on behalf of forces whose goals are to optimize life. Whether a given condition qualifies as a disease would have little legal significance in a culture where law exists primarily to defend the life or power of the sovereign. But when law exists to maximize the potential of populations—and their constituent individuals—then an understanding of the conditions that afflict them matters greatly. The questions that are asked within the law are as much (or more) about managing life as they are about enforcing death; the law must determine which conditions matter most to life and which conditions most interfere with maximizing its forces.

The legal questions asked about infertility thus aim (in the words of Foucault) at *qualifying, measuring,* and *appraising* infertility. Is infertility the inability to have a biological child, or is it the underlying physiological cause of this inability? If the underlying causes are shared by a couple rather than being confined to one member, is the disease rightly situated not in their individual bodies but in the *function* of reproduction that they share? In order to qualify as a major life activity, must a given function occur with a particular frequency or have a certain inherent meaning? Is reproduction a *major life activity,* and if so, does infertility represent a disruption to that activity? These questions of definition seek to pin down the nature of infertility so that legal institutions can employ it to manage life more effectively. For this reason, questions drawing on the stasis of procedure are as significant as those drawing on definition.

Once infertility as an entity is defined, it can become the object of questions about implementation. If infertility is an illness, must treatment for it become mandatory? What sort of treatment should be mandated: that which aims at the underlying physiological problems or that which aims at the function of reproduction? These are the questions that RESOLVE sought to have answered through legislation at the state and federal levels.

As this book goes to press, thirteen state legislatures, including Massachusetts, have enacted laws mandating some form of insurance coverage for infertility, and legislation is pending in other states.[2] Texas (1987), Connecticut (1989), and California (1989) have each passed a "mandate to offer," in which insurance companies are required only to offer the coverage to employers, who can choose whether or not to buy it. A "mandate to cover," in which insurance companies *must* cover treatment, has been passed in Maryland (1985), Arkansas (1987), Hawaii (1987), Montana (1987), Rhode Island (1989), New York (1990), Illinois (1991), Ohio (1991), and West Virginia (1999) as well as in Massachusetts.

Restrictions, which illustrate the methods by which the law enforces reproductive ideals, vary from state to state. Some states (Arkansas, Hawaii, Maryland, and Texas), for instance, specify that infertility must be covered only if it is attributable to particular causes, such as endometriosis, or if the patient has experienced infertility for a specified amount of time (in some cases, five years). The laws of Montana, Ohio, and West Virginia apply only to health maintenance organizations and only to preventive health services. Arkansas has a dollar amount cap, while Hawaii and Illinois allow insurers to limit the number of attempts. Some states (such as California and New York) explicitly exclude in vitro fertilization, while others (for example, California, Illinois, and Texas) exempt religious organizations if a procedure creates an ethical conflict. Several states restrict coverage to married couples, either by requiring that the egg and sperm be those of the married couple receiving treatment (Arkansas, Hawaii, Maryland, and Texas) or by including only married individuals in the definition of infertility (Rhode Island). Appendix B describes the coverage provided by individual states.

While no federal laws currently mandate coverage for infertility treatment, the federal government has been discussing the condition since the 1970s. In addition to deciding in favor of regulating IVF clinics, Congress has created National Infertility Awareness Week (it began in 1989), has commissioned reports on infertility (U.S. Congress, 1988, 1989), and has considered bills requiring coverage for federal employees. During the national health care debates of 1994, both Clinton's proposed Health Security Act and the alternative plans proposed by the House and Senate included coverage for infertility, with the Clinton proposal excluding coverage for IVF. In 1999 and 2000, Congress introduced three bills requiring coverage: one would cover federal employees (HR 2774; U.S. Congress, 1999b), and two would encompass all health insurance plans (HR 2706, U.S. Congress, 1999a; and S 2160, U.S. Congress, 2000). As of this writing, all three bills were still pending in Congress.

The Massachusetts Mandate: Making Private Anguish a Public Issue

By 1985, mandatory insurance coverage for infertility was RESOLVE's primary goal (Simons 141). Although some courts were finding in favor of insured infertile individuals, advocates did not see relying on case law as a viable option, first, because other courts were coming to opposite conclusions, and second, because some insurers were responding to the cases by explicitly excluding coverage for infertility (Cole 723). Instead, RESOLVE advocates believed that defining infertility as a medical entity in the law would guarantee insurance coverage, promoting better health care for the infertile. Law is here understood as a resource upon which individuals can draw to guarantee what is perceived to be fundamental rights. But the advocates hoped for changes beyond the legal. By hoping that authorizing a medical definition would lessen the stigma of infertility, RESOLVE advocates also displayed a belief in law as a resource for changing cultural attitudes. In August 1985, RESOLVE, led by advocates Martha Griffin, Susan Crockin, Karen Sweet, and Bob Sweet, persuaded Democratic state senator Edward Burke to sponsor a mandate for coverage in Massachusetts. The bill, introduced in 1986 and again the following year, passed by voice vote in 1987.

By bringing infertility into the legislature, RESOLVE advocates did not intend to engage in public debate. Instead, the advocates had already defined their problem and its solution and looked to law to validate them. The mandate needed to stabilize infertility in such a way that answers to questions of policy and procedure could be understood as inevitable. Such stabilization would be impossible if the definition of infertility were opened to debate. As a means of limiting the debate, RESOLVE avoided media attention. The first RESOLVE of the Bay State president, Martha Griffin, and others in the organization felt that the media shared the popular idea that treatment for infertility was optional. Griffin hoped that by avoiding media attention, the organization could keep the focus on infertility as a medical issue. As she put it, "We didn't want it to seem like some cause for a bunch of affluent yuppie couples. It is a medical condition" (Cullen 8). The bill, in fact, received scant media attention. As with other legal reforms, such as those dealing with child custody and support (see, for example, Coltrane and Hickman), this strategy of "quiet passage" (Cullen 8) has been cited as a key reason that the Massachusetts mandate was approved so quickly and with so little opposition.

Those present at the public hearings report that very few people opposed the mandate apart from representatives from the insurance industry and the Catholic church. For its part, RESOLVE of the Bay State sought alliances with neither prolife groups, which might have been attracted by the way the legislation had been troped as "family building," nor women's health groups. The decision not to align with either side in the abortion debate avoided a potential schism in its membership; the decision not to align with women's health groups, in particular, kept reproductive technologies from being linked any further with abortion in the minds of Catholic lawmakers. Against the advice of their senate sponsors, RESOLVE of the Bay State also avoided alliances with physicians' groups, from a belief that the testimony of physicians, as a group who stood to gain financially from the mandate, would seem self-serving. Individually, physicians did testify at the public hearings, to discuss either infertility as a medical entity or their own infertility.

Because RESOLVE didn't align itself with outside groups, it needed to rely heavily on the personal stories of the infertile themselves. Recognizing the stigma attached to infertility, however, RESOLVE advocates avoided asking ordinary members to testify. Instead, they requested testimony from infertile people already connected with the medical or legal system on the assumption that these individuals would not be inordinately burdened by the additional stress of making a public statement. A married couple, both physicians, testified at a hearing before the Joint Health Committee, bringing with them their son, who had been born a year earlier after IVF. Noting that their privileged economic position allowed them access to advanced medical care, the couple testified that "the ability to have a family should not be limited to the small number of couples who can afford the costs of treatment. Everyone deserves the chance to be treated for the medical problem of infertility and to have the chance to have a child" (Massachusetts General Assembly 4).

A legislative aide has been remembered as one of the more powerful speakers. Testifying during public hearings the first year the bill was introduced, the aide identified himself and his wife as an infertile couple. The aide told the legislators that on his salary (a figure that would have been known to those in the chamber), he and his wife could not afford the advanced reproductive technologies necessary to have a child. The following year, on the bill's second try, the aide testified again, this time to announce that he and his wife had saved enough money for only one try at IVF. Fortunately for them, he declared, their one chance resulted in a child.

Although RESOLVE of the Bay State did not ask members to testify in public, it did encourage its members to tell lawmakers about their own personal experiences of infertility. The November 1985 chapter newsletter, for example, included a special message from the president urging members to attend a meeting in which they would learn how to contact state representatives about the upcoming bill. In her president's message in the fall 1986 newsletter, Griffin repeated the call, stressed the importance of strategy, and reminded members that lawmakers are public servants: "As most of you know we have made considerable progress in our legislative effort to get infertility covered by health insurance. . . . Please get those letters out and follow up with a phone call. Don't be intimidated by the process. Your legislators are there for you and infertility is your problem" (1). This call was an appeal to members who understood (or were coming to understand) infertility as a problem that could be approached in a public, legal way rather than as solely personal, private anguish. The call also treated the law as a resource to be called upon to enforce perceived rights.

In the campaign that followed, RESOLVE members sent letters to representatives in which they described their own stories of infertility. These personal stories, the advocates reasoned, would illustrate the cost of infertility in a way that the testimony of experts never could. One lobbyist remembers the campaign:

> I think they got every single person in their membership at some point in time or another to write a letter. The letter was your personal story, and those letters were xeroxed and sent to every single committee member, every single congressperson, and there are a lot of them. I mean hundreds and hundreds. They were just inundated with this stuff. . . . It was personal stories, one after another after another. You can't deny people's pain. You can deny a lot of things, but not personal pain.

By bearing witness in this way, advocates and members of RESOLVE demonstrated a faith not only in narrative as a persuasive force but also in the power of law to alleviate pain and suffering. In the case of infertility, there is no one from whom to exact revenge for the pain caused; instead, reparation is understood as an entitlement provided by a network of institutions designed to encourage the general well-being of a government's citizens.

When the bill finally appeared in October 1987 before then-governor Michael Dukakis, letters and telegrams urged him to sign. Some shared detailed narratives of their treatment history with the governor, describing the pain of being "reminded everyday" of their childlessness. One simply stated: "Give the middle class a chance for parenthood" (Santiesteban). The governor signed the bill into law.

Naturalizing Desire: Medical and Moral Discourses in the Debate

The grassroots strategy of RESOLVE and its ability to largely define the terms of the debate played a significant role in the success of the Massachusetts mandate. The mandate was also successful for reasons that, while related to RESOLVE's strategies, go beyond intentionality. The case law on insurance coverage for infertility indicates that even a conceptual framework that accepts infertility as a medical condition might not regard treatment for infertility as "medically necessary." In order for treatment to seem necessary, infertility must be understood as a barrier to an activity deemed fundamental to life. Two interrelated discourses helped to achieve this end. First, the focus on infertility as a medical condition made the married, heterosexual family seem natural. That is, the medical definition of infertility obscured the ways in which the condition and its treatment are profoundly social. Second, the naturalized family in turn bolstered the argument that treatment for infertility is a medical necessity. In other words, male/female unions are seen as natural because of their function in procreation; therefore, the inability to procreate within that union is an aberration and should be corrected.

While other state mandates listed particular reproductive procedures that would be covered by insurance, the Massachusetts mandate took a different form. RESOLVE wanted to make sure that infertility was defined as a "medical entity"; its name (*An Act Providing a Medical Definition of Infertility*) and the supplied definition (drawn from the definitions used by physicians) reinforce this purpose. RESOLVE and its sponsors also ensured that the bill was introduced by the Health Care Committee, not by the Insurance Committee, where it might otherwise have found a home.

As I argued in Chapter 1, it is impossible to separate infertility from its cultural and social context. This approach means not that infertility is a medical entity with cultural and social ramifications but that the classification of infertility as a medical entity is itself a social and cultural act. Arthur Greil, a sociologist who has studied couples experiencing infertility, distinguishes between a reproductive impairment (that is, a physiological characteristic such as blocked fallopian tubes or low sperm count) and infertility, which he defines as "a dynamic, socially conditioned *process* whereby couples come to define their inability to bear their desired number of children as problematic and attempt to interpret and correct this situation" (7, emphasis in the original).

Infertility, then, is qualitatively different from the absence of the physiological ability to have children. It is, instead, an unfulfilled desire. Jean and Michael Carter, in a book that describes the process by which they became "no longer infertile," write:

> *Medically* speaking, you are defined as infertile when you have been trying to get pregnant without success for a certain period of time, usually about a year. At that point you are labeled officially infertile and most doctors will advise some sort of medical investigation to determine the source of the problem. . . . Thus, it seems if you have ever been labeled as infertile and haven't been able to have children, you will always be infertile. For us, however, the most important part of this definition is "trying to get pregnant." If a couple never did try to get pregnant, then they would not be called infertile, whether or not they actually could, in theory, have children. And, following that logic, when a couple is no longer "trying to get pregnant," they are no longer infertile. They no longer have the *medical problem* called infertility. (14, emphasis in the original.)

The language of the Carters illustrates the social nature of infertility treatment, which is obscured by the standard medical definition of infertility and the one adopted by the Massachusetts mandate. An early version of the definition, which was limited to married couples, was protested by the Women's Bar Association of Massachusetts as being "a social rather than a medical construct" that "clearly discriminates against couples who may be living together and unable to conceive and single men and women who become aware that they are infertile and wish to seek treatment prior to marriage" (Talmadge 1). Their suggestion that any mention of marriage be omitted was heeded, and the definition that ultimately appeared calls infertility "the condition of a presumably healthy individual who is unable to conceive or produce conception during a period of one year." Although the definition itself locates the illness (and therefore, presumably, the treatment) within individuals rather than couples, it continues to obscure the social nature (and social purpose) of medical treatment for infertility.

Downplaying the social nature of infertility and emphasizing its physiological characteristics helped place the condition within the realm of medical science so that insurance for it could be seen as justifiable. Reproduction by the heterosexual couple was understood as a natural event; the inability to reproduce within a heterosexual relationship was an abnormality that medicine should be able to address. The placement of this issue within the realm of medicine may have helped lawmakers understand infertility as a disease, but it did not automatically make treatment for infertility seem "necessary"—something that should be mandated. This was especially true for Catholic lawmakers just before the public hearing in 1986, when the Vatican issued an encyclical equating in vitro fertilization with abortion.

Moral discourse on the importance of "family" may have bolstered the argument that treatment for infertility was necessary and may have made it possible for Catholic lawmakers to overlook the Vatican's objections to IVF. Drawing on profamily arguments, Catholic and non-Catholic lawmakers in support of the bill made more formal statements to the Church, condemning the Vatican's position on IVF. In a letter to Cardinal Bernard Law of the Archdiocese of Boston, Sherwood Guernsey, a non-Catholic supporter of the bill, emphasized that IVF is meant to occur within the institution of marriage.[3] He argued that IVF should not be coupled with surrogate mothering, another practice condemned by the Church, because IVF, unlike surrogacy, "offers [infertile married couples] the opportunity of having their own child, born of the wife's egg and the husband's sperm."[4] Catholic lawmaker Edward Burke, the senate sponsor of the bill, reiterated this position in his own letter to Cardinal Law. He wrote, "If you have not yet had the opportunity to meet with a married couple holding their newborn child as a result of invitro [sic] fertilization, I suggest that it would be most difficult for you in good conscience to tell them they have done something immoral." After the bill was passed, Burke adopted language that would resonate with the Catholic church by describing the bill as "a prolife bill. It helps married couples have kids" (Cullen 8).

The definitions of family that circulated during this debate were narrow and commonly focused on the presence of children. An effort to have children was then troped as family building and the inability to do so amounted to no less than the frustration of an important social institution. The notion of family was further delimited by the medical definition of infertility itself. By obscuring the social nature of infertility, procreation within the heterosexual family unit is made to appear natural, whereas procreation within any other relationship is not. Many insurance companies now distinguish between medical infertility and social infertility, refusing to cover the latter. A heterosexual couple who cannot conceive, for whatever reason, are considered medically infertile. A single woman or a woman in a same-sex couple with physiological impairments that prevent conception could also be given a diagnosis of medical infertility, but at least part of her condition would be considered social. That is, the lack of sperm is considered a product of social choice, and procurement and storage of sperm are not usually covered by insurers.

The lawmakers were also influenced by accounts of the plights of individuals. One RESOLVE member who took part in the effort by talking to individual legislators at the Massachusetts State House remembered that Catholic lawmakers were not interested in the mandate unless it affected them personally or unless they were heavily lobbied. When first questioned, she says, they argued that "this isn't the way the church wants you to get pregnant" or "it's not natural." But she found that most of those she approached were willing to listen to her story, especially because she was a volunteer whom "they didn't know from Adam" rather than a paid spokesperson. Listening to the stories of frustrated dreams was particularly hard when a constituent would notice a family photograph on a lawmaker's desk. These lawmakers were often at a loss to explain how they, with pictures of their own children sitting before them, could declare a family-building bill immoral.

The face-to-face encounters with their infertile constituents had another persuasive human dimension. Frequently, those who join infertility support groups or otherwise begin to affiliate with other infertile people are struck by how normal everyone looks. One woman, after seeing for the first time a particularly good-looking couple in her support group, reasoned that they must not be "really" infertile. She was shocked to learn that this "good-looking couple" had been undergoing medical treatment for several years. The personal stories told in lawmakers' offices and the testimony given by couples helped to eliminate the idea that people who could not have children had, in the words of Martha Griffin, "two heads and four arms."

Especially helpful were the statements of the legislative aide who testified during both years the bill was debated and whose wife became pregnant after one cycle of IVF. Griffin, then president of RESOLVE of the Bay State, explains that the testimony of the legislative aide was helpful in "normalizing the experience, and seeing how unfair it was, seeing the inequity part of it. . . . He represented, to them, normality, so he was very influential, very helpful, and he had friends." Seeing the results of infertility treatment was just as compelling. After the bill's passage, Sherwood Guernsey, one of the representatives who sponsored the bill, noted that "mothers brought babies in here. That affected people in here" (Cullen 8).

Insurance as a Technology of Normalization

In the case of the Massachusetts mandate, law functions as a restorer of individual rights: "the 'right' to life, to one's body, to health, to happiness, to the satisfaction of needs, and beyond all the oppressions or 'alienations,' the 'right' to rediscover what one is and all that one can be" (Foucault, *Sexuality* 145). RESOLVE sought to establish fertility as a natural right so that legal intervention could be understood as inevitable. With courts coming up with various definitions of infertility, RESOLVE saw legislative action as a way to authorize a singular medical definition that focused on the inability to procreate rather than on any underlying conditions that led to this inability. With this definition stabilized in statutory form, the regulatory apparatus of insurance could be engaged to shape and carry out the policies that would follow.

Insurance arose, alongside the discipline of statistics, during the industrial revolution. Adopting the worldview of statistics, insurance creates its own reality by imposing order on events (such as illnesses or accidents) that would otherwise appear haphazard (Ewald 142). Individuals are known by their place in actuarial tables of populations, and resources are distributed accordingly. Insurance creates its own kind of justice; unlike legal judgments that seek the cause of damages, insurance "refers no longer back to nature but rather to the existence of the group, a social rule of justice that the group is free to determine for itself, and on its own terms" (Ewald 147). In other words, while law traditionally attempts to assign responsibility so that the responsible party can make reparations for harms (by serving time or paying fines, for instance), insurance imposes a *collective* burden that is based not upon responsibility but upon membership in the group. Each person within the collective has a right to agreed-upon reparations if events that are insured against do occur.

The collective nature of insurance makes it both a lens through which to examine the harms that a society understands as deserving of reparation and a mechanism by which social change can occur. Deborah Stone argues that "insurance tends to beget more insurance" because it "creates *social mechanisms* that tend to increase what gets perceived as insurable and deserving of collective support" (13, emphasis in the original). During the debate over the mandate, legislators were lobbied to make them understand both fertility as a natural right and infertility as a burden that should be shared collectively, as are burdens associated with other natural rights. Advocates for the mandate were arguing from a standpoint of equity, so that inequity, as well as infertility, emerge as an adverse event against which insurance should protect people. In their appeals to lawmakers, RESOLVE advocates and private citizens relied on this trope in at least three different ways: they argued that it was unfair not to be able to have children (because normal people are able to do so), that some people received covered treatment while others did not, and that childless couples had to contribute to the pool of insurance for pregnancy and dependents when those with children did not have to contribute to their infertility treatment.

The Massachusetts mandate might thus be regarded as a case in which "insurance . . . offers a new *rule of justice*" (Ewald 147, emphasis in the original) intended to ameliorate the unfairness of infertility. Addressing the unfairness of infertility, however, is different from addressing infertility itself. Although the medical treatment for which mandatory insurance coverage provides is meant to enable people to have biological children, the coverage does not guarantee this outcome. Instead, because medical treatment does not always result in pregnancy or live birth, the coverage only guarantees (in many instances, at least) the *opportunity* to become biological parents.

Law here functions to identify inequitable relationships so that they can be made more equitable through the provision of opportunity. To perform this function, the law operates as an appraiser of difference: it must determine how the infertile can be differentiated from the fertile, the first step in normalization. Legislators and judges debate which conditions can be contained within the category of infertile and refine the category through qualification so that it can be communicated to other institutions. Categorization permits the law and other institutions to determine how those falling into the category of infertile can be treated more equitably. To be treated more equitably, however, does not necessarily mean being moved into the category of "fertile." Although the provision of equitable services is ostensibly intended to make the abnormal into normal subjects, I argue that it serves instead to reinforce the distinction between the two categories. Because the medical services for which the mandate provides do not guarantee a live birth, some members of the category of the infertile will never become fertile. Even many of those who do have children through medical treatment continue to think of themselves as Other, however, both because they have been medically and legally categorized as such and because the experience of infertility extends beyond the inability to have a desired biological child.

As I will argue in the next three chapters, infertility also indexes abnormality along other axes. Those who pursue medical treatment for infertility desire not only a biological child, but also success, order, and control. For many of the women in this study, medical treatment for infertility creates double binds as they attempt to fulfill these desires. These double binds are not necessarily resolved when a couple has a biological child. Some of those who have a biological child continue to feel caught between success and failure, order and discontinuity, control and constraint, while some of those who do have a biological child find other ways to reduce or eliminate the pull of these competing demands. It is to these competing demands that I now turn.

3

Success and Failure

I believed.
I believed in hard work, in determination, in fairness, in / deserving.
And, more and more, I cried.
—Peg Beck, "Periods of My Infertility"

In the true sense of the term, the middle class is defined not merely by the desire for material betterment but by a conscious, calculating effort to move up the ladder of success.
—Robert Bellah et al., *Habits of the Heart*

"A normative order," writes legal theorist Lewis A. Kornhauser, "divides our options in three: what we *must* do, what we *may* do, and what we *must not* do" (213, emphasis in the original). The Massachusetts mandate, as part of the normative system of the law, gives infertile individuals the option of pursuing medical treatment through economic support from their insurers. In the liberal story of the law, medical treatment is viewed as a *right* that the infertile may exercise if they choose to do so; this right creates a corresponding *obligation* for some other individual or institution, in this case, the insurer. Different normative orders may have competing notions of obligations, rights, and prohibitions that compel individuals to negotiate their differences. For example, from the perspective of another normative system—the middle-class—these same women adhere to an ethic of success embedded in the tradition of individualism. "In this conception," write Robert N. Bellah et al., "individuals, unfettered by family or other group affiliation, are given the chance to make the best of themselves, and, though equality of opportunity is essential, inequality of result is natural" (148–149). In this cultural narrative, success is achieved through hard work and persistence, a determined and conscious effort—which anthropologists David M. Schneider and Raymond Smith (20) take as the defining attribute of the contemporary American middle class—to make the most of life's opportunities and to create opportunities where none is seen. In this normative order, the person who desires to be successful is almost *obligated* to take advantage of opportunities.

The position of contemporary middle-class American women at this nexus of normative orders creates a conflict for them. To some degree, some middle-class white women, enculturated with narratives of success, experience the Massachusetts mandate an obligation as much as a right. Seeing insurance coverage as an opportunity to achieve the longed-for goal of pregnancy, some middle-class white women view medical treatment for infertility as an opportunity they cannot refuse. This conflict of options may not be as obvious as when, for example, the normative order of the law *requires* a behavior that the individual's moral values *prohibits*. Instead, the conflict is a matter of how the individual reads the text of the law. In other words, while a formalist would maintain that the statute clearly provides for an individual right, an interpretivist would maintain that not every individual understands the statute in the same way. And as Kenneth Burke reminds us, an individual's interpretation of concepts cannot be separated from situations in which that individual acts. The experience of middle-class white women thus both highlights the fuzzy boundary between rights and obligations (and the material consequences) and illustrates that this boundary is not the same for all legal subjects.

This chapter examines the topos of success for the middle-class white women in this study. Many of these women have experienced the myth of American success as reality. Those who have achieved success in education, career, and relationships sometimes attack the goal of fertility with the same tenacity. For some, the hard work of infertility pays off in the form of a pregnancy. For many women, however, pregnancy comes only after repeated failure, and for others, it does not come at all. Failing, often repeatedly, to achieve a pregnancy can shake a woman's sense of self-worth and her belief in the essential fairness of the world. She might come to see medical treatment for infertility as a right that can restore what she perceives to be a fundamental injustice, or she might come to redefine what it means to be successful and the ways in which success can be achieved.

This chapter shows that for some middle-class white women, unlimited access to reproductive technologies, as provided for by the Massachusetts mandate, appeals to their desire to "do all they can" in pursuit of a goal, sometimes making it difficult to determine when they have done "enough." As a result, these women sometimes become caught in a double bind: driven by both a sense of entitlement and a sense of obligation, they are drawn to a solution characterized as much by failure as by success.

Success and Failure in Medical Treatment for Infertility

Metaphors of success and failure saturate infertility treatment. Women might be termed "good responders" or "poor responders"; they might be told they have "premature ovarian failure," an "inadequate luteal phase," or an "incompetent cervix." One researcher studying infertility has noted, for example, that women in an artificial insemination program who decided to stop treatment were called "psychological dropouts," "poorly motivated," and "knowledge failures" (Schoysman-Deboeck et al., quoted in Sandelowski, "Compelled" 37). Self-help books echo this theme in their titles: *How to Be a Successful Fertility Patient* (Robin) and *The Pregnancy Prescription: The Success-Oriented Approach to Overcoming Infertility* (Melnick and Intrator). For good reason, metaphors of failure are of particular interest to feminist critics concerned with the pathologizing of women's bodies, who maintain that the portrayal of female bodily processes as abnormal promotes arguments for medical intervention (see, for example, Martin).

Metaphors of success and failure have particular resonance for women who are achievement-oriented, providing goals to which they can aspire. The process of infertility treatment is broken down into stages that provide opportunities for reaching these goals and for having what may be interpreted as microsuccesses. Initial workups often uncover nothing at all unusual or problems that can be addressed through limited interventions, such as fertility drugs or the timing of intercourse to coincide with ovulation. A drug might be prescribed to help a woman regulate her menstrual cycle. In many cases, the abnormal cycle is regularized by the drug, and the woman feels she has had a microsuccess. Even if she does not become pregnant, the woman often has no reason to stop treatment or to decide not to move to a more advanced treatment. Success at one stage compels her to move along to the next (Sandelowski, "Compelled" 39).

The same logic works during advanced interventions, such as in vitro fertilization. Unless a woman is in or is entering menopause, her ovaries can usually be stimulated into producing at least a few eggs. Retrieval of more than a few eggs is usually seen as success and compels optimism about the next step. The eggs are mixed with sperm and are allowed to incubate into embryos. While the fertilization of more eggs is considered more successful, simply getting one to fertilize means a chance at pregnancy. One or more embryos are then transferred to the uterus, and the woman waits to see whether a pregnancy test is positive. If the woman is pregnant, she waits to see whether the fetus can be brought to term. If the woman does not become pregnant or if she miscarries, she must decide whether to make another attempt.

Good results up to the point of implantation often create an incentive to try again. Paula, a woman who felt that she could stop treatment after eight IVF attempts, says that her physician was encouraging her to continue because she is a "good responder" and has had "spectacular" results. "The problem," she said, "is that everything worked except I didn't get pregnant. And so they kept trying again." Good results thus create a double bind: microsuccesses can compel someone to stay in treatment even when they have failed—sometimes repeatedly—with the outcome that matters most: a live birth. For Sheri, fertilization occurred in six out of eight cycles. These good results prompted her to continue. She says: "I think when you have fertilization your hope is more and your belief is there. You can say, well we have to make use of it. If there is no fertilization ever, we might have stopped after three, four, five, six cycles. I don't really know. We didn't have to make that decision." Even while the embryos were not implanting, the results seemed promising enough to keep going. Sheri interprets the good results as more than an incentive, however. Saying "we *have to make use* of [the fertilization]," she indicates a belief that to stop after such good results would be to waste an opportunity. In the face of such promise there is something of an obligation to continue.

The effect of the gradually progressive nature of treatment is not lost on patients, but they do not necessarily stop once they know that they may become caught up in treatment. Betsy and her husband, who had a low sperm count, were discouraged enough when fertilization failed to occur in an IVF procedure that they decided to stop and adopt. Betsy thinks, however, that she would have continued had fertilization occurred. She says: "It became very clear to us that it probably wasn't going to work for us. And maybe it would've, but we felt like we sort of reached, for us what was enough of a decision, and I didn't want to keep going through it. But I think that if I'd been given more hope I would have kept going. For a while anyway. . . . Where do you draw the line?" With her question "Where do you draw the line?" Betsy indicates an awareness of the pull of treatment, as well as a sense that success at one stage does not guarantee success at another, that fertilization does not necessarily mean pregnancy, and that becoming pregnant does not necessarily mean a live birth. The line is unclear because the only outcome that really matters is never certain even when all the steps leading up to it give reason for optimism.

Patients and physicians do not always agree on definitions of success. In some cases, a physician may not tell a patient whether her results were successful in medical terms. Susan, for example, recalls that for her first medicated IUI, "I responded with one follicle on each side and I was thrilled. I said, wow, this is cool. We used drugs and now I've got two. It's great." Susan did not realize at the time, and was not told by the medical staff, that two follicles are not considered a successful result in medical terms. Without knowing the medical interpretation, Susan considered the results successful and was optimistic that she would eventually become pregnant. Only after an IVF cycle resulting in a pregnancy and miscarriage and two more cancelled IVF cycles did she learn that her results had never been good. She says: "I didn't know that you could have a bad response. I thought I had had good responses. Nobody told me . . . that I was a poor responder all along. Nobody ever told me that."

Learning that she was a "poor responder" made Susan question not only whether to go on with more treatment but also whether she should have stopped sooner. "I don't know that it would've made a difference," she says, "but again, it might have. Any of these things might have triggered us to look at other options sooner." Susan's reaction illustrates how the normalizing process works at individual stages of treatment. Her physician considered her body's production of only two follicles so far below the norm as to be poor, but Susan found the results encouraging enough to continue with further treatment.

Other women disagreed with the evaluation of their physicians that they were doing well and should continue. Lisa eventually stopped treatment after five cycles of IVF and adopted a child. She recalls talking with her doctor in a follow-up visit after the fifth cycle failed. She remembers that "when he came in he said, 'Oh, you had a good cycle, and ya-da-da, and let's try again.' I said, 'I didn't have a good cycle,' I said, 'take a look.'" The doctor, she says, eventually admitted that she might want to think about trying another strategy or stopping treatment altogether. Lisa scheduled another cycle but decided in the interim not to go through with it.

For those accustomed to success, the inability to have a child can be a frustrating experience. For some women, infertility is the first major failure of their lives. Leslie, who had four miscarriages before carrying her son to term, says it is "because everything has come fairly easy, in a sense. Am I the brightest student in school? No, school's another issue. But . . . having a baby was the hardest thing I've ever been through." Although Leslie does not regard herself as a great academic achiever, she still sees her life as one in which her successes have come relatively easily. Some women compared themselves to their relatives, noting with frustration that they were unable to accomplish what others seemed to do effortlessly. Jennifer, whose husband had had a vasectomy, was undergoing artificial insemination by donor. She says: "We're really frustrated that [it's not happening]. This unexplained sort of thing. None of this stuff runs in my family. . . . My first cousins breed like rabbits. My mother came from a family of seven. The joke was all my grandfather had to do was take his tie off."

Other individuals feel rage. At a workshop on adopting after infertility, a woman told a story about wanting to attack a pregnant woman with a knife. Responding to her, the facilitator said, "You're angry because you're having to pay for what everyone else gets for free by making love." Embedded within this response is an assumption of entitlement. Rather than understanding the inability to have a child as a matter of divine will, personal responsibility, or bad luck, the facilitator sees it as a fundamental injustice. In this worldview, people have a right to be able to have children "for free" by making love; those who cannot do so justifiably become angry about the disparity. As the legal scholar Lawrence M. Friedman argues about the expectations of modern legal culture (what he calls "the republic of choice"), "when we face situations that are *not* of our choosing, it is not right that we should suffer adverse consequences" (100, emphasis in the original).

Many of the middle-class white women in this study were drawn to medicine as a resolution for infertility not only because it has been constructed as the preferred path but also because it resonated with their experiences. At one level, descriptions of treatment draw on metaphors of success and failure, which imply that individuals can play an active role in the outcome. At another level, the regime of treatment provides a variety of opportunities for those accustomed to working toward goals to believe that they are progressing toward pregnancy. Defining success in biomedical terms, they become frustrated when persistence does not guarantee the results that they had hoped for.

Working Hard at Infertility Treatment

In their classic text of class and gender roles in America, the anthropologists David M. Schneider and Raymond Smith write that while the American "lower and upper classes are at rest, relatively speaking," the middle class is characterized by "calculating attempts . . . to move up the ladder of success by the solid virtues of thrift, hard work, and calculated self-interest" (19–20). Many of the women in my study saw treatment as something at which they had to work in order to succeed. On an obvious level, RESOLVE's own name indicates the importance of determination and persistence. According to Merriam Webster, the verb "resolve" can mean "to deal with successfully" or "to find an answer to," senses that hint at the problematic nature of the issue in question. Infertility might thus be regarded as a problem, a puzzle, or a conflict that can be approached, known, and understood. Merriam Webster also defines the word "resolve" as a noun meaning "fixity of purpose: resoluteness."

The way to deal successfully with infertility, from this perspective, is with determination and perseverance. Many women in this study demonstrated perseverance through a willingness to try (or at least to consider) any medical treatment by continuing with medical treatment in spite of low success rates and by becoming active participants in their own care. For Sheri, this persistence manifested itself in her refusal to consider *not* parenting. "Childfree," she says, "is not an option." Ellen, a single woman who eventually had a daughter by artificial insemination, describes her determination this way: "I'm gonna have a child, no matter what. . . . I'm really determined to do this. I get more voracious about it daily. I'm like a fucking Amazon warrior. . . . I'm ready to go to the mat. Whatever it takes, surgery, in vitro, let's do it, and let's do it now." The metaphors Ellen uses illustrate the depth of her desire. Her hunger is increasingly voracious; she envisions herself as a warrior engaged in a fierce wrestling match, "ready to go to the mat." Unwilling to wait for her desire to be fulfilled, Ellen wants the most aggressive treatment available. Other women also envisioned themselves as facing a formidable challenge. Stephanie, for example, says, "It's this quest and it's like the holy grail and you just gotta get it." Similarly, the leader of a workshop on living without children after infertility said of herself, "I thought of myself as this heroine going through this trial and nothing was going to stand in my way."

Regarding infertility treatment as effort, most of the women in the study took an active role in their own care. Far from being passive recipients of whatever measures their physicians advised, most of the women in this study learned a great deal about infertility and used that knowledge to make decisions. Women learned by reading RESOLVE literature and books on infertility, talking with others going through treatment, belonging to support groups, reading information on the Internet, talking to their physicians, and attending symposia and workshops. Some women did not begin doing intensive research until after their first or second cycle of treatment did not work; perhaps these women had hoped that they would become pregnant right away and would not need to do further research.

As an organization, RESOLVE advises members to become active, informed patients. Patients are treated as consumers of medical care who should thoroughly investigate their options before choosing a path. In one newsletter published by RESOLVE of the Bay State, the president writes: "We are advocates of self-help; those who succeed in resolving infertility also succeed in becoming informed consumers of medical care, psychological counseling, adoption and related services. . . . You can break the monthly cycle of failure by gaining control over small decisions. Each decision you make can be an informed one if you learn from others who have been there before you" (Jette 1). In this worldview, knowledge is the key to success, and the individual is capable of (and responsible for) working to obtain this knowledge.

The message appeals to those who understand education as a route to success, who see problems as conquerable through a steady application of learning, and who see themselves as capable of understanding complex medical concepts. Knowledge is held not only by the so-called experts but also by those who have firsthand experience. As a result, the woman who wants to learn sees that learning takes place both in support groups and in more formalized settings, such as seminars and symposia; she places herself in a position to learn from both experts and peers. Sheri, for example, sees herself as capable of understanding her own medical condition even more than her physicians do. She says:

> I used to [have] a consistently 28-day cycle. Here and there maybe day 29. But it would never fluctuate, and now I could have a 54 day cycle.... It makes me think, boy these drugs are really manipulating stuff inside, so, it's a little scary. Not scary enough that I say no, but it makes me very aware. And it makes me become more educated about myself. I look at these doctors and they've got 2200 patients and I'm just one of them. But I know my own story best.

Unwilling to rely solely on the opinions of individual physicians about the possible dangers of fertility drugs, Sheri learns more about them herself. Educating herself becomes a means of self-advocacy.

Self-advocacy for Sheri also meant educating herself about procedures and facilities, a process that eventually led her to switch clinics in order to get care from an embryologist with a good reputation for doing a particular procedure. The change, however, required Sheri to relinquish a certain amount of control over her own care. She explains: "[Leaving the facility] was a hard decision and I think also an emotionally challenging decision because I had had three years with this facility.... I could tell them what to do.... Sadly, every person in there knew me, along with the pharmacist." Sheri's drive for success and her understanding of herself as an important component in that success led her to become more educated in her treatment. But the knowledge she gained through this process led her to a decision that placed her in a double bind: leaving the clinic she had been with for years meant leaving an environment she felt she could control because of her knowledge of the clinic, whereas not leaving meant ignoring the new knowledge that she had gained about another facility.

For many of the women in this study, much of the work of infertility treatment is doing battle with insurers about coverage, sometimes even if the insurer is legally obligated to pay for treatment. Less than three years after the mandate passed, the newsletter published by RESOLVE of the Bay State included an article informing readers of the current problems in compelling coverage (Crockin, "Insurance"). In Sheri's case, her husband's company was self-insured and did not have to cover treatment. After voluntarily covering it for some time, the company decided to change the amount that employees were required to contribute and to place a dollar amount cap on the benefits. When they learned of the change in policy, Sheri and her husband felt compelled to fight it even though they would need to identify themselves as infertile. She remembers that it was "pretty bad to have to do that, but it was not going to happen being a silent partner in the team." She recalls spending a month making phone calls, gathering information about what other companies covered as "reasonable and customary" treatment for infertility before sitting down with benefits administrators at her husband's place of employment. At this meeting, the employer's representatives reiterated that they were in line with what other self-insured companies offered and were under no legal obligation to offer any coverage. Sheri eventually bought her own insurance that covered the treatment.

When trying to compel insurers to cover treatment, experts advise persistence. Two booklets, one developed by RESOLVE and one by the infertility drug company Serono Symposia, advise infertility patients to become their own "insurance advocates." Both tell patients to research their insurance plans to determine what is and is not covered, to understand what coverage is legally required in their state, to keep records, and to ask that denials of coverage be put in writing. The booklet produced by RESOLVE, written by a financial counselor who specializes in infertility, also gives detailed advice for becoming a persistent self-advocate. Early on, the author counsels patients, "Don't take NO for an answer. . . . Remember, you have a right to the coverage as stated in your contract and a right to pursue your claim, so don't stop asking questions and don't take no for an answer until you are satisfied" (RESOLVE, *Infertility Insurance* 3, emphasis in the original). If necessary, he advises patients to contact their insurance commissioner or to hire an attorney to compel an insurer to cover procedures.

Lawrence M. Friedman argues that the tendency to "make use of, enforce, and invoke rights . . . in particular against the *government* and other bulky institutions" (97, emphasis in the original) is a mark of the modern citizen. Getting coverage, either from an insurer who is legally obligated to cover infertility or from one who is not, requires a kind of persistence that probably comes in part from knowing your rights, from having a sense of your rights and the belief that they are not usually violated, and from the sense that you are right and that the law will come to your aid if necessary. This sense might not exist for those for whom the system does not always seem to work—people with a lower income, those with no formal education, and people of color, for instance.

Compelling coverage also requires time, access to a telephone for much of the working day, a certain literacy, an ability to extract information from unwilling sources, and a knowledge of how to negotiate the chain of command. Many of the women in this study also demonstrated an unwillingness to take no for an answer. Sheri made certain that she talked to the highest-level person available, contested many bills, and researched the coverage provided by other insurers. She spent a lot of time on the phone (something she could do, she said, because she worked at home). Similarly, Stephanie hired an attorney to compel her insurer to send her to a clinic that would treat her at age thirty-nine, and Ellen began throwing away bills that she was convinced she did not have to pay.

For those accustomed to working hard to obtain a goal, persistence is more than just a strategy; it is an expectation. Those who really want to succeed at treatment will educate themselves and work hard. For these individuals, treatment for infertility becomes something of a job, where one must perform well in order to be rewarded. But persistence itself is not enough. As Sheri says, "I don't look at that as something to be proud of. . . . Some people look at me and say, oh my god, she's done eight [in vitro fertilization cycles], wow. And I think it is nothing to feel successful about." For Sheri, persistence is no achievement without success.

Investing in Infertility Treatment

Many of the women in this study did not wait a full twelve months before seeking medical intervention. They expected not that pregnancy would occur immediately but that it would occur eventually, within some "reasonable" amount of time. At the point where people are first attempting pregnancy (through intercourse, for married heterosexuals, and through insemination by a donor for single women and those in same-sex relationships), a certain amount of effort is expected before the reward of pregnancy can be attained. Sheri and her husband waited only three months before having his sperm analyzed, "because it seemed a pretty easy thing to do." In Sheri's mind, three months was a reasonable amount of time to attempt pregnancy before being successful.

This paradigm is extended when couples begin medical treatment for infertility and when single women and lesbian couples move to more advanced reproductive procedures. With faith in medicine to put things right, individuals and couples tend to hope that they can be quickly diagnosed and cured over a relatively short period. Some might expect to become pregnant after the first month of treatment or might have friends or family with similar expectations. Stephanie, for example, who was in treatment for five years before having twins through IVF, remembers "telling somebody and they'd say, oh yeah, my cousin took pills and she got pregnant the next month." Most of the women in this study, however, like those in other studies on infertility (see, for example, Sandelowski, "Compelled" 36), expected treatment to last at least several months.

Sheri, who had friends with infertility problems, envisioned her own medical treatment on the basis of her friends' experiences. She remembers: "I had a bunch of friends who were in treatment, so it wasn't something that was new to me. And I was very involved in thinking I understood what they were doing. And saying uh huh, uh huh, oh. And then of course they got pregnant. . . . My vision was doing IUI. I thought, . . . I'll go in and we'll do a few IUIs and we'll be all set." For Sheri, a few IUIs fit with her expectations regarding the amount of effort necessary to get pregnant. Even though she might have hoped to become pregnant on the first attempt, she assumed that she would have to do "a few" before becoming pregnant.

Some fertility specialists recommend that people think in terms of courses of treatment rather than individual tries. A physician at a Boston-area clinic comments:

> Often one has to be thinking . . . , if we're gonna give it a good college try we really need to be thinking in terms of three cycles. But you know, the medical aspects of it and the reality of people's lives and how they make decisions are two separate things. So if you said, I want to win megabucks, I would say, you're gonna have to keep playing megabucks, but you may decide that that's not a good way for you to spend your money or your time. And you want to go back to college and get a better education and earn the money instead of trying to win the money. So it's analogous: if your goal is to win megabucks then you're gonna have to play. But that may not be the best decision for you because the odds are low. Whereas for some of these folks the odds are going to be very high with IVF and they should keep trying. If they can see their way clear to do it, emotionally, financially and in terms of their time.

There is a sense, then, that patients must decide to invest a certain amount of resources (for example, time, money, emotions) in the business of becoming pregnant but also that, as with all business decisions, infertility treatment is a gamble. In her description of the decision-making process, this physician appeals to middle-class understandings of the business world. According to this worldview, taking risks can make sense if the odds are good and if the cost of failure is not too high. A smart investor, however, must sometimes move to lower-risk ventures (for example, by getting an education and earning money rather than playing the lottery). As in other areas of business, the individual or couple in infertility treatment makes such decisions based on the probabilities for success, on an assessment of the costs involved, and on an evaluation of the potential benefit. In a cultural climate where children are understood as priceless, however, no risk is too extreme for some doctors and their patients (Becker and Nachtigall, "Born" 514).

Many of the women in my study used metaphors of investment and risk to describe their treatment options and decisions. They talk about "spending" time and money (if not their own, then that of their insurance company); about "investing" energy and hope; about the emotional costs of particular approaches or treatments; and about risks and "chances" for success. One woman, who decided she would quit after three cycles of treatment, became pregnant with twins on the third cycle. She described the event as "hitting the jackpot." A facilitator at a workshop on living without children after infertility tells the audience, "You are not obligated to go through this for the rest of your life. . . . There is a point at which you are shelling out too much capital and not getting any return and it's time to change your investment." While most of the members of the audience might have had insurance coverage for their treatment, there was still a sense that treatment "costs" something.

Financial costs are a consideration even when insurance is picking up the tab. Lynne, for example, had been undergoing treatment for a little less than a year, at the expense of her insurer. Yet she still thought of her treatment options in terms of investment, saying, "if [medical treatment] doesn't work, then [you] may be faced with the adoption route, and you have to sort of say, what's a better chance? Where . . . is my money better spent?" Lynne knew that adoption would cost her money out of pocket, and so deciding to stop treatment and adopt would be a certain increase in cost for her. She realized, however, that success (when defined as parenting) is not guaranteed with either medical treatment or adoption.

Similarly, Sheri's insurance company had paid over $38,000 over four years for her medical treatment. While Sheri and her husband had paid only $600 in out-of-pocket expenses, she still had a sense that money had been spent, on their behalf, by the insurance company and the clinic. As a savvy consumer, she wanted good value. After her insurer refused to cover about $1,000 worth of expenses, for example, she wrote to ask a physician to waive his fees for a particular procedure. Sheri remembers: "I wrote him a letter and I said I'm having difficulty paying this. And the truth is we could have paid it. I mean we could have. But I thought, there's no way. At least they've gotten $38,000 from us, from our insurance company. We're not walking away free. The other is, we haven't had success, and I think, I was feeling a little bit damaged that we keep going there. They're sucking in all this money, and we're walking out with nothing."

While the $38,000 did not come directly from Sheri's pocket, she still felt ownership of the money. If it hadn't been for her treatment, the clinic would never have been paid by her insurer. As a result, she felt entitled to some results. In asking the doctor to waive his fees, Sheri was not getting the results she was hoping for, but she was, in some sense, seeking a rebate. Because they had not had good results, she reasoned, they shouldn't have to pay the money that her insurer would not provide. Her physician agreed to waive the fees.

Not all women in my study, however, felt the same sense of entitlement as Sheri. Lisa, who eventually stopped treatment and adopted, felt less inclined to demand good treatment, because the money was not coming out of her own pocket. She says: "If there had not been this amount of coverage available to me and if I had not been speaking with [a friend who was also in treatment], I don't think I would have made all these attempts. And I certainly would have given them more feedback. I had spoken to them when they made [a mistake], but I think, if I had been spending my own money I'd have been even more vocal."

Single women and those in same-sex couples are often even more financially depleted before they are diagnosed with medical infertility. In most cases, these women must pay for both office procedures and sperm until a physician has determined that there is an underlying physical problem preventing pregnancy. At that point, many single women and those in same-sex couples continue to pay for sperm while their insurers pick up the cost of any medical procedures. Before they reach this point, however, some of these women have undergone up to a year of inseminations purchased out of pocket.

Kim and her partner were lucky in that their health care provider did not charge them for office visits even before her partner was diagnosed with an ovulation disorder. Still, because they had to pay for the sperm, they spent $3,000 on thirteen attempts at artificial insemination before her partner became pregnant. Later, they decided to have a second child. When Kim became pregnant on her first attempt, she was relieved because they had already depleted their "baby money." She says: "We started saving in one account, baby money, so that we would have savings just to use to get pregnant. And we continued doing that while we were trying to get pregnant with the first child. We built it up and then we used that money. But we didn't do anything like that with the second one. We were just using our own money." The pregnancy with their first child did not deplete finances set aside for other uses, but the second pregnancy did. Had it taken longer than one month, the second pregnancy would have become a financial burden.

Several women spoke of their emotional "reserves." Susan felt that medical treatment had so depleted her emotionally that she would not have enough emotional energy left for adoption. One reason that women, in particular, become emotionally exhausted is because of the cyclical nature of infertility treatment, a process some call a "roller coaster," a "merry-go-round," or a "whirlwind." At the beginning of each new treatment cycle, a woman's hopes are raised as she contemplates the possibility of becoming pregnant. Along the way, results might make her more or less hopeful that the procedure will work. If a pregnancy test at the end of the cycle is negative, or if the cycle is cancelled for some reason, she might become depressed, frustrated, or angry. For most assisted reproductive procedures, the woman's emotional state can also be affected by the hormones she is taking to stimulate ovulation. Some women experience severe mood swings as a result of the hormones, intensifying the already emotional event.

For many women in this study, time is also a precious resource. Sheri wanted to start trying to have children soon after getting married, although her husband wanted to wait two years. She says, "I cried and said, it has to be a year. And I don't think it was really age related for me or for him. I just think there was something about, I don't know, trying because you never know." Although Sheri says that her urgency was not age related (at the time, she was thirty-one), it is clear that she either wanted to allow enough time to get treated (if there was a problem) or to avoid any problems altogether by trying when the odds were better (that is, when she was younger).

Time is precious especially as a woman gets older and sees menopause approaching. Ellen, single and forty-one by the time she started artificial insemination, wanted the most aggressive treatment available so that she could become pregnant before entering menopause. Similarly, Anne, who became pregnant after her fifth home-based artificial insemination, was annoyed that her clinic did not advocate intrauterine inseminations (which have a higher success rate) over home-based inseminations. Their clinic, which caters mostly to lesbian couples, aims as part of its philosophy to help women become pregnant at home, where they are more likely to feel comfortable and in control, rather than in a medical environment. Anne, however, felt that this approach meant that many women were not given access to the procedures most likely to produce results. She says: "Why didn't they tell us this, because people are spending a lot of money. They're investing a lot of energy. A lot of times people are older and don't have a lot of time to be screwing around with it." Because most of these procedures are not covered by insurance, the investment at risk is monetary as well as temporal.

For women who have embryos in storage, the passage of time has different implications. Sarah, who had one child without assistance and had twins by IVF, had frozen an embryo that was not transferred back to her body during her last in vitro procedure. She knows that she can use that embryo, even after menopause, to have another child. The issue for Sarah, then, is not whether she will wait so long that she no longer has viable eggs but whether becoming pregnant later in life is a wise decision. She contemplates becoming pregnant again: "I could imagine having more. I happen to really greatly enjoy pregnancy and breast feeding. And part of it also is letting go, getting older, coming to the end of your fertility. It's difficult. So I still fantasize about it, but the realistic voice takes over: we don't have any more bedrooms, we already have three kids to put through school, we're already running in the red just doing day care. I'm going to be 40 in November. My husband's going to be 44. Do I really want to extend the period where I can't live my own life another two years?" For Sarah, then, time is also a resource that can be used up. Time must be managed so that her other resources (for example, money and space) are not depleted.

How women interpreted the wisdom of their investment (of time, energy, and money) often depended on whether their investment paid off (that is, whether they became pregnant and had a child). Their interpretation may also reflect the economic class of the patient. In her study of middle-income and low-income women, for example, Margarete Sandelowski found that the middle-income women were more likely to find waiting for one year before treatment as "a waste of precious time"

("Compelled" 36). In my study, some of those women who did not become pregnant talk about having "wasted time" by undergoing treatment. Lisa, a woman who eventually stopped treatment and started adoption proceedings, says that "I think it just wasted several years that maybe I could have been putting my effort somewhere else." Susan, who also eventually adopted, speaks of wasting not only time but also energy and optimism. Stephanie, however, who had twins through IVF, says that she would not undergo medical treatment for another child but would do it again if she had none. She says, "Would I do it again . . . for a third child? No. Would I do it again if I didn't have children? Oh, yeah. I'm an idiot." Stephanie's response is not unusual for those who have children through assisted reproduction. While they look back on the treatment as difficult and painful, the end result—a child—makes it seem worth the effort.

Deciding That Enough Is Enough

A frequent theme in the RESOLVE literature, at meetings and symposia, and in self-help books on infertility is the problem of deciding when "enough is enough." When insurance does not pay for infertility procedures, individuals and couples often have compelling financial reasons for stopping treatment. If they do not stop, they may wipe out their life savings, may indebt themselves beyond recovery, or may forgo other financial goals such as a home or a secure retirement. When coverage is virtually unlimited, as in Massachusetts, however, patients often have to find other reasons for stopping and for evaluating whether the other costs are worth the results. Lisa, who stopped treatment and adopted a child, put it this way: "There's always a question, I think, what price to achieve a goal?"

RESOLVE's stated goal is helping each individual or couple come to this decision, in their own way and in their own time. Some people may have difficulty conceiving and never seek medical care, reaching "resolution" without ever becoming part of the cycle of medical decision making. There is an assumption in RESOLVE, however, that those unable to conceive will seek medical care, at least for diagnosis. Diagnosis frequently leads to at least some medical procedures, such as hormone therapy, so that the infertile are rarely in a position to ask whether the initiation of medical treatment is appropriate. Instead, the question remains: when to stop?

For women in my study, deciding to stop medical treatment sometimes meant redefining success. For some, the process meant realizing either that they should try a different path to the same goal or that they needed to reevaluate the end goal itself. Sheri was accepting adoption as a different way to achieve the success of parenting. She says: "I have a friend who after three months of finishing her home study just brought home a baby a couple of days ago. . . . So, it's like my first reality of somebody I actually know, who's a friend, who [is] going to be with this child. So I think that reality might be a good one for me to be part of to believe. Because all the other babies I know are all IVF babies. And that's my belief. We know it works. Just hasn't with us." Sheri had seen a lot of other people go though infertility treatment and end up with a biologically related child. From her observations, then, it was possible to be successful with medical treatment. Seeing the problem of infertility solved in another way—through adoption—made it possible for Sheri to see that she could be successful by other means.

Accommodating the idea of success by means other than medical treatment can mean revisiting the goals that originally motivated a woman (or couple) to start treatment. Sheri found that she needed to separate her desire from her goal: "in the end, . . . wanting it so badly, sometimes you get confused about what is it you want." When I contacted Sheri again after a year, she had done one more IVF cycle and had decided to stop treatment and adopt. The decision had been easy, she said, because she realized that her goal had always been to be a parent rather than to be pregnant. If she continued in treatment, she could go another year without having a baby. Still, she reflected that had their results been better all along, she might still be doing treatment. "I still believe it can work," she says, "but it doesn't look like it will work for us."

Of the women who eventually adopted children, several mentioned having to refocus on the goal of parenting rather than on the goal of pregnancy. Lisa, for example, realized that she really wanted to become a mother, through the biological route or through adoption. She says: "Every once in a while I think, well it would be nice to have a child, a biological child, but it's not an issue for me anymore. And I think going through this infertility stuff and being surrounded by it, I was sort of submerged in that whole thinking in those terms of achieving a pregnancy, and I think now my major thought is, that I just want to be a mother. And it's not as important to me." Here Lisa both adopts terminology used by the medical profession ("achieving a pregnancy") and uses its definition of success to refocus on her initial goal (becoming a parent). Now, no longer "thinking in those terms" (that is, those of the medical establishment), Lisa is able to evaluate her resolution as one that fulfills her needs.

Only one of the women I interviewed was no longer pursuing either medical treatment or adoption. Lynne had been undergoing treatment for about a year when I first spoke with her. Five months later, she was no longer trying to have a child. Instead she was working on a graduate degree and interviewing for a new job. "Children," she said, "have fallen way down on our list of priorities. Perhaps we've done this on purpose to rationalize away the emotions or perhaps it's just coincidence."

As these women learned, infertility treatment does not work for everyone; not everyone can "achieve" a pregnancy. Betsy, who adopted two children after trying in vitro fertilization for male factor infertility, thinks that the medical establishment does not help infertility patients consider all their options, especially the option of stopping. She says, "It just feels like there's sort of this attitude, if you just keep at it, we'll get you pregnant. And the truth is, that's not true. That's a lie." Similarly, Sheri found that hard work doesn't always pay off. She says: "[Deciding that the next cycle will be our last] definitely was a hard decision, I think because we were trying so hard and it hasn't worked. And I think if this next cycle were to work, I think I'd just forget that I even did any of these cycles. If it doesn't work I'm not going to forget that I did these." The decision to stop medical treatment and consider adoption is difficult because of Sheri's belief that hard work should bring rewards. As with other hard-won goals, she believed that having a biological child would make her forget how hard it had been. But if that goal were not realized, the memory of all that medical treatment would not go away. Implicit in this reasoning is the idea that hard work is something that is inherently valuable and can be exchanged for something else of value. In this case, the hard work of medical treatment could be "exchanged" for a child in the sense that it would be erased from memory. But if no child resulted, she would have nothing to show for the work of medical treatment.

For many of those accustomed to succeeding when they have worked hard, failure at infertility treatment is unacceptable. According to Gay Becker and Robert Nachtigall:

> The medicalisation process effectively limits acceptable outcomes to one, the biological production of a child. Alternative social solutions, such as remaining childless, adoption, and other modes of incorporating children into daily life, such as fostering others' children, are apparently viewed as more undesirable once a biomedical approach is initiated because they symbolise a dual failure: the failure to conceive and the failure to be cured. ("Eager" 468)

In other words, an individual or couple might be unwilling to stop treatment because it means that they have failed not once but twice. For many, the second failure is as much a failure of willpower and determination as it is the failure to be cured. This fear of failure helps to create a double bind. Unwilling to succumb to a failure of perseverance, a woman might continue with medical treatment even if success by this route looks unlikely.

Resisting this double bind, for some of the women in this study, meant reevaluating the opposing choices. If a woman defines success only in medical terms, then stopping treatment short of pregnancy and birth cannot be reconciled with her desire to succeed. If she can define success differently—by deciding on a goal other than pregnancy—then medical treatment can be ended without the perception of failure. As these women have demonstrated, however, embracing new goals is not a simple process.

The Massachusetts Mandate: Encouraging Persistence

Although some women who do not have children through assisted reproduction say that they regret having undergone treatment because of the wasted time or energy, many others feel differently. They feel that having the ability to participate in the treatment made it possible for them to "do all they could" in pursuit of their goal of having a biological child.

At several points, Sheri indicated that she was motivated in part by the desire to believe that she had done all she could. When discussing her decision to switch clinics after repeated failure at her first, she says, "If it is successful, I'll of course say, this is the best thing I ever did. And if it's not, I'll never question, I really should have changed." Similarly, a leader of a discussion on living without children said that having surgery to remove fibroid tumors "made me feel that I had done all that I could." She went through another six years of treatment after the surgery, and her husband explained that "we wanted to exhaust every mainstream possibility" to avoid having any regrets later.

Margarete Sandelowski, who has studied infertile women in the working and middle classes, notes that the fear of having regrets later is a motivating factor particularly for those in the middle class. She writes:

> For couples in my research, giving up and then regretting it was much more powerful as an incentive for persisting in treatment than any cultural mandate to reproduce. Especially for middle-income respondents—both unused to waiting for (as one economically less privileged woman put it) "God [to be] ready" for them to have babies and accustomed to setting and meeting goals—infertility was either the first obstacle they had ever faced or the first one they found difficult or impossible to overcome. Indeed, for them it was quitting, not persistence, that seemed to require explanation and justification. After all, if winners never quit, then quitters can certainly never win. ("Compelled" 41)

Similarly, Becker and Nachtigall found that the women in their study (almost all of whom were middle class and white) "felt unable to pursue other options until all possible avenues of medical treatment had been exhausted" ("Eager" 462). Even then, quitting can be seen as failure; as the leader of a workshop on adoption noted, "Those of us who are high achievers hear, 'you failed.'"

A critique of the mandate as an instance of liberal legal thinking might note that not all infertile individuals seem similarly able (or likely) to persist when negotiating the contractual relationship of insurance. Certainly those without health insurance are unable to take part in this relationship. Even those with health insurance are most likely to be "successful" in getting coverage when they have a sense of their rights and know how to demand them. A woman like Sheri, who works out of her home, has the time and the mental and physical resources to get what she feels she deserves. But women like Sheri might be more likely to put so much of their energy and faith into the "resolution" provided by health insurance that they not seriously consider other options until medical avenues have failed.

The Massachusetts mandate might thus be regarded as creating a double bind for the middle-class woman. Susan, who eventually adopted a child, explains: "Insurance coverage is a blessing and a curse. . . . It has allowed us the chance without worrying about financial strain, but it also confuses the end, so it causes emotional and relationship strain, and it makes it harder to answer, when is enough enough? If we didn't have insurance coverage, maybe one try at IVF, maybe no tries, maybe we would have taken that money and just gone to adoption."

Insurance thus acts as an incentive for those who are accustomed to taking advantage of opportunities for success. For some individuals and couples, this incentive might be transformed into an obligation. Margarete Sandelowski says that the infertile "can suffer the opprobrium of failure, not just because they fail to reproduce, but because they fail to *try* to reproduce. . . . American couples with the financial means and the medical, psychological, and social profile to be accepted into treatment programs . . . now bear a new set of obligations distinctively associated with their privileged access" ("Compelled" 32, emphasis in the original). With this dual sense that they are exercising rights and fulfilling responsibilities, some middle-class white women experience the Massachusetts mandate as both a resource and a problem. Without insurance, most individuals and couples must stop medical treatment when they deplete their resources. With insurance, many women are able to feel that they have "done all that they can" to have a biological child. Determining the point at which they have done enough, however, is a new and challenging territory.

The Double Binds of the Drive for Success in Infertility Treatment

In a culture and century dominated by significant medical advances, Americans most often understand their own infertility as a medical problem that both deserves medical attention and can likely be alleviated. The Massachusetts mandate embodies both this faith in the medical approach and what Lawrence M. Friedman calls "a heightened sense of entitlement" (60). Understood as an injustice, infertility is seen as deserving a remedy that is at least partially provided by a social safety net. But the mandate is not simply a resource from which individuals can draw in order to fulfill their personal goals. It is also a means by which those motivated by the drive for success feel compelled to enter—and remain in—a regimen of treatment that is defined as much by failure as it is by success.

Middle-class white women who experience infertility, for whatever reason, sometimes face the first major failure of their lives. Those who are goal-oriented and accustomed to achievement through hard work might enter into medical treatment with high hopes, fueled by a belief in technology and a faith in their ability to see treatment through to a successful conclusion. Many of them will become pregnant and have children. In 1997, for example, infertility clinics reported 24,582 babies born from 71,826 cycles of IVF, ZIFT, and GIFT (U.S. Centers for Disease Control 9–10); these numbers do not include those who will become pregnant through less advanced means, such as induced ovulation or IUI. It is the hope of becoming one of the successful, perhaps, as well as the fear of failing to persevere, that keeps many patients going, even when the odds seem to be against them.

At least for the present, however, many individuals and couples will never have children as a result of treatment for infertility. For this reason, we might consider contemporary treatment for infertility as much about failure as it is about success. I argue, however, that medical treatment is in large part about failure for other reasons. Individuals enter into medical treatment because of reproductive failure; the very existence of the medical approach presupposes that those who seek it out have failed to reproduce on their own. More important, the medical regimen itself gives patients many opportunities for microsuccesses, even when the only success that really matters—a live birth—remains elusive.

Along the way, constant monitoring and intervention—the normalizing process of infertility treatment—raise the possibility of multiple kinds of failure; infertility, after all, is understood as a complex process often caused by more than one factor. Finally, and perhaps most important, the focus of infertility treatment on the production of a pregnancy, rather than on correction of the underlying anomaly, helps to distinguish both success and failure. While this approach results in more pregnancies (and therefore more success in medical terms), it emphasizes the failure of the individual or couple to procreate without assistance. No matter how hard they worked at infertility treatment or how much faith they have in medical science, those who have children with assistance often continue to regard their children as miracles; they understand that they are still unable to have children without assistance. Regardless of whether treatment results in a child, the infertile at some level have failed both to *be* normal and to *become* normal.

In the previous chapter, I argued that legal arguments supporting insurance coverage for infertility rely on the claim that medical treatment is not only reasonable but necessary. Such a claim is essential if insurers are to be required to cover the treatment. While individuals are certainly under no formal or legal obligation to seek the treatment for which the mandate provides, many of the middle-class white women in this study perceived it as an opportunity they could not refuse. The preferred pathway to parenthood is the one authorized and provided by this coverage: the biomedical path. When a woman follows this path, she tends to measure success in biomedical terms, but the biomedical model is one defined by failure as much as by success. Her desire to succeed, coupled with a desire to follow only one path, creates a double bind that is not necessarily resolved by the conception and delivery of a biological child. Most likely still unable to achieve pregnancy "naturally," she may feel she has not reentered the realm of the normal. The distinction between the normal and the abnormal, then, has been emphasized rather than eliminated.

4

Order and Discontinuity

The biological clock ticks on with speed,
Where is the extra time we need?
—Maria McNaught, "Dream Baby"

Exercise, having become an element in the political technology of the body and of duration, does not culminate in a beyond, but tends towards a subjection that has never reached its limit.
—Michel Foucault, *Discipline and Punish*

To many, bringing a child into the world is an expected life event that marks the entrance to adulthood (Greil 64). The inability to complete this event is often experienced as disruption in the way that life is supposed to be ordered, both temporally and psychically (Becker, "Metaphors"). Those unable to have children may feel frustrated by their inability to carry out their life plans. Infertility can also be experienced as a break in generational continuity, as becoming a parent establishes a link that connects past and future generations. As a former president of RESOLVE of the Bay State puts it, "The potential threat to genetic continuity deprives infertile people of the *illusion* of immortality that comforts fertile contemporaries" (Berson, emphasis added). The infertile, then, may feel burdened by the desire to create the future, a desire that they seem unable to fulfill. Those who seek medical treatment for childlessness are in some sense attempting to restore the normal sense of continuity—what they see as the natural order—that they have lost.

This chapter takes the view that our conceptual systems—our ways of making sense of the world—are themselves metaphorical. We impose structure and frameworks on the world in order to make sense of it by categorizing, ranking, arranging, organizing, and delimiting. In other words, we develop concepts by imposing relational orders that attempt to interpret patterns or structures as well as rank, prioritize, or otherwise organize the items in those patterns. In *The Order of Things,* Foucault maintains that "there is nothing more tentative, nothing more empirical (superficially, at least) than the process of establishing an order among things; nothing that demands a sharper eye or a surer, better-articulated language; nothing that more insistently requires that one allow oneself to be carried along by the proliferation of qualities and forms" (xix–xx). This process of ordering is continual and recursive, based on interactions with the external world and on reassessments of our language-based experience. This chapter also presupposes that order is a culturally contingent concept, that the "fundamental codes of a culture—those governing its language, its schemas of perception, its exchanges, its techniques, its values, the hierarchy of its practices—establish for every man [sic], from the very first, the empirical orders which he will be dealing and within which he will be at home" (Foucault, *Order* xx).

The sense of order as continuity is a characteristic of American culture at the turn of the millennium. Contemporary Americans share the belief not only that "life should be predictable, knowable, and continuous" but also that the individual plays the primary role in maintaining continuity (Becker, "Metaphors" 401). In this climate of individualism, the infertile individual feels compelled to act to restore order. Understanding herself as both capable of and responsible for regaining control of a chaotic event, the infertile middle-class white woman may draw on those resources that may have served her in the past and those to which she may feel entitled: law and medicine.

These resources are not without their own narratives of order, however. Medical treatment for infertility, as part of the discourse of science, is infused with what Lyotard has called "the principle of a general progress in humanity" in the West during the nineteenth and twentieth centuries (77). According to this principle, humanity moves forward through advances in science, technology, the arts, and other arenas of knowledge. In infertility treatment, the potential of such advances sometimes encourages hope that successful treatments are just around the corner. The narrative of progress sustaining these hopes, however, has no defined end goal. Advances in knowledge are instead part of a process of continual improvement. As in the narratives of evolution (biological and social), progress points toward an infinite horizon that can never be reached. Individuals undergoing treatment for infertility are caught between these two narratives of order. On the one hand, the narrative of continuity helps to construct the end goal of pregnancy, because parenthood through pregnancy is part of the natural continuity of life. On the other, the narrative of progress that sustains medical treatment means that successful intervention is always on—or just over—the horizon. In other words, the narrative of progress in medicine can compel the infertile to stay in treatment until the end goal of pregnancy is reached. Understanding the maintenance of continuity as an individual responsibility, the infertile may feel required to submit to continuous improvement through treatment. The Massachusetts mandate, by providing almost unlimited access to this treatment, makes this continuous improvement a preferred path.

In this chapter, I describe the double binds created by such narratives of order. Expecting the ability to become biological parents, to plan the timing of children, to provide grandchildren to their own parents, and to establish their own genetic legacy for the future, those who are unable to conceive may not know how to continue with their lives. With infertility experienced as a disruption in expected life plans, medical treatment offers a remedy, a means by which the "natural" order can be restored. Yet for some of the middle-class white women in my study, medical treatment for infertility—and especially the virtually limitless treatment for which the Massachusetts mandate provides—places them in a double bind. While individuals and couples hope to be able to restore order, to "get on with their lives," infertility treatment is often experienced as limbo, a process that offers hope around every corner while simultaneously delaying the moment at which they might choose nonmedical solutions. For some, the biological clock speeds up while the process of medical treatment stretches out into eternity.

Reproductive Life Plans

The narrative of continuity informing the decisions of many of the women in my study includes shared values about the appropriateness of the timing of children. Some women remembered wanting children all their lives, while others developed the desire as adults. All the women, however, shared a sense that there are more and less appropriate times to have children and that the most appropriate times are after becoming part of a stable relationship or after establishing a career. Their shared values resonate with those that seem to be common among white middle-class women in contemporary America, who do not generally have children without a partner (although there is a greater trend to do so) or before establishing a career. In this value system, individuals prepare for careers through education and training, ideally meet mates in their twenties or thirties, and then consider having children.

Ellen, for example, a forty-two-year-old single attorney, had always wanted to have children. When we first spoke, she had undergone nine inseminations (artificial insemination and IUI) over the course of a year. Her doctor was not hopeful that she would become pregnant, and she was contemplating asking for more advanced intervention, such as IVF. If she did not become pregnant after exhausting all of her medical alternatives, Ellen planned to try to adopt a child, even though she considered it prohibitively expensive and knew that she might need to borrow the money from her parents.

Even though she was contemplating adoption, Ellen very much wanted to see what she called "a little me" in the form of a child. For Ellen, like many others, this biological connection creates a sense of continuation with the future as one's genetic material moves "forward" even after one's death. With heterosexual couples, biological connections can also bind two people together with each other. Ellen reflects that "there's a time that you recall that your mother looks at you and goes, oh, that's just like your dad or that's just like me." While she would not experience that kind of connection with a partner, she wanted to feel that connection with a child.

Biological connections are also sometimes seen as securing one's own future. Anne, a thirty-five-year-old woman with a same-sex partner and a daughter through artificial insemination, says: "I think I started feeling mortal in some ways, like what would I be like when I'm old and would I be alone, and seeing my parents, my mother (my father's passed away), seeing my mother and her aging and me taking care of her in some ways, and her doing that for her parents. That seemed like something that was wonderful about the human race, that we can do that for one another." While the presence of children does not guarantee help or companionship in later years, some people see this as one reason to have children (Carter and Carter 98).

Ellen's desire to have children became stronger as she turned thirty-five. She had hoped to find a man with whom to have a child, but none of her relationships had worked out. As she approached forty, she began to consider having a child on her own. Her fortieth birthday meant to her that her time was running out and that she could not afford to delay any further. "I think when you turn 40," she says, "you start realizing what is important in life and what isn't." For her, family became much more important. Friends, she says, come and go, but "your family is always your family." Turning forty made her realize that if she wanted to build her own family (in her case, by having children), she would have to do it alone.

Like other women in this study, Ellen saw thirty-five as an important marker in a woman's reproductive life. Although there is some disagreement among fertility specialists about when women should expect a decline in fertility, specialists tend to agree that advice and treatment for infertility should differ according to the woman's age. A 1982 study published in the *New England Journal of Medicine,* for example, shows that fecundity (the "capacity" for procreation, as opposed to fertility, or "actual" procreation) begins dropping off after age thirty (Fédération CECOS, Schwartz, and Mayaux). In an editorial in the same issue, fertility specialists argue that the results of this study indicate a need to change the counseling given women seeking help for infertility (DeCherney and Berkowitz). Similarly, an informational video on infertility recommends that couples in which the woman is over thirty-five seek medical intervention after only six months of trying to become pregnant rather than waiting the full year advocated by the standard medical definition (*Infertility*). And the authors of a book on infertility for lay audiences suggest that while "there is nothing magical about age 35" (Tan, Jacobs, and Seibel 30), women over thirty-five should seek medical intervention sooner than other women "because fewer years are left if treatment is needed" (37).

Physicians, social commentators, and the infertile themselves question whether women should be advised not only to begin treatment earlier but also to try to have children earlier. In their 1982 editorial in the *New En-*

gland Journal of Medicine, for example, DeCherney and Berkowitz argue that "individual and societal goals may also have to be reevaluated," suggesting that "perhaps the third decade should be devoted to childbearing and the fourth to career development, rather than the converse, which is true for many women today" (425). In the pronatalist tract *The Birth Dearth,* Ben Wattenberg uses the tactic of fear to persuade women to have more children earlier. Arguing "that for most people—men as well as women—a life without offspring is likely to be, at least, less happy and less fulfilling than a life with children" (108), Wattenberg says that delaying childbearing increases the likelihood of no childbearing. "Fertility delayed," he argues, "is fertility denied" (106).

While Wattenberg does not envision a world where women must choose between work and family (but, rather, that more innovative child care policies and career paths will enable more women to combine both), there is a tendency in the popular imagination to see career and family as two paths that a woman cannot pursue simultaneously. In a society where women find it hard to have children and a full-time career, the expected life course seems like a binary: either follow the career path, having children later and taking the risk that it might be more difficult or impossible, or choose the path of their mothers by having children first and a career, if any, later. This choice, which appears rooted in biology, is sustained in advertising, the popular press, and institutional policies: because women bear children, they must choose between careers and children. While feminists have pondered various solutions to this double bind (see, for example, Rothman, "Women"; Ruddick), little mainstream discussion seeks to distinguish between the biological ability to have children and the rearing of them.

The nuclear family model that dominates white, middle-class America presumes that children will be sent to day care or that one parent will stay home with them. Because women tend to earn less than men, and because white American women lack the type of "women-centered networks" that sustain child rearing in African American communities (Collins 119), members of this group continue to feel as if they must make the choice between career and children. Susan articulates her concern about this choice when she contemplates the advice that she would give to young women:

I do want to tell women, don't take it for granted. . . . And then I thought, wait a minute. How can you say that to young, up and coming women who have been brought up on women's [liberation]? I want to tell them, don't deliberately wait, but at the same time . . . we don't want a generation of women just having babies at 18 because they're afraid they can't at 35, and being dependent and not going to college and not being able to support themselves and perhaps picking partners who are not really in their best interest. . . . How do you get that message across without totally confusing women about what to do with their lives? . . . It really is a dilemma.

For Susan, women must make a choice about the ordering of their lives. She wonders whether a forty-five-year-old friend who had two children early in life did things in the right order. "They're grown now," Susan says of her friend's children. "She's in graduate school now. She's looking forward to the next twenty and thirty years of career and really the freedom that that brings in her mid-forties. Maybe having them sooner and then having a career makes more sense."

The feminist movement of the 1960s and 1970s has been blamed for misleading women into thinking that they can successfully delay childbearing long enough to establish a career. In his tract, Wattenberg lists women's liberation as one of the causes of the "dangerous" decline in Western birthrates (126). The popular press has also played a role. The media, argues Susan Faludi, picked up the 1982 *New England Journal of Medicine* report about fertility and aging and began exaggerating its claims and blaming feminism for the trend (27–28). Though infertility was more prevalent among lower-income women, the "epidemic" of infertility was attributed to middle-class professional women who did not delay their own personal fulfillment (29). In the press, she says, medical professionals talked about endometriosis as a "career woman's disease" (29) and warned women that too many abortions might prevent women from having children later (30). These claims, however, were not backed up by reliable medical evidence.

Women's prior use of birth control to delay childbearing is sometimes seen as the cause of infertility. Blame is often directed not at the manufacturers of ill-tested products but at individual women themselves and at the feminist movement that advocated birth control. Ellen reflects on her decision to get a Dalkon Shield:[1] "We had one friend who was like, Ms. Feminist Health Center and she used to come in and lecture us: 'Forget the pill, that's bad for you. IUDs are the birth control of the future.' This is the early seventies, and we all bought it. We thought this woman was fabulous. She was . . . the woman we all wanted to be. And she was beautiful, and smart, and the feminist's feminist, you know. So we all got IUDs." When Ellen became ill with pelvic inflammatory disease, thought to be a cause of infertility, she remembers being seen by a "monster": "He started screaming at me, going, 'This is what you young girls get for doing this, you're never going to have any children.' And he was literally screaming at me. And I'm sitting there, back in this vulnerable position with my feet up in the stirrups, and I couldn't walk too. And he's screaming at me." This physician did not question the wisdom of placing such products on the market but instead faulted individual women for using them. He seemed to believe that women who did so deserved whatever consequences befell them. For Ellen, the news that she might be infertile because of the IUD did not bother her then. She remembers thinking, "this is actually quite good news because I don't have to use any birth control anymore. . . . I don't have to have any more IUDs, no more pills, no more diaphragms. This is actually not bad news." Her pelvic inflammatory disease only became bad news when she decided she wanted a child.

Paula, forty-four, had a similar experience with the use of an IUD. She says she never felt her "biological clock" ticking and from early on worried about bringing children into the world. At age twenty-nine, she had her first IUD inserted. During the process, she was asked whether she wanted to have children. She recalls answering, "I'm sure not, more or less, you know, no." She believes that that openness with her physicians has now made it more difficult for her to get aggressive treatment, in spite of her age. Because she had been with the same health care provider since she was twenty-one, all of her records are available to those now helping her with infertility treatments at age forty-four. She says: "They had three inches in my folder and they knew that I had IUDs for 15 years, including the Dalkon Shield. . . . So that was a disadvantage because they had my whole chart. They could say, 'Well you didn't want to have kids when you were 29 anyway. . . . ' I was always very open with my doctors. . . . They just knew everything about me. It's embarrassing. I've realized since then that it's none of the doctor's business." Paula believes that she is now being penalized by the health care system for her past decisions about birth control, made at a time when she did not want children. Her health care provider did not get her into an IVF program immediately when she first sought infertility treatment (even though she was already forty) and did not tell her that they did not perform IVF on women over forty-two, information that would have helped her plan her decisions. She wonders whether her doctor's decisions were based on the life plans she had held (and shared with her doctor) as a younger woman.

Women who do not attempt to have children until their thirties or forties and then have difficulty conceiving are sometimes seen as having taken a selfish risk with consequences that they must now accept. But the women in this study exhibited resistance to such thinking. Susan reflects: "People say, you shouldn't have waited so long. Well, excuse me. I really didn't have the partner at the time that would have been more optimal." Like Susan, Ellen had had an abortion in her twenties and balks at the suggestion that she should have had children sooner. While she knew she wanted children, Ellen did not feel ready for them in her twenties. "I wasn't ready for the responsibility then," she says, "and I wasn't financially solvent." In this value system, there are prerequisites for having children, including being able to care for them financially.

For Susan, another prerequisite was not only being in a relationship but being in a stable one. "[My first] marriage wasn't particularly stable," she says. "I knew that that's a mistake to bring a child into an unstable marriage." Both heterosexual and lesbian women expressed the desire to make sure that a relationship was solid before having children. Lauren, who, with her same-sex partner, has a daughter through artificial insemination, says that "folks aren't just getting together one year and deciding to do this the next. Almost everybody [in our baby support group] had been together in a relationship for quite a number of years before they decided to do it."

While the women in my study did not share a lifelong expectation of having children, most of them did share a belief that they could plan their reproductive lives, that they could prevent pregnancy until the time was right to have a child. A diagnosis of infertility disrupted these beliefs.

Infertility as Disruption

If Americans expect to plan their reproductive lives, infertility disrupts that expectation and the narrative of continuity that informs it. In American culture, a common metaphor for infertility, as for life, is the "journey," illustrated in titles of books (Fleming's *Motherhood Deferred: A Woman's Journey;* and Cooper and Glazer's *Beyond Infertility: New Paths to Parenthood*) and workshops ("Life on Hold: Restructuring Your Life," "Secondary Infertility: The Next Step," "Stopping at One: Feeling Complete as a Family of Three"). In most cases, the journey of infertility is a detour from the expected life course that individuals and couples feel they should not have had to take. Like a detour on a road, the unanticipated detour of infertility leads the traveler to unforeseen obstacles. The infertile may not feel fully prepared, mentally or physically, for what lies ahead.

In the meantime, the infertiles' lives are "on hold," or "in a rut," and their dreams are "deferred." They are prevented from "getting on with their lives." This sense of limbo is described by a former RESOLVE of the Bay State president in her regular newsletter column: "Time is a funny thing—so constant and precise according to clock and calendar, but totally subjective in experience. We all know, for example, what it's like to feel the same two hours 'linger for an eternity' or 'flash by in an instant' depending on the circumstance. Infertility is one of those time altering circumstances. It speeds up the tick of the biological clock with agonizing predictability and stretches out the waiting until the moments and months seem to last forever" (Silverstein, "President's Message" [Winter 1991]). This passage illustrates the dual nature of infertility's effect on perceptions of time and order. When women sense that they will soon be too old to bear children, they feel pressed to move quickly through medical treatment. But the cyclical nature of medical treatment means that much time is spent waiting: for test results, for ovulation, for the next menstrual cycle.

With the expectation that one's life should and will follow a certain course, the inability to have children can be experienced as a profound disruption. Stephanie describes her reproductive plans as a science, saying: "I always knew when I was going to get married. I always knew when I was going to have children. I was always going to start trying to have kids when I was 30. I mean I had this planned down to a science. . . . I got married in time, but I didn't start getting pregnant in time, and when it didn't happen, I just didn't know how to live my life." Not only did she have a sense that children for her were inevitable and that they would come after she married, but she had also established a timetable for when this would occur. When her expectations were not met, the disruption was profound. She was unable to imagine a life different from the one that she had thought she would lead. Her sense that her life was going awry intensified as she found herself surrounded by friends with children. Stephanie says: "All my friends were having kids and I was the first one of my friends to get married and I was the last one of my friends to have kids. All my friends went on and they were like on their second and then their third." While women around her were following what she perceived as the normal life course, Stephanie found her own life incoherent. Her friends "went on," surpassing her and leaving her "last." Ellen, too, believed that she was at least partly influenced to have a child by the fact that most of her friends were married and had children.

For women especially, infertility can affect career and other long-term decisions. Judy, a thirty-three-year-old homemaker, had hoped to wait a while after being married before having children. Just before the wedding, however, her doctors diagnosed her with endometriosis and advised her to start trying right away. "I was just floored by the whole thing," she said. "I had gone to college and I thought that our plan would be that we would wait a while." In Judy's case, the sense of disruption came not after trying and failing to become pregnant but after learning that she would not be able to time her reproductive decisions as she had hoped. Many women are reluctant to move or make career changes because a pregnancy might be "just ahead." Infertility compounds the sense of disruption when it stalls a woman's professional life as well as her personal life. Stephanie recalls: "I left a job because of it. . . . I couldn't work a regular job. I mean, I was never there. You are always given tests, I couldn't work, I couldn't . . . have a life. I had no life left. You couldn't go on vacation, because . . . it was so all-encompassing."

While not all women were able to give up their jobs, a few expressed a willingness to do so if necessary. For some, the availability of insurance coverage in Massachusetts influenced career decisions. Because of the Massachusetts mandate, some couples moved to the state in order to be covered; others decided not to pursue job opportunities in other states where they would not have had coverage for their treatments.

Recurring cyclical events sometimes serve as painful reminders to the infertile that their lives are not "progressing." As markers of the passage of time, holidays can heighten the sense that a person is not "where they thought they would be." For those who are already stressed, holidays provoke memories of past holidays that might have been more joyous. At gatherings, family members and friends might ask questions about a couple's reproductive plans (if they are unaware of the infertility experience) or might offer unwelcome advice (if they are aware). Holidays that are particularly child-oriented, such as Christmas and Hanukkah, can bring the infertile into contact with children, which often intensifies feelings of isolation or unfairness.

In a regular column in the chapter newsletter, presidents of RESOLVE of the Bay State commonly organize their messages around an upcoming (or recent) holiday or change of season. Contributors, as well, frequently refer to a cyclical event as having particular symbolic importance. Commonly, the theme is used as a way to offer support and strategies for coping with a particular time of the year or an event or for reevaluating goals and priorities. In an article devoted to helping members cope with the holidays, for example, a social worker suggests possible responses to remarks considered insensitive. When asked to participate in Mother's Day events, the infertile woman is advised to use a response such as this one: "Please don't ask me to cook a Mother's Day dinner for my sisters. They're honored every day of the year by the presence of their children. I'm afraid there will never be a Mother's Day for me. I would feel like Cinderella if I gave the dinner you're suggesting" (Bombardieri 4). Mother's Day, as might be expected, is a pointed reminder that a woman has not fulfilled a desired role.

As reminders of the passage of time, the fall and winter holidays, coming so close together, can be seen as an ordeal to be either endured or avoided. One woman, writing in the newsletter of RESOLVE of the Bay State, recounts a Christmas Eve: "We had just completed our last IVF attempt and came home to see my baby sister's new baby and my brother's two young children. We went to a Christmas Eve service and suddenly I was faced with the minister's sermon, entitled 'Do You Want to Hold the Baby?'" (Ciganovic). Christmas and Hanukkah, coming at the end of the year, serve as reminders that another year is about to end. For the same reason, New Year's seems to be a particularly painful time. In one of her president's messages, Martha Griffin writes: "It was always New Years which fostered that lump in the throat feeling: that desperate feeling. I would attach each of the unanswered 'hopes' of the year past to the new year, only to be struck by the reality of no pregnancy: no child, just another year older and closer to menopause" (Untitled). Several years later, another president offered words of hope at the same time of year: "For those of you awaiting resolution," she writes, "I wish you speedy days, short nights and hope and light to guide you through these difficult times" (Silverstein, "President's Message" [Winter 1991]).

The change of seasons is similar in effect to the advent of holidays. As one president of RESOLVE of the Bay State writes: "Summer can be just as difficult a time for those dealing with infertility as the winter holiday season. Simply going to the beach can be a painful reminder that our dreams of building sandcastles, looking for shells or exploring tidal pools with a child of our own have not yet been realized, while all around us moms and dads are spending happy moments together. Everyone else seems to be the ideal family on vacation" (Crockin, "President's Message"). Without their heavy winter clothes, pregnant women seem ubiquitous; schools have let out for the year, making it all the more likely that the infertile will see children at any time of day. Spring, however, is more closely linked to the ability that seems to elude the infertile. Martha Griffin writes that spring is a "reminder of how all other living things seem to be able to blossom, and without medical intervention" ("President's Message" [May 1985]). Several women in this study contrasted themselves to nature in spring, noting their inability to perform an act that seems so basic to all other living things.

Just as spring provides reminders of generational continuity, so do the expectations of grandparents. "Many parents," write Jean and Mike Carter, "see grandchildren as the 'pay-off' for the hard work of parenting" (108). For some, such as Ellen, parents never make any direct statements about their desire for grandchildren. Ellen recalls that her parents never pressured her, although she does remember her mother commenting that Ellen would "make a great mother." The experience of Ellen, who is single, may be similar to that of women in same-sex relationships, whose parents generally do not expect (or hope for) their children to reproduce. For parents of adult children who decide to have children outside of marriage, learning of a pregnancy might be experienced as something that must be accommodated. In fact, several lesbians in this study noted that anticipating the negative reaction of families made them think twice about becoming parents.

Parents of people in married, heterosexual relationships, however, tend to expect grandchildren and often experience a "courtesy stigma" when none is born (Goffman 28). That is, those who are associated with the stigmatized individual (in this case, the infertile person) sometimes experience effects of the stigma even though they do not suffer from the stigma themselves. Parents sometimes ask directly or complain that a son or daughter has not done the duty of providing grandchildren. Knowing the intense desire of their parents for grandchildren, some couples do not tell their families about their infertility in the hope that it will all be over soon. Ellen had been inseminating for a year but had not planned to tell her parents unless she ended up adopting a child. Then, she said, she would tell them that she had tried to have a child biologically. Susan, too, did not tell her parents about her years of medical treatment until she became pregnant. Lynne and her husband told his parents after she had a surgical procedure for infertility. She says:

> You tend to feel like they think that we're selfish, that we're so wrapped up in our lives that we don't want to provide a grandchild. You have no idea how they're really looking at it and I read in books that a lot of times it's just as hard for the grandparents to . . . accept the idea of no grandchild just as the parents. In a way they have to go through their own mourning, so I wanted them to know early on, rather than to say, "Hey, we're at the end of the road, and guess what?"

Lynne's fear that her in-laws would think that they were "selfish" is common in American thought. In the 1970s the voluntarily childless became more visible and vocal in a movement that positioned not having children as "a better lifestyle—better for individuals, better for couples, better for the planet" (May 182). While some in the childfree movement sought more engagement with public life, others saw their lifestyle as one with more opportunity for leisure time and material gain. For these couples, the cult of domesticity had remained, "but now the children had dropped out of the romantic picture" (May 185). Those who did not have children were seen as selfish in wanting more of their material resources and time for themselves and in "denying" grandchildren to their parents.

Self-help literature on infertility, including that published by RESOLVE, often offers advice for dealing with one's parents during infertility. In the newsletter of RESOLVE of the Bay State, a social worker writes that many parents long to become grandparents because they can enjoy children without being fully responsible for them (Beck, "Family Affair"). In addition, they might hope for their own son or daughter to take on the role of parent because of the importance they attach to that role. Infertile individuals or couples can experience additional stress as they try to please their parents or help them fulfill a desire. Infertile couples are sometimes racing against their parents' biological clocks as well as their own. As infertile couples age, so do their parents; the passage of time increases the likelihood that a child will never get to know its grandparents.

As when experiencing topological detours, the infertile will sometimes, at the end of the journey, reflect and conclude that the trip was ultimately worthwhile. The detour may have forced the infertile to think about the value of paths they would not ordinarily consider. They may recall the journey as being one that has ultimately strengthened them because of its difficulty. As one columnist in the newsletter of RESOLVE of the Bay State writes, "Infertility helped me discover strengths I never knew I had. It gave me the confidence to tackle other hurdles in my life ('Well, if I can survive the pain of infertility, I can conquer a little stage fright!'). And it sure taught me how to communicate my needs to doctors!" (Wolfson 15). A former president of RESOLVE of the Bay State offers this advice to those going through infertility: "For those of you now venturing forth, take heart. There are thousands of us who have set out before you and returned transformed, each with a different tale to tell" (Silverstein, "Hero" 1).

Not all the women in this study experienced infertility as a highly disruptive event. Diane, whose husband had a son from a previous marriage, was going through infertility treatment but had accepted the possibility that it would not work. "We are trying to have children of our own," she said, "but if it doesn't work, it's not the end of the world. We have a happy life now, and it would just mean we get to take more vacations!" Diane's sense of her future was not intimately entwined with having children; her world would "not end" if she did not become pregnant. Her life, in fact a happy life, would continue. It may be that Diane, who was very close to her stepson, felt that she had already experienced parenthood sufficiently. Or she may have found other ways to fulfill desires commonly associated with having children, such as the desire to nurture or to be creative.

Similarly, like heterosexual couples who become pregnant within time frames that seem normal, single women and those in same-sex relationships may not experience social infertility as disruptive if they are able to become pregnant within a time they consider normal. Lesbians are perhaps more likely to experience the decision to parent initially as disruptive, because they work against norms that, in the popular imagination, connect lesbians with sexuality and hence disconnect them from maternal qualities (Lewin).

Medical Treatment for Infertility as a Process of Continual Improvement

If infertility disrupts the expected life course, medical treatment offers the opportunity to put life back on track. Some who enter medical treatment become pregnant with very little intervention; others move on to advanced technologies. Through reading and talking to others, infertile individuals often have a sense of the progression of treatment. Many see IVF (and its cousins, GIFT, ZIFT, and ICSI) as the most advanced and invasive procedures, measures not to be tried until other procedures have failed. Some individuals or couples, however, are unwilling to take the more conservative course, preferring to skip what some physicians might consider standard protocol and move on to the procedure most likely to be effective even if it is more invasive or expensive.

At the beginning, Ellen sensed that she would try six months of home-based inseminations and IUI before "going to stage two on this." After a couple of home-based inseminations, however, Ellen was ready to move on to IUI because she had heard it had a greater chance of success. "Let's go high tech," she said. "Let's just shoot it right in there and hope for the best. . . . Do it and get it over with." After switching facilities and doctors, Ellen remembers the physician's assistant explaining the standard protocol of ovulatory regulating hormones and inseminations. Ellen's response was emphatic: "I said, no, I'm way beyond that. I said I've been doing that for six months, let's move on here. I'm ready to do in vitro." Other individuals and couples expressed the desire to move on quickly. Susan and Paul tried to persuade their doctor to go directly to IVF rather than IUI. Similarly, Anne, who became pregnant through artificial insemination, and her partner wanted to try IUI for their second child because they had since learned that IUI had a higher success rate.

The use of more advanced technologies, of course, does not guarantee pregnancy. In fact, an individual or couple in the earlier stages of treatment might be more hopeful than someone using more advanced interventions. Because of the way that treatment generally proceeds, someone undergoing less aggressive therapy can still imagine pregnancy being "just around the corner," "just ahead," or "around the next bend." Even those using more advanced technologies may remain hopeful, however, both because physicians can alter any number of variables with each cycle and because (in Massachusetts) much of the treatment is paid for. Paula, for example, had undergone eight IVF attempts and was considering stopping. Her physician, however, wanted her to consider using an egg from a donor. She is ambivalent about using a donor egg but feels compelled to do so. "With all this high technology," she says, "you always go to the next step. It always escalates." Even though she has gone through eight tries with no pregnancy, she feels that new developments offer additional hope.

One woman, a leader of a workshop on living without children after infertility, remarked, "A part of me always was sure that there would be an eleventh hour miracle." The infertile also continue to hope because of a pervasive belief in the progress of science. Believing that new advancements that can help them are just over the horizon, infertile individuals may stay in treatment.

Sheri and her husband, for example, went through a treatment called ICSI, in which a single sperm is injected into an egg. Because part of their diagnosis was poor sperm quality, ICSI held promise for them. This procedure did not exist, however, when they first entered medical treatment. They learned of ICSI during treatment and had to wait months before it was approved for use in the United States. As they waited, Sheri continued with another treatment even though she felt it was not working. She says, "We also could choose not to [continue with other treatment]. But we of course chose to. So, time I think has been a factor too. What we're doing now did not exist when we started." Their experience demonstrates what Margarete Sandelowski has called infertility treatment's "inherent quality of never being enough" ("Compelled" 31).

New technologies can act as a lure until an individual or couple has had a child or has come to terms with ending treatment. Ending treatment can be difficult when, as the leader of a workshop on childless living says, "the medical community keeps holding out carrots to us." The attraction of new technologies, however, is not just that they provide continued opportunities. When the individual is seen as responsible for providing individual and generational continuity, and when economic support provides for mechanisms that might lead to this continuity, the infertile may feel compelled to exhaust all possibilities. With continual development of new technologies, the infertile may never be able to exhaust them, instead submitting themselves to a process of continual improvement. This may be why the ability to continue with medical treatment is sometimes seen as a matter of endurance. Ben Wattenberg, in *The Birth Dearth,* argues that "97.5 percent of all couples *willing to go the last mile* to conceive—can conceive" (125, emphasis added). Wattenberg does not take into account the fact that individuals or couples have no way of identifying the last mile. New technologies, as well as economic and symbolic support for them, have extended the journey so that it is harder for the infertile to know when they have reached the end.

At the End of the Medical Journey: Adoption or Childless Living

In contemporary American culture, the journey of infertility is expected to follow more or less the same path: medical treatment first and, if medical treatment fails, adoption or the decision to live without children. Ellen thought that she would try adoption if she did not become pregnant through medical means, but she did not consider adoption first. When I caught up with Ellen again after almost a year and a half, I learned that she had become pregnant three months after our first meeting and had had a daughter. She was contemplating trying to have another biological child or, if that failed, adopting a second child. For most Americans, adoption and childless (or childfree) living are seen as options to consider *after* medical treatment has failed or has at least been ruled out as the first avenue of intervention.

In an informational video on infertility, a physician places adoption at the end of the infertility journey: "If couples have explored everything, including the possibility of donor sperm or donor eggs, there still is the possibility that they will indeed have their own child, because adoption is an option. That's a wonderful and marvelous way to have a family" (*Infertility*). Although the doctor positions adoption as "wonderful," it is something to be considered only after all medical avenues (including donated genetic material) have been considered or pursued.

Similarly, in much of the RESOLVE literature, adoption is seen as something you "move on to" or "make the leap to." Medical treatment is something you "move on from"; there is rarely a question that a person won't seek medical treatment first. A brochure produced by a fertility drug manufacturer (Serono Symposia) and entitled *Pathways to Parenthood*, for example, contains descriptions of medical interventions alone and thereby illustrates the prevalent belief that the real path to parenthood is biological. Similarly, in a talk entitled "Making the Leap to Adoption," part of an all-day symposium on infertility sponsored by RESOLVE, the speaker discussed a three-part strategy for getting ready to adopt a child. The first step is to extricate from treatment, the second is to resolve losses, and the third is to prepare for adoption. Being able to extricate from treatment means recognizing that it requires planning for its early, middle, and end stages and that some things will "move us forward," while others "hold us back." In this model, medical treatment is the natural first step in resolving infertility, and any subsequent steps must deal with the failure of medicine to put things right. The speaker, a social worker, offered plenty of advice for helping the members of the audience identify the end of their own medical journeys. She advised listeners to create a personal checklist to identify the point at which they feel as if they have done everything or enough, to think of a course of medical treatment, and to get into a special routine to handle the bad times. These processes function not only as methods for decision making but also as means of restoring order in a situation that is interpreted as increasingly chaotic. The checklist is a way for an individual or couple to use their own criteria for the steps that need to be taken and for determining when to take them. Similarly, thinking of medical treatment as a course implies a beginning and an end. Each individual or couple must determine how long their course will last. The special routine, as well, establishes an ordering effect as individuals or couples "go through the motions" of preestablished steps that require no additional decisions. During these processes, metaphors are used not only to describe disruption but also to make sense of it and help to recreate order (Becker, "Metaphors").

Before "moving on to adoption," the individual or couple is advised to "grieve for the loss of your imagined biological child" (Carter and Carter 87). Prospective adoptive parents are asked to give up the image of the imagined child so that they will be able to accept an adopted child who, like any human being, cannot live up to ideal standards (Carter and Carter 87). The imagined biological child is seen not as an actual child but as the "loss of potential" (Bonchek 6). In this sense, the child embodies what "might have been"; to "move forward," the infertile must abandon these hopes for the future. The individual or couple contemplating adoption must also come to terms with cultural assumptions about the "quality" of children produced by those with an unplanned pregnancy. Some members of the white, middle-class infertile population "live such organized lives" (in the words of an adoption advocate) that they have a hard time understanding how anyone could become pregnant without planning it. Perhaps this is one reason why the Open Door Society (an adoption advocacy organization) prefers to talk about birth mothers "making an adoption plan" for their children rather than "giving their children up" for adoption. Finally, those considering adoption must be willing to endure a different kind of limbo as they wait for a child to be placed with them.

The process of adoption has its own sense of proper rank and chronological order. The home-study system, used by adoption agencies to assess potential parents, is a method of ranking that favors traditional models of parenting. As Elizabeth Bartholet writes:

The system ranks prospective parents from top to bottom in terms of relative desirability, which is assessed primarily on the basis of easily determined objective factors. These factors reflect the system's bias in favor of a biological parenting model as well as a socially traditional family model. So heterosexual couples in their late twenties or early thirties with apparently stable marriages are at the top of the ladder. These are the kind of people who could, if not for infertility, produce children, and who should, in the system's view, be parents. Single and older adoptive applicants—those in their late thirties and forties—are placed lower on the ladder, along with people with disabilities. Gays, lesbians, and the seriously disabled are generally excluded altogether. (*Family* 70–71)

While gays and lesbians are no longer excluded from adopting children in Massachusetts, the system of ranking prospective parents remains. Children are also ranked in terms of desirability, with healthy white infants at the top and "special needs" children (that is, older children and those with disabilities) at the bottom. Children at the top of the ranking are matched with prospective adoptive parents at the top of their ranking, creating "a market system . . . in which ranking produces buying power" (Bartholet, *Family* 71). In some seminars, prospective adoptive parents are advised to identify ideals they would be willing to give up in order to parent. They are asked whether they feel it is necessary to have an infant, a child who resembles them, a child of the same race, and a child who is apparently physically and mentally healthy.[2]

For various reasons, some who consider adoption will ultimately decide instead to live without children, a lifestyle that is variously termed "childless," "childfree," and "living without children." Several women in this study who were still undergoing medical treatment were reluctant to call this lifestyle "childfree," seeing in that name the connotation that children are something bad for you (like sugar or caffeine) that should be eliminated. Those who have embraced the "childfree" label focus on its positive implications. For a social worker writing in the newsletter of RESOLVE of the Bay State, "the difference to me relates to a more positive feeling that an infertile couple can still choose not to have children, yet feel whole, fulfilled, and complete" (Covington 8). For Jean and Michael Carter, the term "childfree" means "changing negative into positive" (30), "taking advantage of the advantages" (31), and "taking control of your life again" (33). Like others, the Carters recognize that many people, especially those undergoing medical treatment for infertility, find the possibility of being fulfilled without children threatening to their own value systems. Because medical treatment takes such persistence and dedication, those who have chosen another path appear to be rejecting the values that sustain them.

Those who choose to live without children are often seen as having decided *against* adoption. The Carters write that there is an "implication that adoption is the *next natural step* after infertility and that not adopting is an aberration" (86, emphasis added). The Carters (and others) argue, however, that adoption and childfree living are two separate paths that must be evaluated separately.

"Natural" Order and the Limbo of Medical Treatment for Infertility

Often the disruption of life plans cannot be put right in ways that an individual or couple had wished for. Hoping for a child that is biologically related to both, members of a heterosexual couple might pursue the medical avenue for years before realizing that a biological child is not an inevitability. At this point, they might take the advice of a RESOLVE counselor, who says that "moving on" means reevaluating expectations and the sense of what is necessary in order to lead a fulfilling life. Whereas a child related to both partners would once have seemed the only acceptable option, a couple might come to consider having a child related to only one partner (through donor sperm, donor egg, or surrogacy), adopting a child, or living without children. Taking stock of such options means reenvisioning how one should lead one's life—or as a former president of RESOLVE of the Bay State puts it, "to take a radical vision and grasp it close to your heart, until it becomes warm and familiar and finally part of you" (Silverstein, "Hero").

The Massachusetts mandate recognizes the cultural logic that infertility is a disruption in the normal, natural course of life. Those with health insurance are given almost unlimited opportunities to get their lives back on track through medical intervention. In this sense, the mandate is consistent with American values about the importance of biologic relatedness and about preferred life paths. The legal sanction of a medical definition of infertility symbolically reinforces social preferences regarding the resolution of infertility. Social infertility is not covered, with the result that the mandate indicates when (and with whom) it is appropriate to have children. In omitting comparable coverage for adoption, the law privileges medical resolutions. And because only those employed and with insurance are covered, the mandate reinforces the social order: there are financial prerequisites for parenthood. More broadly, the mandate is also a statement about the role of law in restoring order in private lives. The law affects not only the public sphere but also private decisions. Through the vehicle of health insurance, law appears to be helping white middle-class families put their private lives back in order. The way things should be appears natural, and so insurance appears to be reinforcing what nature intended.

The mandate's preferred solution to the disruption of infertility—the medical model—seems less to ameliorate this disruption, however, than to emphasize its contours, creating a double bind for those who follow this path. Like new reproductive technologies, the Massachusetts mandate has extended the medical portion of the journey of infertility, sometimes beyond menopause.[3] Some of the women in this study feel that insurance coverage confuses the end of medical treatment. No longer fettered by severe financial constraints, those covered by the mandate must craft new road signs to direct their way. The medical avenue has the appeal of offering hope for a biological child; women envision pregnancy as possibly "right around the corner" with the next cycle of treatment. Even those who have tried every medical treatment that is currently available feel lured from time to time by the development of new technologies. With a faith in progress, they may hope for a moment when fresh advances will make it possible for them to have children. This "never-enough" quality of reproductive technologies (Sandelowski, "Compelled"), plus the removal of economic barriers, makes it easier for a couple to see a biological child as eventually inevitable and thereby encourages them to postpone the point at which they consider other ways to fulfill their desires.

Like the double bind of success and failure described in the previous chapter, the double bind of order and discontinuity sustains the processes of normalization by emphasizing the differences between the two poles rather than resolving them. To most of the middle-class white women in this study, a normal life course has a sense of continuity between the past and the future. Wanting to control the timing of reproduction and often to make a connection between other generations, those who discover an inability to reproduce feel disconnected from what they regard as the normal course of events. Medical treatment offers hope to restore order, but it also creates a sense of discontinuity. Those for whom pregnancy remains elusive sometimes feel caught in limbo as they hope for positive results. For them, rather than restoring a sense of continuity, medical treatment has made their lives appear to be on hold. Pulled by the desire to regain normalcy, the infertile enter into a routine that is far from normal and that emphasizes how far from the normal life course they have veered. This normalization works not only to shape individual lives but also to create cultural expectations regarding the best way of approaching disruptions in the life course.

5

Control and Constraint

At times I feel like a harp string drawn tight and pulled by the slightest breeze that blows.
—Leah Rugen, "Waiting Room"

Law has entry into minute aspects of the life of the body and has the potential to regulate women's activities whilst appearing most liberal and benevolent.
—Carol Smart, *Feminism and the Power of Law*

As members of the first birth control generation, many American women of childbearing age understand fertility as something that can be controlled. As Celeste M. Condit argues, the birth control pill has been touted as providing such near perfect control over pregnancy that women no longer see children as being timed by the failure of the method (as was more the case with the condom and diaphragm). Instead, women using the birth control pill envision it as providing them with a switch—which they control—that turns fertility on or off. In addition, the birth control pill, unlike the condom or diaphragm, protects a woman at the time of intercourse whether or not her partner consents. In this way, argues Condit, "individual women . . . wrested virtually complete control of procreation, not only from biology but, perhaps more importantly, from individual men. In a crucial way, therefore, the pill made the social demand for control or 'choice' *appear* as a biological and physical possibility" (70, emphasis in the original).

Like citizens of other liberal democracies, middle-class white women in America share some expectation of being able to control their private lives. In the liberal tradition, the private sphere is envisioned as an apolitical space in which individuals, as long as they do not interfere with the rights of others, should remain unfettered to pursue their own ends. On the other hand, the state's activities, and the promotion of social change, are seen as properly confined to the public sphere. In this tradition, to have reproductive freedom means being able to make decisions, without outside interference, about whether and when to have children. The state's role in these reproductive freedoms is to guarantee them, to remove any barriers that might prevent individuals from freely exercising reproductive choices. The Massachusetts mandate, from a liberal perspective, is a law that removes economic barriers, making it possible for at least a majority of the state's infertile to seek some medical treatment for the condition.

While the "origins" of Western feminism might be said to be located in the liberal tradition, and while some liberal ideals (especially the ideal of individual rights) continue to appeal to feminists of many stripes, liberal political philosophy's dichotomy between the public and private is a target of much feminist criticism. As social theorists Elizabeth Frazer and Nicola Lacey argue, feminists critique both the existence of a boundary between the public and private sphere and the implication, which follows from this assumed boundary, that the private sphere is an apolitical space. The state intervenes in the most private of decisions through regulations about, for example, who may marry whom and who should have custody of children in divorce settlements.

In addition, nonintervention, as well as intervention, has political motivations and implications, despite protests to the contrary. When states rule, for example, that rape within marriage is not a crime because the matter is within the private sphere, outside the realm of state interests, the state is both validating the activity by looking the other way and declaring the marital relationship apolitical. This move to render the private sphere apolitical reveals an understanding of power as an entity that is transferred, in its entirety, between only the state apparatus and the individual, denying its operation in culture more broadly construed (Frazer and Lacey 76). Reproductive freedom, in this framework, is limited only by the negative power imposed by the state and not by other forces, such as the discourse of scientific progress, politics within interpersonal relationships, or cultural norms.

In this chapter, I take the position that individuals do not simply control the private sphere while the state controls the public. I also assume that control over reproduction is not exercised solely by individuals and the state; it is affected by a host of other material and discursive forces. And just as the domain of control is complex (as is the question of who exerts it where), so is the notion of control itself. Drawing on Foucault, I understand control as an example of the microphysics of power. "Power," according to Foucault, "is everywhere" (*Sexuality* 93). It operates both at a macro level, as the "complex strategical situation in a particular society" (*Sexuality* 93), and at a micro level, as the "meticulous control of the operations of the body" (*Discipline* 137). In the form of this "meticulous control," power is the means by which discipline, and by extension, normalization, are accomplished. Like other forms of power, control is characterized by an ability to produce (not just repress) and by the possibility of transformations and reversals. Understood in this way, individuals are capable of controlling as well as being controlled but not in a stable, predictable way.

While I argue in this chapter that the Massachusetts mandate is exerting control over the private sphere while appearing to do otherwise, my goal, generally speaking, is not to determine who *has* control in any given circumstance. Rather than looking at control as an independent entity that can be held, to greater or lesser degrees, or as a cognitive representation existing only in the mind of individuals, I examine the concept of control as a topos shared by one particular group (middle-class white women). In other words, looking at how members of a certain group imagine "control" can tell us something about the shared cultural values of that group. As legal theorist Lawrence M. Friedman reminds us, the "*sense* of control and the possibility of control are as important as the actual control" (98, emphasis in the original).

The white, middle-class women in this study share (to a certain extent) the idea that being in control is possible, desirable, and normal. For these women, being in control means being able to make choices; controlling one's fertility means choosing whether and when to have a child. Those expecting to be able to turn on their fertility by stopping birth control may experience infertility as a loss of control or as a confirmation that control has always been an illusion. For some, the sense that they lack control may have filtered into other areas of their lives; they may have begun to doubt their own competence in their relationships or jobs or the certainty of things they previously took for granted. Medical treatment can both alleviate and exacerbate the loss of control experienced by the infertile. Those who seek medical treatment often experience both an increased sense of control over their own destinies (because they have been able to do something toward resolving the difficulty) and a loss of control over their own bodies as they encounter the routines of intervention. In this way, medical treatment for infertility can place women in a double bind: to gain the control they feel they have lost, many women submit to a regime that can be experienced as constraining. The double bind may not be resolved by the birth of a child. While those who have a child may feel that they have reestablished some control in their lives, the experience of infertility seems to leave many feeling that control is simply an illusion. Resisting the double bind, for those who have biological children and those who do not, may mean redefining what it means to be in control.

Infertility as Loss of Control

Many heterosexual women, having controlled their fertility during early years of career and marriage, assume that they will have the same control over pregnancy. Lynne, for example, was twenty-three when she and her husband married; they started trying for a child two years later. After three months, she asked her gynecologist for any "secrets"; her doctor told her that it sometimes takes a while and that she should come back in six months. Lynne remembers: "I never suspected I would have a problem. . . . You grow up as a woman expecting that as soon as you don't use any protection, it's gonna happen. So when three months go by, you start to really wonder, is something wrong, even though they say it takes up to a year."

As an adolescent Lynne may have been exposed to messages from public information services or from her parents when they debunked the myth that a woman cannot get pregnant the first time she has intercourse. She came of age in an era when there was a wide array of choices in temporary birth control. Like many women, she took her fertility for granted, used birth control, and expected pregnancy to occur when she stopped. Monica, another woman, had been living with her future husband for two years before getting married. Soon afterward, they decided to start trying to have a child. Monica describes her expectations this way: "I was in a relationship for five years in my 20s when I was pursuing my MBA and doing other things. So I guess I felt comfortable postponing that decision until my 30s, and then I got caught. Like everything. I thought I could just turn it on."

Like other women in this study, Monica regarded fertility as a "switch" that was either on or off. She had turned it "off" during the years she was completing her education and starting her career, and she assumed that she could turn it "on" when she was ready to have a child. Susan, who eventually adopted, wanted "to tell women, don't take it for granted, you can't depend on it to be there when you want it, and you don't have control over it like you do over conception."

For Sarah and her husband, the assumption of fertility held true for their first child. Sarah, who had been married for three years before she began trying to have a child, became pregnant after only two months of unprotected intercourse. She says: "And it was absolutely textbook, no problems. . . . She was born vaginally, everything was perfect. And of course, since everything was just perfect, we figured well, we'll have three kids in five years. One would be born when she was two and a half and one would be born when she was five. And we'll pick the month. Little did I know." Sarah's first pregnancy went as she had expected, a "textbook" case of planning for and having a child. With this good experience serving as evidence that she had control over her reproductive future, Sarah and her husband planned to have more children. They envisioned controlling not only the number of children they would have but the timing (down to the month) of the children's births.

Sarah felt able to control this decision in part because she had charted her cycle—even though she had not had previous problems conceiving—and the charting had gone as she had expected. "I took my temperature for a couple of months," she remembers, "and it all happened, everything it was supposed to do. It was great." When attempting to have a second child, Sarah began charting again. She recalls: "A couple of months went by and nothing happened. Which isn't that unusual but I was charting things very carefully and it really seemed to me like it should be working. . . . The charts were working right, everything was doing exactly what it was supposed to do. It just wasn't happening. . . . All this stuff was happening, and it wasn't happening. It was devastating." Nothing about the charting process itself, or the readings, had changed from the time of her first pregnancy. Both times, the charts were working "as they were supposed to." The difference was in whether the "perfect" charts translated into a pregnancy. When she became pregnant the first time, Sarah had a feeling of control over her fertility and considered the charting to be something that had helped her to gain it. But when she could not become pregnant the second time, the same charts were a source of frustration.

In Sarah's case, her first pregnancy gave her the feeling that she should be able to control her fertility. In other instances, a woman might expect to control her fertility because she has been in charge of other areas of her private life. Leslie, for example, had four miscarriages before having her son. She reports being frustrated "because it was mother nature taking its course." She says: "I had no control over it whereas everything else I have done, I've had control. I could get married when I wanted to, and who I wanted to get married to, but having a baby, I had no control." In Leslie's experience, a person generally has control of her or his private life. In her attempts to have a child, an uncontrollable force ("mother nature") intervened, making it impossible for her to predict or determine what lay ahead. Women and couples frequently experience this sense of uncertainty early in the experience of infertility. Unless friends, family members, or acquaintances have had similar experiences, or unless a previous medical condition indicated future fertility difficulties, those having trouble conceiving are unlikely to have anticipated that fertility would become a problem.

In this study, some of the women in same-sex couples also expected to control when their children would be born. Kim, whose partner became pregnant after almost two years of inseminations, says that "we expected it to take a few months to get pregnant, but we didn't expect it to take twenty-two." Still, when Kim decided to get pregnant with their second child, they thought in terms of controlling when it would happen. She says:

> Our first one was going up to two. . . . I was of the style of having them very close together. I could see having them eighteen months apart. . . . My partner liked the idea of our first child being able to verbalize how she felt about it all. She was more interested in them being three years apart. But when we actually were trying to figure out when to do it, we were also considering that I didn't want to be very pregnant in the summer. . . . And we also, it sounds crazy, we were considering school age for our kids to enter school. We knew that if this child was born before April 1, that would be a lot better, save us a full year of day care.

Even after her partner had had twenty-two months of inseminations in the attempt to conceive, Kim was hopeful that they would be able to control when the second child was born so that the timing would be optimal for their first child, for her comfort, and for their finances. For Kim, this assumption held true. She became pregnant on the first attempt.

Not all women in this study automatically assumed that they would be able to control becoming pregnant. The women who did not assume fertility tended to be those who had some physiological condition that led them to believe that once they began trying, they would have trouble. Lisa, for example, said, "I had known ahead of time that I was going to have some difficulty because I never had a regular cycle. I asked a lot of times whether it was going to be possible for me or not." Similarly, Donna, who was diagnosed with polycystic ovarian disease while in college, had told her soon-to-be husband that she might never be able to have children. Both Lisa and Donna anticipated that they might have to seek medical intervention to become pregnant. Donna and her husband tried for a year to see whether she would get pregnant "just by chance"; they sought treatment and eventually had a child through IVF. Lisa started immediately with a gynecologist when she decided to become pregnant; after five IVF cycles, she decided to adopt instead. Unlike most of the other women in this study, Lisa and Donna did not experience the initial sense of uncertainty when pregnancy did not occur. Not anticipating control over pregnancy, they did not feel out of control when it did not happen.

The Uncertainty of Medical Treatment for Infertility

For many white, middle-class Americans experiencing infertility, medicine offers a way to regain control. Comfortable with scientific solutions and medical authority, many Americans look to medicine as a resource for understanding and correcting a range of problems (Conrad and Kern; Stein). Susan felt great hope when she started IUI after a battery of tests. She says, "I can't tell you how optimistic I was. This is what we'd been waiting for." Others expressed similar attitudes, feeling more in control when taking action, in the form of medical treatment, than when trying for pregnancy on their own.

In some cases, those who seek medical intervention come away, early on, with knowledge that provides an end to the uncertainty. A woman whose mother had taken DES when pregnant, for example, might have severe uterine malformations that would prevent her from becoming pregnant or carrying a child to term. In the most extreme cases, medicine may not be able to help this woman have a child. In addition, until the introduction of ICSI, those who discovered that the male partner in a relationship had virtually no sperm would have little medical recourse. Individuals and couples in these situations, knowing the cause of the infertility and understanding the inability of medicine to "put things right," may be able to move on with their lives and begin taking control of decisions again.

Most people who seek medical help for infertility, however, do not receive such clear-cut answers. Reproduction is a complex process, and infertility is often a multivariate problem requiring months or even years of investigation before the cause and solution can be determined. Most often, then, the first visit to a physician does not end uncertainty but begins an investigational process that extends the uncertainty, at least for a time.

After her initial visit to her gynecologist, Lynne waited a year before returning because her husband was unemployed and they were in no hurry to have a child under those financial circumstances. Both Lynne and her husband had the basic tests run, and the only problem appeared to be that Lynne had irregular cycles. Her doctor prescribed an ovulatory regulating hormone and told her to return in six months. Especially for young women, this treatment regimen seems common. If initial test results do not indicate any obvious problems, or a problem that is relatively simple to correct (such as an ovulatory problem), a doctor might encourage a couple to keep trying after certain simple interventions. In Lynne's case, the intervention was hormonal therapy.

When physicians cannot identify any reasons for an inability to conceive, a woman or couple is described as having unexplained infertility. In such cases, a doctor may recommend not only further diagnostic tests but also procedures designed to produce a pregnancy, such as IUI or IVF. A physician at a Boston-area clinic believes that unexplained infertility is one of the easiest diagnoses to treat. With treatment, those with this diagnosis have about the same chances of conception, per cycle, as the general population (about 25–30 percent). Because the chances of success are greater than for all other known categories of infertility, he argues that it is better to be uncertain about the cause and patient about outcome. Patients, however, find the uncertainty troubling. Susan, for example, who was initially diagnosed with unexplained infertility, wanted her doctor to find something wrong with her so that it could be fixed.

Those with social infertility sometimes have a hard time getting any medical intervention. One of the confounding factors for single women and those in same-sex couples is that there are fewer facilities willing to perform artificial insemination on this population. Even though increasing number of physicians believe that it is discriminatory to deny services to single women and those in same-sex relationships, several women in this study experienced difficulty in finding someone to perform inseminations. Ellen, a single woman, called several doctors before finding any that would agree to the procedure. She recalls their saying, "Oh heavens, no, we would never do that. How can you think of doing such a thing?" Some women felt confined to the couple of Boston-area facilities that provide services primarily to single heterosexual women and lesbians. Having a local program that caters mainly to this population is an advantage probably not enjoyed by women who live in more rural (and more conservative) areas; however, not having a range of choices can also be interpreted as confining.

Interventions, however, can also lead the patient to feel a loss of control. If intervention does not produce a pregnancy, individuals and couples can experience further frustration. When medication and intercourse did not result in a pregnancy, Lynne began medicated IUIs. When this procedure did not succeed, she decided to take a break from treatment. She intended to ask for the same procedure when she resumed, hoping that it would work. She says:

> Last cycle, everything was working, just for some reason [it] didn't work, which blows your mind. . . . At that point, you're thinking, wait a minute, [a sixteen]-year-old in the back of a Chevy, and here I am needing A or B and you're telling me it's not working? . . . Their explanation was when you're putting so much medication into a body, to sort of regulate the hormones, there's gonna be other things that'll go out of whack. And you just can't have total control of everything. All you can do is just sort of play a game of odds.

Lynne voices frustration that the doctors do not know what is going wrong. She feels a lack of control when she cannot accomplish what others (for example, "a sixteen-year-old in the back of a Chevy") do without effort. Still, Lynne also expresses a belief that it is not possible to understand and control everything.

The idea that infertility treatment is "a game of odds" is common among women undergoing these procedures. Those undergoing treatment for infertility use other metaphors of uncertainty and aimless motion to describe the experience. A woman writing in the newsletter of RESOLVE of the Bay State uses the metaphor of a boat on a rough sea, saying, "We felt alone, caught in a storm, adrift" (Fragola 8). Some call the cyclical nature of treatment a "merry-go-round" or a "treadmill," often noting that they feel or felt unable to get off or even to know when the ride was over. Others talk about treatment as a "roller coaster" with emotional highs (usually at the beginning of a cycle or when good results have come in) and lows (frequently at the end of a cycle). Still others describe being "caught up in a whirlwind."

Uncertainty in medical treatment for infertility frustrates the desire for knowledge, often understood as a prerequisite for control. Within this logic, one must understand something before successfully controlling it. Because treatment does not always provide the knowledge patients hope for, control appears to remain elusive. Encouraged to enter treatment by a faith that medical technology will provide answers, some women are unprepared for the uncertainty they often encounter. If a woman has a diagnosis, moving from diagnosis to pregnancy is not as straightforward as she might have expected. While those with unexplained infertility have a greater chance of success than those with most other diagnoses, they often find the uncertainty about the cause of their condition unsettling. They begin medical treatment in the hope that it will help them to regain a sense of control as well as to become pregnant; they often remain in treatment despite the unexpected uncertainty it offers.

Medical Treatment as Constraining

Medical treatment for infertility imposes routines and rituals that can supply comfort in the face of apparent chaos. Those in medical treatment, however, may also experience a loss of control because the regimen can enter into so many parts of their daily lives. The power of the medical regimen is "modest"; it draws on what Foucault calls the "simple instruments" of observation and judgment (*Discipline*, 170). This regimen is nevertheless powerful because it acts regularly and on the micropractices of the body. Regular routines are disrupted or replaced by monitoring and interventions (performed at home and in clinics) intended to diagnose the cause of infertility or to create a pregnancy. As the site of pregnancy, the woman's body is the object of most observations and interventions. In the least disruptive scenario, a woman may monitor her ovulation in order to time intercourse or insemination. In the most disruptive scenario, she may take daily injections of hormones for up to two weeks out of the month and make frequent trips to a clinic for blood tests, injections, ultrasounds, and other procedures.

For infertile heterosexual couples, babymaking is a private routine between a man and a woman, often undertaken with great excitement and anticipation of the child they hope to be creating. When pregnancy does not occur, and the couple seeks medical treatment, they often get caught up in a more public, externally regulated regimen. At the beginning stages of treatment, heterosexual couples are sometimes advised to time intercourse, with or without accompanying hormonal medication. For these couples, infertility treatment can transform sexual intercourse from lovemaking into work that must be performed on a controlled schedule. Susan describes it this way: "For the first two years, we kept trying every midcycle. It would be like, eleven o'clock, and I'd say, "Honey, we have to do this," and he'd be like, "I've got to go to bed." I'm like, "Honey we have to do this. It's day eleven." It was such a horrible chore. There was no pleasure involved in it. . . . It wasn't a lovemaking episode, it was, we have to have some sperm in there."

For Susan, intercourse had lost its spontaneity and its connection to sexual desire. Intercourse had to be performed for a purpose ("to have some sperm in there") on a particular day (midcycle, or "day eleven"). Lovemaking, which had once been important to both Susan and Paul, was no longer under their control. Those who use technologies that join the egg and sperm outside the body sometimes suspend sexual intercourse altogether during treatment. Some women are unable to disconnect lovemaking from babymaking; others, feeling "violated" by the medical procedures, do not want any further "invasion" by their partners.

Those involved in more advanced interventions sometimes describe clinics and procedures as making them feel like "objects" or "numbers" being controlled rather than like human beings with a say in the process. Women describe being "poked" or "prodded" like a "piece of meat," being "invaded," and being "pushed" or "pulled" along. Some tests, seen as "humiliating," make women feel "vulnerable." Some of the women in this study describe certain clinics as "factories." Lisa, for example, says:

> Going through [this particular clinic] was really going through like a mill. It really felt like they just push you through. It didn't feel like there was any individual attention to what was going on with me. And you have to go in early in the morning, get your ultrasound done and wait for that. Then you have to go upstairs and have your bloods drawn. And then you have to walk your bloods down, and then you have to be home at three or four. Just the way they dealt with me, personally, did not feel personable. . . . I felt like I was just being pushed through one more cycle, one more cycle, one more cycle, one more cycle. You can start now, you can start now.

As Lisa describes it, the individual patient has no control over her treatment in this clinic. She must have particular procedures done at certain times of the day. She moves through the facility, having tests done or samples taken in one place, then transporting them with her to other places. She must be at home at a certain time to receive test results. She is told when to start treatment and is encouraged to stay within the "mill." Cheryl, another woman, talks about disliking the same clinic because it controlled her schedule; she says that it "doesn't even start seeing you until after eight [A.M.], which means that there's no way you can get to work at a decent hour." Like Lisa and Sheri, other women felt a tension between wanting a larger, specialized clinic and wanting the kind of personalized attention that you get with a smaller facility. Sheri, who was going to try a procedure that was new at the time, did not want to go to what she calls a "rinky dink size place [because] they're never going to get to be doing [the new procedure]." She also felt that the training at a larger facility was more likely to be better. "I don't want to be the first patient," she says, "or the 20th." For many, however, going with the larger facility sometimes means getting lost in the crowd.

Single women and those in same-sex relationships can experience most of the same medical routines that heterosexual couples do. Like heterosexual partnered women, these women usually chart their menstrual cycles to be able to time insemination, sometimes regulate their menstrual cycles through hormones, and often undergo IUI. They may also undergo more costly and invasive procedures, such as IVF, especially if they are diagnosed with medical infertility. Unlike many heterosexual couples, however, they can choose sperm of known "good quality" and change donors if they do not become pregnant, avoiding the manipulations that heterosexual couples sometimes go through in order to compensate for the "low-quality" sperm of the male partner. Single heterosexual women and women in same-sex couples share with heterosexual couples the option of choosing artificial insemination by donor rather than use the sperm of a male partner, friend, or relative. In this process, individuals or couples select donors from a list that contains information such as physical and social traits and whether the donor would allow a biological child to contact him later.[1]

Like single women and married couples, women in same-sex relationships experienced some of the routines of medical treatment as constraining. Several of the women in this study who went through a local program for artificial insemination geared primarily for lesbians were happy with its political agenda but unhappy with what they saw as a rigid protocol and a disorderly bureaucracy. In order to save money on shipping costs, the facility orders sperm once a month, meaning that those who are inseminating must plan what they want in advance and will almost always end up with extra sperm if they become pregnant. In addition, the facility is closed on weekends, so that women who ovulate on a weekend must pick up their sperm samples before the end of the day on Friday in order to do the insemination on Saturday or Sunday. For some, the clinic's rigid program contributed to a feeling that they did not control the timing of their inseminations even though they were performing them at home.

While single women and those in same-sex couples follow a different routine in babymaking and one that is separate from sexual intercourse, the medical regimen can nonetheless be grueling and disruptive. Ellen reflects that "none of this is easy. I mean you really have to want this to go through all of this crap. Because it's not a casual thing at all." Although generally expected, the routine of charting (or using ovulation predictor kits), taking hormones, being inseminated, and then waiting to see whether pregnancy occurs takes its toll. To Anne, "the whole thing. . . . becomes so much your whole life, trying to get pregnant. You live in these two week periods of waiting to ovulate and then waiting to not get your period. And even just the inseminating part, just timing it, it's stressful." In addition, after repeated inseminations, an individual or couple may suspect an underlying physiological condition that is preventing pregnancy.

Whether single or married, heterosexual or lesbian, undergoing minimal intervention or advanced procedures, women are often prescribed hormones. Many of the women in this study described hormonal therapy as altering their personalities and impairing relationships and decision making. Judy describes her reaction to a drug used in the mid-1980s: "I got all of the typical side affects. I experienced weight gain, moodiness, depression. I actually ended up getting facial hair growing, and my voice changed. . . . So the whole year that I was on it, it was very, very difficult, especially the first year we were married."

Some women found that their emotional state changed in ways affecting other relationships. Stephanie describes her reaction and its consequences this way: "My hormones were just raging and that was really hard for me. I'm . . . one of those people who's on an even keel most of the time and I'm real jolly and I'm always in a good mood. I was just a bitch for years, and I lost a lot of friends. . . . I've never lost friends like that before. I've always had really long-lasting relationships, and my friendships just kept falling apart and it was like, what are we doing wrong? Well, I was not nice." Stephanie, like other women, was also concerned about the long-term effects of hormonal therapy and what she perceived as the willingness of physicians to prescribe large dosages for long periods. Similarly, Monica, who believed that some doctors "don't care if they kill you, trying," reported being advised to see a psychiatrist for antidepressant medication rather than reducing the dosage of her hormonal medication.

Whether because of medication or because of the regimen of treatment, many of the women in this study expressed the feeling that infertility and its treatment could take over their lives. The charting of the menstrual cycle, the daily doses of medication (some of which have to be administered through injection, often done by a partner), trips to the clinic (often daily) to have blood drawn, and periodic clinic visits for ultrasounds can consume much of a woman's nonworking day. This intense schedule makes it difficult for the woman to separate infertility treatment from the rest of her life, with the result that some women begin to feel (or appear to others) obsessed with becoming pregnant.

Stephanie, for example, who eventually had twins through IVF, says: "Nobody understands how desperate you get, unless you've been there. The desperation that I felt was so bizarre. There are days now when I think, what was I so desperate about. This is it? . . . You can't stop and for me, . . . I was possessed." While Stephanie says that she would do it all over again if she did not have children, she expresses here a discrepancy between the level of her desire ("possession") and the end result (children).

Other women expressed concern that they not lose control. Lynne, who believed that infertility tends to "take over your personality," was concerned about becoming obsessed. She says: "Some people, their whole life has really been built around having children, and it's anything goes. . . . I don't feel that way, and I will go up to IUIs, which to me is like wow, this is really advanced. . . . We started looking already into the adoption issues." Lynne and her husband had decided that they would do three intrauterine inseminations, which seemed like a lot more medical intervention than they had hoped to need. To pursue even more advanced techniques, such as IVF, seemed to Lynne to verge on obsession. Paula, who had already done several IVF cycles, was worried more about her emotional investment than about which technologies she used. She says: "I read those . . . magazine articles where people get obsessed about things. And I don't want to get obsessed. I get really easily obsessed. I'm very, very organized. I just didn't want it to take over my life."

Paula was afraid that the pursuit of pregnancy would become all-consuming. Similarly, Susan, who eventually adopted, was afraid of being desperate. After it began to seem that Western medicine would not work for her, Susan went to see an acupuncturist who claimed to be able to cure infertility. While Susan (like other women in this study) felt that seeking help from non-Western medical sources was a reasonable thing to do, her experience with the acupuncturist made her feel desperate. She remembers:

> He said that the soul of my aborted child from twelve years ago hadn't released and was preventing me from getting pregnant . . . and he would do a ceremony where the two of us could connect and release each other and prepare the way. . . . Well, I walked out of there . . . and I said to my husband, we're getting desperate . . . Acupuncture by itself, I don't think is desperate, but when this guy started talking like that, that there was some hokey pokey going on, in these other realms, I said, oh my god, I'm getting desperate. I don't want to be desperate. . . . Sell me some swampland in Florida and snake oil while you're at it.

Susan's sense of desperation came from her feeling that she was becoming ever more willing to be duped. At the end of her medical treatment, Susan began to believe that Western medicine had promised more than it had delivered. Here she expresses the desire not to be so desperate that she becomes the target of others selling false hopes.

Medical treatment for infertility thus operates on the practices of everyday life, altering sexual habits, schedules, and moods. The loss of control is no longer just about the inability to control reproduction. While in treatment, women may feel constraints on their time, relationships, abilities, and bodies, constraints that can exacerbate rather than alleviate their frustration.

Infertility and "Choice"

In *Sweet Grapes: How to Stop Being Infertile and Start Living Again,* Jean and Michael Carter write that "if we had to come up with one basic necessity for transforming childless into childfree, it would be choice; you have to choose childfree in order to live childfree" (55). For some women undergoing infertility treatment, choosing to be childfree (or even child*less*) does not seem possible. They envision infertility as something that has been done *to* them, something over which they have no control. They did not choose to be unable to have a child, and they are working very hard at trying to conceive. How, then, can being childfree be a choice, when the alternatives seem closed? In this vein, how can adoption be a real choice for those unable to have children biologically?

These reactions show that the relationship between infertility and choice is complicated and intimately connected to the notion of control. Those who feel that they have lost control of their reproductive capacity may react by trying to regain that capacity. This is especially true for those who have experienced a sense of control over other areas of their lives. For many white, middle-class Americans, regaining reproductive capacity means seeking medical treatment to correct the problem. Lynne, for example, sees infertility as a condition in which something is wrong with the body that needs to be repaired. She says, "More or less I look at it as my body doesn't work. If I had a kidney problem, you would fix it." While Lynne compares infertility to kidney dysfunction, others have compared it to cancer, high blood pressure, or diabetes.

Given such comparisons, infertile people unsurprisingly often experience "choices" as having to do with medical decisions about a medical condition. A woman or couple decides whether and when to make an initial visit to a physician, whether to continue with higher-tech medicine, which fertility clinic to use, what course of treatment to try, and when to stop. Each of these decisions is made in an effort to cure the medical condition. In contrast, consider the concept of choice in the prevention of pregnancy or birth. Although pathologized, the condition of pregnancy is generally not regarded as a medical abnormality that must be prevented.[2] That is, unless a woman's life or health is in danger, it is not medically necessary to prevent birth. Efforts to prevent pregnancy (through contraception) or to eliminate it (through abortion) are thus troped as choices rather than as medical decisions.

Herein lies an ironic source of tension between feminists critical of assisted reproduction and those in favor of increased access to these technologies. Most feminist critics of advanced reproductive technologies argue that women do not freely choose assisted reproduction because they are compelled by society and culture to become biological mothers at any cost (see, for example, Corea, *Mother,* "Brothel"; Rothman; Rowland; Spallone and Steinberg). Feminist critics of reproductive technologies, however, are also likely to be proponents of a woman's right to choose abortion. In other words, women are seen as more able to choose abortion freely than infertility treatment. Those in favor of increased access to reproductive technologies cite this apparent contradiction when advocating for their position. The comparison of abortion and infertility is itself contradictory, however; abortion is seen as a reproductive choice, while treatment for infertility is seen as medically necessary. In other words, troping infertility as a *medical problem* to a certain extent compels a *medical solution.*

Jean and Michael Carter, however, believe that infertile people can choose how to deal with the condition of being unable to have children and that this choice can help them regain control over their lives. Those who want to parent by adoption must come to see that they have made the choice rather than merely settling for second best. And those who decide not to have children can transform being child*less* into being child*free.* As the linguistic turn implies, making this transformation means turning a negative (not having desired children) into a positive (not desiring children) as a way of resisting the double bind. The Carters write:

> So choice plays a crucial role in the transformation from childless to childfree. It is a way of regaining control over our lives, of affirming who we are. When we look at choice in this light, the contradiction of the paradox begins to disappear. It would be a *real* contradiction to say that you could choose to be childless when you couldn't have children. To be child*free* though, *demands* a choice. The transformation from acceptance of childlessness to childfree occurs through the process of making a life decision. It is not simply resigning yourself

to your fate. It is not the stoic acceptance of what you can't change. No, it is the act of making a decision to create a positive change. (59–60, emphasis in the original)

In the remainder of their book, the Carters explain how couples can come to see living without children as positive. Among other things, making this transformation means using birth control (to eliminate the hope of becoming pregnant), discovering the reasons for the desire to have children (so that these desires can be fulfilled in other ways), reenvisioning the future to create new goals and dreams, and establishing a network of friends who can provide human interaction and support.

One woman in my study had read the Carters' book and had taken this idea of making positive choices to heart. Betsy, who eventually adopted two children, describes how she and her husband used the book not to decide to remain without children (although they both considered this option) but to adopt:

> The book really makes you think about what your choices are and that you can feel like this is all being done to you. . . . [Jean Carter] says, yeah you don't have a choice of getting pregnant, but you do have choices. You have a choice to adopt, you have a choice to live childfree. You can make a positive choice. . . . I was reading it when we went to the social worker [at the infertility clinic], and her attitude was sort of like, "Oh, why are you reading that book? You know, you're thinking of not having children?" . . . It's true that the authors chose not to have children, but the book kind of brought you to think about your choices. You know, your choices are beyond infertility treatments. And I just didn't feel like [the social worker] really had any understanding.

Betsy immediately recognized herself in the Carters' story. She had come to feel that her infertility was "done" to her, that procedures were "done" to her, and that she had no control over the outcome. Recognizing that all her choices did not have to be medical decisions ("your choices are beyond infertility treatments"), Betsy resisted the double bind of control and constraint. The reaction of the social worker at her clinic, however, illustrates a point of view that is perhaps common among those in infertility care. According to this point of view, a patient should be dedicated and single-minded; a patient who would consider living without children is not sufficiently determined. The social worker's reaction also illustrates that at least some patients are receiving the message that their choices are limited to medical decisions.

Women in this study found other ways to regain a feeling of control. Leslie, who had four miscarriages before having her son, credits a miscarriage support group for helping her to feel in control. The group helped her, she says, "because I . . . was stuck, I didn't know where to turn or who to go to. And I just support women's groups if you're having problems, because emotionally you can talk to them. And they said, well you got this test done, and this test done, try this doctor, I have this doctor." For Leslie, then, feeling more in control came from learning more about her options as well as finding more emotional support in dealing with the difficulty of her situation. Other women also acknowledged that becoming more knowledgeable about their conditions and their options made them more able to participate in medical decisions. Christine, who had several miscarriages before carrying a child to term, says that she would advise others to "read everything. Try to doctor yourself. Try to find anything that sounds remotely like you, and you carry it off to the doctors."

Others felt more able to control how they handled the stresses of infertility treatment by participating in a popular stress reduction program, offered by a major infertility center for women undergoing infertility treatment. The goal of the program is to help women cope with the stresses of treatment through medication, exercise, and diet. Sandra, who had been in treatment for two years before starting the program, became pregnant soon afterward and attributed her success to it. Another woman, writing in the newsletter of RESOLVE of the Bay State, said that the same program made her feel more in control. She writes, "I did not get pregnant and the pain was just as great, but I knew I had given it my best effort" (Ciganovic 3). The historical trend of attributing infertility to women's psychological problems has made such programs problematic. While support group facilitators and therapists do not usually claim to help women become pregnant, at least one study reports increased pregnancy rates for those who take part in psychological intervention (Domar et al.).

Mandating the Control of Infertility

A backlash movement, and one commonly seen in the popular press, holds that infertility is a disease of choice. Women's inability to have children at will is seen as the price to be paid for delayed childbearing, previous abortions, and sexual promiscuity. There has been a historical trend of blaming women for their inability to conceive (Sandelowski, "Failures"). According to this way of thinking, pregnancy is a natural state that women consciously or subconsciously control, at least until age makes conception impossible. The Massachusetts mandate was, in part, an effort to control these assignations of blame by locating infertility in the physical bodies of both women and men. By defining infertility as a medical condition, the reasoning went, women could be treated for it without the accompanying stigma. As Susan Sontag shows in her analysis of the metaphors used in describing cancer and tuberculosis, however, medical diagnoses do not necessarily absolve the afflicted of blame.

The mandate was also an effort to control the inconsistent treatment that women received and the inconsistent and inadequate coverage of treatment by insurance companies. Before coverage, the infertility industry was only in its infancy, so that women only rarely received treatment beyond surgery. Some procedures might be covered some of the time by some insurers, while other procedures were never covered by any insurer. The mandate did more than create access to existing technologies, however; like other health insurance initiatives, it helped to develop these technologies (Stone 29). Twelve years after passage of the Massachusetts mandate, infertility clinics are a common feature of the health care landscape in the state. Clinics have established records, practitioners have built reputations, and relationships between insurers and clinics and between clinics and other medical practitioners have been cemented. This network has set a standard in Massachusetts (especially in the eastern part of the state, where most of the clinics are located) that routinely includes advanced reproductive technologies.

In order to achieve the goal of mandatory coverage, treatment for infertility could not be seen as optional. Before the mandate, insurers frequently likened infertility treatment to plastic surgery, a comparison that infuriated women who did not (for whatever reason) see motherhood as optional. The comparison also infuriated those who might have considered motherhood optional but wanted to be in control of that decision. As Elizabeth Heitman argues:

> Many middle-class white women experience infertility as a frustrating foreclosure of choice. They seek to regain personal control over their lives and bodies through medical intervention. By contrast, many poor and non-white women who have endured other hardships and who consequently may not focus on issues of personal control, may experience infertility more in terms of general adversity. If infertility is one in a series of negative, seemingly irreversible events in a woman's life, she may be more likely to attribute it to fate or God's will than seek to address it through science. Women with such beliefs are less likely to seek medical treatment irrespective of their rates of infertility. (94)

In other words, rather than regarding infertility as just another insurmountable barrier to fulfillment, middle-class white women are more likely to view it as an aberration. Infertility has taken away their choices and therefore their sense of control.

Elaine Tyler May argues that "according to the American ethos, if you work hard, earn a decent living, delay gratification, and live by the rules, your life should be in your control" (212). In the late twentieth century, the expectation of control comes partly from the rapid growth of technology and its expansion into more and more facets of our lives. Technology has changed not only whether some things are possible but also whether Americans *expect* them to be possible and to have the freedom to choose them. For Americans, then, technology and law are intertwined as mechanisms by which individual choices can be ensured (Friedman 98–99). The Massachusetts mandate, in this view, provides a way in which people who are infertile may regain what they feel they have lost: the choice to have a biological child.

But the mandate also creates double binds for many of these same women. They may feel compelled to pursue medical treatment for infertility rather than some other options. While many do not consider their desire for medical treatment a function of limited choices, others do, particularly in retrospect. They may later regret having spent so much time in medical treatment and may wish that some professional had presented other options to them sooner. Or from the beginning, they may feel unable to decline the medical option primarily because it is covered by insurance. In addition, in order to regain the sense of control that they have lost, these women submit themselves to a regimen of treatment that often makes them feel constrained.

Many of the women in my study certainly felt that insurance coverage gave them more choices (especially medical ones) and that entering into medical treatment made them feel that they were taking positive action toward resolving their problem. Many of the same women (and others), however, experienced a lack of control during medical treatment. They submitted their bodies to scrutiny and probing, took hormones that changed their bodies and emotions, rescheduled their daily activities around the routines of tests and procedures, and disrupted their sex lives, often month after month. Perhaps accustomed to believing that they could control their lives, they placed their faith in technologies that they thought would help even though these technologies often fail.

Unlimited medical treatment can thus frustrate those who desire control by demonstrating that fertility is something that cannot be absolutely planned, predicted, and achieved. Even those who have children through assisted reproduction are transformed by the experience. Perhaps once believing that they controlled their lives, those who have children through assisted reproduction are not necessarily restored in this belief. Once control has been turned over to medical professionals, the uncertainty of the outcome and the constraints of the procedures may do more to convince them that control is elusive if not an illusion altogether.

As with the desire for success and order, the desire for control helps to sustain the processes of normalization in infertility treatment. As part of the ethos of normalcy for many of the women in this study, the desire for control compels them to enter into and remain in medical treatment even when it is experienced as constraining. The resulting double bind creates a tension between the control the woman wishes to regain and the constraint she seeks to avoid. Because normalcy is wrapped up with the desire for control, this tension sustains the difference not only between these two opposites but also between the normal and the abnormal. Treatment for infertility, then, does not so much resolve these oppositions as sharpen them.

Epilogue:
The Cultural Work of the Double Bind

> We do not seek partiality for its own sake, but for the sake of the connections and unexpected openings situated knowledges make possible.
> —Donna J. Haraway, *Simians, Cyborgs, and Women*

In this book, I have explored the mundane example of health insurance for infertility to see what it can tell us about the normalizing processes of contemporary life. I now speculate on what this example can tell us about the cultural work of the double bind and how double binds might be engaged.

In the late 1980s, when the Massachusetts infertility mandate was being debated, Americans lived with a sense that the world was becoming increasingly unstable. In response, they turned toward home and family as their last bastion of control. One way to control childlessness was to medicalize it: to define it in medical terms with medical solutions. As a medical condition, infertility became, on the one hand, an intensely personal and private experience and, on the other hand, an experience that could be approached and known by the medico-industrial complex. The medicalization of infertility had contradictory effects; it sharply distinguished between the normal and the abnormal rather than erasing their differences.

While the increased attention to treatment conferred greater normalcy on infertility (by making infertility more visible), the vast array and greater accessibility of treatments made it more abnormal to refuse treatment and accept the condition. Medicalization located the problem within an individual's physical body (rather than with Divine Providence or with a woman's subconscious desire to avoid pregnancy). In so doing it intensified feelings of personal abnormality for individuals, but it also made the condition, when seen as something that affects the entire population, a problem that demanded attention from governments and other institutions.

In Massachusetts, public attention took the form of mandatory insurance coverage for the condition. From a liberal feminist perspective, the mandate can be seen as having given women more choices in their reproductive decision making. A biological child has become more affordable for some women in middle and lower economic brackets as they have gained access to opportunities that had previously been the privilege of the wealthy. I have argued in this book that the mandate does more than remove economic barriers to medical technologies, however. Itself functioning as a technology of normalization, the mandate structures experience by institutionalizing the category of infertility. In material terms, insurance coverage allows for the creation of new clinics and for further research in biomedical approaches to infertility. In addition, insurance shapes the ways in which physicians and individuals affected by the condition understand the available options. In symbolic terms, authorizing a medical definition of infertility functions for the middle-class white women in my study both as a stamp of approval and as a map of a preferred path. Accustomed to seeing the law as means of ensuring individual rights, and bolstered by a faith in medical technology, these women experienced the mandate as providing opportunities that could not easily be refused.

The category of infertility, once institutionalized, reifies the distinction between fertile and infertile. The process both stabilizes these categories and positions them as authoritative. Those unable to have biological children are caught within this framework. Consider the example of Jean and Michael Carter, the authors of *Sweet Grapes: How To Stop Being Infertile and Start Living Again,* who decided that they were "no longer infertile." Neither fertile nor infertile, the Carters sought a third category that would help them to understand their cultural position: "no longer infertile." Unable to inhabit the first category because they could not have biological children, and unwilling to inhabit the second because they no longer desired children, the Carters nonetheless felt compelled to define themselves in relation to both categories. All those who once desired to have biological children and discover that they cannot do so—whether they have children through treatment, leave treatment without children, or never enter treatment at all—are affected by this cultural expectation and categorization. But the influence of these categories also extends beyond the infertile themselves. As Carol Smart argues, "the process of 'normalization' may fall heaviest on the infertile, but no one escapes the power of the renewed medico-legal discourse on normal family life" (112).

The medical definition of infertility authorized by the Massachusetts mandate has helped to create a new standard of care and is reshaping what constitutes a normal family. As RESOLVE hoped, the medical model has informed the new standard. This metonymic process—"the *reduction* of some higher or more complex realm of being to the terms of a lower or less complex realm of being" (K. Burke, *Grammar* 506, emphasis in the original)—is a necessary part of normalization, which must eliminate any "superfluous models" (Ewald 150). The normal model for the family is constituted as the biological family, but the proliferation of advanced reproductive technologies means that a number of medical options can now be considered normal within this model. The vast range of technologies for assisted reproduction—through surrogacy, donated eggs, and artificial insemination by donor—all afford pathways to biological parenthood, to a semblance of normalcy. At the same time, however, the pregnancies that they produce are to some degree *only* a semblance of normalcy in that they are not the result of "natural" intercourse. In other words, the family conceived through assisted reproduction is simultaneously normal and abnormal.

This is the work of normalization: it is not so much about reforming the abnormal (which would eliminate the need for normalizing power) as it is about distinguishing between the normal and the abnormal (which would sustain the need for continual improvement). To achieve this work, a technology of normalization (such as the mandate) creates a tension between the categories to be differentiated. In the case of infertility, the tension occurs not only for the women who seek medical treatment but also for a culture that has come to understand this treatment as reasonable and necessary. In America at the turn of the millennium, infertility is a cultural category that deserves attention and response. Medical treatment helps to mark the outlines of that category by perpetually distinguishing it from fertility. In this way, the medical treatment of infertility is a disciplinary exercise, which "by bending behavior towards a terminal state, . . . makes possible a perpetual characterization of the individual either in relation to this term, in relation to other individuals, or in relation to a type of itinerary" (Foucault, *Discipline* 161).

At the level of individual bodies, medical treatment can be understood as a way of relating the infertile woman to the fertile woman she might become. At the level of populations, the existence of the entire disciplinary apparatus of reproductive endocrinology creates a cultural expectation that those who are unable to have biological children can be categorized as infertile, as different from the fertile population. But while the regime may help them become pregnant, these people will never return to the category of the fertile. As the convict who leaves the prison is more of an "ex-con" than a "law-abiding citizen," the infertile are not so much reformed as distinguished by what they are not.

The distinguishing of opposites essential to normalization is achieved in part by the rhetorical mechanism of the double bind. Throughout this book, I have examined the double bind in the example of infertility, but it can teach us about other normalizing processes. Within other processes of normalization, the categories that are placed in opposition will differ, as will the double binds that individuals find constraining. In the case of infertility, the category of *fertile* is held in tension with *infertile*. As I have argued in this book, however, the condition of infertility is impossible to separate from its cultural context. The middle-class white women in this study experienced infertility as the play of other oppositions—between success and failure, control and constraint, order and discontinuity—that create double binds. As long as women feel the pull of both sides of these double binds, the tension necessary for this process of normalization to continue is maintained.

Kathleen Hall Jamieson argues that the double bind is imposed by the powerful on the less so; while men may be affected by double binds, she says, it is women who have been historically less powerful and who have thus borne more of their weight. She notes that women have felt the effect of double binds for centuries, forbidden from masculine activities and behavior yet judged by masculine standards. While the double binds that I have traced do not seem peculiar to gender, they are experienced in ways that are profoundly gendered. For the women in this study, for example, the definition of success often includes the ability to reproduce, a faculty that women, more than men, are likely to see as central to their identity. How one defines success, and how that affects the experience of infertility, may also be related to class and race. Accustomed to being rewarded with success after putting in hard work, many of the middle-class white women in my study experienced infertility as an obstacle to be overcome through effort. Although I do not have evidence of how people in other groups experience the double binds I have identified, I suspect that normalization works through different sets of double binds, depending on one's subject position. As part of the pursuit of parenthood, for example, the women in this study were pursuing success, control, and order. Their experience of normalcy as middle-class white women is entangled in these goals as well as in the ways they define them. Members of other groups may pursue these same goals with similar or different definitions, or they may pursue different goals altogether.

Normalization can thus be regarded as a matrix of double binds created not by one individual for imposition on another but by intersecting institutional and cultural discourses. Each individual experiences normalization according to her or his relationship to these discourses and according to exigence (for example, the inability to have a desired biological child). The number of possible configurations of double binds may be as infinite as the number of possible exigences and possible subject positions (inflected by gender, race, class, nationality, sexual orientation, ability, and any number of other identifiers). If so, normalization works through one set of double binds for a middle-class white woman defined as infertile and a different set for a working-class Latino man defined as homosexual or a working-poor African American girl defined as learning disabled. In this conceptualization, understanding who is being caught by double binds is not as simple as identifying the powerful and the powerless. Foucault's notion of disciplinary power may be helpful here. Rather than being possessed by individuals, disciplinary power "functions like a piece of machinery" (*Discipline* 177); it is the entire "apparatus" that observes, measures, compares, and distributes individuals in a normalizing system. While everyone is caught within these apparatuses, each individual experiences them in a particularized way.

Understanding the role of the double bind in the processes of normalization thus means situating it within institutional contexts and connecting it to the mechanisms of biopower, which operate at the level of the individual and of populations. The tensions I have identified in this book appeal to a particular kind of legal and medical subject, one who sees both law and medicine as providing pathways to individual fulfillment. The individual is drawn to the mechanisms of normalization to realize personal goals, but the goals being sought are defined primarily in relation to a population. This is the function of biopower: to operate simultaneously at the individual and species bodies to increase efficiency and productivity. In the scenario I am positing, the individual is not a passive subject of biopower but makes decisions and takes actions. The women in my study, for example, decided whether or not to pursue medical treatment, which treatments to pursue, whether to stop treatment, and whether to consider adoption as an alternative. Far from being autonomous agents, individuals nevertheless make choices between competing alternatives.

How and to what extent, then, can individuals disrupt double binds? Jamieson argues that the rhetoricity of the double bind makes it susceptible to disruption or resolution. "Examined as rhetorical frames," she writes, "double binds can be understood, manipulated, dismantled" (20). She offers a range of rhetorical strategies—including reframing, recovering, reclaiming, recasting, rewriting, and recounting—for undoing the binds that constrain women. The strategy of reframing, for example, means changing the perspective from which the opposing choices are viewed. Through these strategies, Jamieson argues, women as individuals and as a group can progress, if only gradually, so that they eventually attain equality with men. Like Jamieson, Bateson and his colleagues believe that resolving double binds is a matter of recognizing their rhetoricity. For the schizophrenic, Bateson and his colleagues advocate a therapeutic treatment that helps the schizophrenic to "communicate about communication, to comment upon the meaningful actions of oneself and others" (258). Through metacommunication, individuals caught in double binds can eventually discern the "real" message and work themselves out of the bind.

In this book, I have shown how some women come to feel empowered by working themselves out of double binds. Betsy, for example, began to see that the choices offered to her were all medical choices. Once she expanded the idea of choice to include nonmedical options, she felt less caught by the desire to be in control in an environment in which she otherwise felt she had little or no control. Susan, who once thought that being normal meant having a biological child, felt compelled to undergo medical treatment until she came to see adopted children as more normal. In each case, the woman "reframed" the oppositions pulling her.

An assessment of the ultimate effect of these strategies, however, especially for the double binds that sustain normalization, must consider the subject positions of those constrained by double binds and the problems of advocacy in the face of diversity. While the binds that tie women in Jamieson's narrative are more or less universal for all women at a particular cultural moment, those sustaining normalization appear to be highly individualized. To negotiate these double binds, individuals would need to be constantly aware of their competing desires as well as open to interrogating and discarding some of them. Even so, I do not believe that all double binds are soluble; some narratives retain such strong cultural force that denaturalizing them is not a project for the individual already stressed by the double bind. In addition, a woman who works herself out of one double bind may find herself in another, unforeseen and perhaps unrecognized.

More problematic, however, is the extent to which deconstructing double binds can work for entire groups rather than individuals. Jamieson's approach is one of progress; as a group, she argues, women can resolve the double binds that tie them so that they can reach eventual gender equality. Writing of the binaries that create double binds for homosexuals, Eve Kosofsky Sedgwick takes a different position. She argues that recognizing binaries as inherently unstable and therefore subject to reversal or disruption does not necessarily eliminate them. "Quite the opposite: . . . ," she writes, "an understanding of their irresolvable instability has been continually available, and has continually lent discursive authority, to antigay as well as to gay cultural forces" (10). More significant for this book, though, is the complexity of the role of the double bind in the normalization process, which appears to work through multiple and constantly shifting discourses. The constellation of double binds emerging from these discourses operates differently on differently situated subjects.

Advocates working on behalf of marginalized subjects confront potentially infinite numbers of these constellations. While deconstructing these constellations appears possible, at least to some extent, reconstructing positive discourses necessary for institutional or cultural change is more problematic. Whose experience should be represented in these reconstructions? Whose experience can be omitted?

Recognizing double binds as irresolvably unstable means seeing them as a condition to be monitored rather than as a problem to be solved. Double binds and the normalizing forces they sustain must be engaged vigilantly, partially, and locally. Such engagement entails attending to the commonplaces that frame the oppositions constituting the double binds. In this book, for example, the commonplace of control gives rise to the double bind of feeling compelled to enter into a regime that offers opportunities to regain control over reproduction while simultaneously making such control appear elusive. Examined as commonplaces, these desires take on a significance greater than the individual. Far from indicating only individual private desire, commonplaces are the knowledge shared by members of a collective. As common sense, this knowledge becomes naturalized, taken for granted as descriptors of reality rather than as arguments capable of being disputed.

One strategy for local engagement, then, is to challenge the commonplaces framing double binds in addition to challenging the terms of the binds themselves. For instance, when moved by the desire to succeed and informed by medical definitions of success, a woman might be drawn into medical treatment for infertility even though it offers just as many opportunities for failure. To challenge the double bind as a binary opposition, the woman might attempt to create a third option by redefining what it means to be successful. To challenge the commonplaces upon which this bind is constructed, however, means also to question the authority of "success." Because the commonplace of success may very well frame double binds in other processes of normalization, such a strategy can move beyond the level of the individual or the situated position occupied by the middle-class, white, infertile woman. I am not suggesting, however, that the challenging of commonplaces can necessarily serve all members of a collective once and for all. To the extent that commonplaces are incapable of standing for the universal—and stable—sentiment of a collective, intervention must remain partial, contingent, and continual. Resistance may be a better strategy than resolution.

Perhaps the most important site for such resistance is within the institutions that give power to the double binds that sustain normalization. In Massachusetts, medicine and law collaborated to authorize a standardized definition of infertility that would enable a standardized approach to the problem. By removing competing models from official discourse, the authorized definition made consistent treatment possible. The double binds experienced by the women interviewed for this study emerge from this standardization. Pulled on the one hand by the topoi of success, order, and control and on the other by the medical model of infertility, the women in this study were often doubly bound. Normalization relies on such homogenization so that communication can occur among institutions. It is at these points where strategic interruption can take place. Interrogating what ends and interests are served in these processes is a local tactic of heterogeneity with the potential to disrupt—if only momentarily—the forces of normalization.

Appendix A: Text of the Massachusetts Infertility Insurance Mandate

The Massachusetts mandate consists of new sections added to several chapters of the *General Laws of Massachusetts* (ch. 175, § 47H; ch. 176A, § 8K; ch. 176B, § 4J). In addition, one sentence was added to ch. 176G, § 4.

The following excerpt is the entire text of ch. 175, § 47H, which outlines the mandate. The other changes specify further requirements for various types of insurers.

> Any blanket or general policy of insurance, except a blanket or general policy of insurance which provides supplemental coverage to medicare or other governmental programs, described in subdivisions (A), (C) or (D) of section one hundred and ten which provides hospital expense or surgical expense insurance which includes pregnancy-related benefits and which is issued or subsequently renewed by agreement between the insurer and the policyholder, within or without the commonwealth, while this provision is effective, or any policy or accident and sickness insurance as described in section one hundred and eight which provides hospital expense or surgical expense insurance which includes pregnancy-related benefits and which is delivered or issued for delivery or subsequently renewed by agreement between the insurer and the policyholder in the commonwealth while this provision is effective, or any employees' health and welfare fund which provides hospital expense and surgical expense benefits which includes pregnancy-related benefits

and which is promulgated or renewed to any person or group of persons in the commonwealth while this provision is effective shall provide, to the same extent that benefits are provided for other pregnancy-related procedures, coverage for medically necessary expenses of diagnosis and treatment of infertility to persons residing within the commonwealth. For purposes of this section, "infertility" shall mean the condition of a presumably healthy individual who is unable to conceive or produce conception during a period of one year.

These statutes were implemented by the *Code of Massachusetts Regulations* (211 Code Mass. Regs. 37.00 [1987]), which further specifies that insurers are not required to cover experimental procedures, surrogacy, sterilization reversal, and egg cryopreservation. Insurers are prevented from restricting access to those with preexisting conditions but may "establish reasonable eligibility requirements, based upon the insured's medical history, and reasonable provider contractor standards."

Appendix B: Legislative Information

This appendix contains information on the state legislation regulating insurance for infertility current as this book goes to press. Table 1 contains information on states that have passed "mandates to cover," which require insurers to cover some form of medical treatment for infertility. Table 2 contains similar information for those states that have passed "mandates to offer," which require insurers only to *offer* the coverage.

Note: The information in these tables is intended for comparative purposes only and is not comprehensive. For complete information about coverage in any state, contact the regulatory agency for insurance in that state. For updates as they occur, see the RESOLVE web site at http://www.resolve.org.

Table 1. Mandates to Cover Some Form of Medical Treatment for Infertility

State and Code	Year Passed	Details
Arkansas	1987	• Covers IVF only.
		• Exempts HMOs.
Ark. Stat.		• Specifies that a woman's eggs must be
Ann. §§ 23-85-		fertilized by her husband's sperm.
137, 23-86-118		• Limits treatment to those with either a
(1999)		two-year history of unexplained infertility
		or one of the following conditions:
		-endometriosis
		-in utero DES exposure
		-male factor infertility
		-removed or blocked fallopian tubes
		(except for voluntary sterilization)

State and Code	Year Passed	Details

Hawaii
 	
Haw. Rev. Stat. §§ 431: 10A-116.5, 432: 1-604 (1993)
	1987	• Covers IVF only.
		• Provides a one-time only benefit.
		• Provides coverage only if other covered treatment options have failed.
		• Specifies that a woman's eggs must be fertilized by her husband's sperm.
		• Limits treatment to those with a five-year history of infertility or at least one of the following:
		  -endometriosis
		  -in utero DES exposure
		  -male factor infertility
		  -removed or blocked fallopian tubes

Illinois 215 ILCS 5/356m, 125/5-3 (Smith-Hurd Supp. 2000)	1991	• Limits the number of egg retrievals depending on whether the pregnancy is for a first or second birth through treatment (four for the first, two for the second). • Provides coverage only if other covered treatment options have failed. • Exempts businesses with 25 or fewer employees. • Excludes religious organizations from offering coverage if it conflicts with their ethical standards. • Defines infertility as "the inability to conceive after one year of unprotected sexual intercourse or the inability to sustain a successful pregnancy."

State and Code	Year Passed	Details

Maryland
 	
Md. Ins. Code Ann. § 15-810 (1997)
	1985	• Covers IVF only.
		• Provides coverage only if other covered treatment options have failed.
		• Exempts businesses with 50 or fewer employees.
		• Excludes HMOs.
		• Specifies that a woman's eggs must be fertilized by her husband's sperm.
		• Limits treatment to those with a five-year history of infertility or at least one of the following:
		  -endometriosis
		  -in utero DES exposure
		  -removed or blocked fallopian tubes

Massachusetts Mass. Ann. Laws ch. 175, § 47H; ch. 176A, § 8K; ch. 176B, § 4J; ch. 176G, § 4 (West 1998)	1987	• Covers "medically necessary expenses of diagnosis and treatment." • Defines infertility as "the condition of a presumably healthy individual who is unable to conceive or produce conception during a period of one year."
Montana Mont. Code Ann., §§ 33-22-1521, 33-31-102 (1999)	1987	• Applies to HMOs only. • Included as part of basic health services; specific infertility services are not specified.

State and Code	Year Passed	Details
New York N.Y. Ins. Law §§ 3216, 3221, 4303 (McKinney Supp. 2000)	1990	• Prevents denial of procedures solely because the condition they correct causes infertility. • Excludes IVF and other procedures designed solely to produce pregnancy.
Ohio Ohio Rev. Code Ann. § 1751.01(7) (Anderson Supp. 1999)	1991	• Applies to HMOs only. • Included as part of basic preventive health services; specific infertility services are not specified.
Rhode Island R.I. Gen. Laws §§ 27-18-30, 27-19-23, 27-20-20, 27-41-33 (1998)	1989	• Includes coverage for "medically necessary expenses of diagnosis and treatment of infertility." • Defines infertility as "the condition of an otherwise presumably healthy married individual who is unable to conceive or produce conception during a period of one year."
West Virginia W. Va. Code § 33-25A-2 (Supp. 1999)	1999	• Applies to HMOs only. • Included as part of basic health services; specific infertility services are not specified.

Table 2: Mandates to Offer Coverage

State and Code	Year Passed	Details
California Cal. Health & Safety Code § 1374.55 (West 1990) and Cal. Ins. Code § 10119.6 (West 1993)	1989	• Requires insurers to offer GIFT but not IVF. • Excludes religious organizations from offering coverage if it conflicts with their ethical standards. • Defines infertility as "either (1) the presence of a demonstrated condition recognized by a licensed medical physician as a cause of infertility, or (2) the inability to conceive a pregnancy or to carry a pregnancy to a live birth after a year or more of sexual relations without contraception."
Connecticut Conn. Gen. Stat. Ann. § 38a-536 (West Supp. 2000)	1989	• Requires insurers to offer coverage for "medically necessary expenses," including IVF. • Defines infertility as "the condition of a presumably healthy individual who is unable to conceive or produce conception, or retain a pregnancy during a one-year period."

Texas
 	
Tex. Ins. Code Ann. Art. 3.51-6 § 3A (West Supp. 2000)
	1987	• Requires insurers to offer coverage for IVF.
		• Specifies that a woman's eggs must be fertilized by her husband's sperm.
		• Excludes religious organizations from offering coverage if it conflicts with their ethical standards.
		• Limits treatment to those with a five-year history of infertility or at least one of the following:
		  -endometriosis
		  -in utero DES exposure
		  -removed or blocked fallopian tubes
		  -oligospermia (too few sperm)

Appendix C: Research Methods

To understand the complex social phenomenon of reproduction, this book employs the methods of multisited ethnography. Ethnography—as a collection of methods (observation, interviewing, and archival research) rather than one method alone—is particularly well suited for projects aiming to examine a phenomenon from a variety of angles. As a particular kind of ethnography, *multisited* ethnography is appropriate for research that interrogates the relationships among institutions and between the local and global where the "global is an emergent dimension of arguing about the connection among sites" (Marcus 99).

In this project, by envisioning the site of ethnography as multiple and emergent rather than as singular and fixed, I was able to follow the object of study as I reached different understandings of it. Approaching this research as "practices of construction through (preplanned or opportunistic) movement" (Marcus 106), I remained at a particular site long enough to trace further connections before moving on. For this reason, I've treated some sites in more depth than others. I have aimed neither at consistency nor at comprehensiveness; I assume that partiality is a necessary feature of this kind of work. In other words, I have sought to represent not a unitary whole but a trajectory that is only one among many possibilities.

Data Collection

One of the primary goals of this project was to examine how various institutional discourses—medical, legal, administrative, and religious—interact with each other and are negotiated by the individuals whose lives are caught up in them. The multisited approach that I adopted for this project took me, between June 1995 and December 1996, to infertility clinics, the Massachusetts state archives, the offices of RESOLVE of the Bay State, the homes and workplaces of the infertile, and the varied locations of informational meetings on infertility and adoption. I attended RESOLVE events (including an all-day educational symposium and several presentations on particular medical, emotional, or social aspects of infertility) as well as lectures and meetings sponsored by other organizations, such as adoption agencies and organizations, infertility clinics, and universities. I also "listened in" on an Internet discussion group devoted to infertility and an Internet mailing list for lesbian mothers.

In addition to this observational research, I conducted archival research at the offices of RESOLVE, the Massachusetts state library, and the Massachusetts state archives. The written texts that I analyzed included legislative records of the debate about the mandate; court opinions from infertility insurance cases (nationwide); articles in newspapers and the popular press about infertility and the Massachusetts mandate; newsletters and other materials from RESOLVE; and promotional materials from adoption agencies, drug manufacturers, infertility clinics, sperm banks, and surrogacy agencies.

To gain a sense of the issue from various perspectives, as well as to understand the historical context of the legislation, I conducted interviews with a lawmaker involved in the legislation, two people who had played a central role in drafting the legislation, several physicians, RESOLVE staff, attorneys, and public health administrators. In addition, I had informal conversations with government employees, community organizers, and clinic employees. My goal was not to be comprehensive—that is, I did not attempt to speak with everyone who had a role in or opinion on the legislation—but to see the mandate from multiple perspectives. These interviews consisted of both closed-ended and open-ended questions that varied, depending on the person I was interviewing. I asked the drafters of the legislation, for example, to tell me how it came into being and to evaluate its strengths and limitations. Some, but not all, of these interviews were taped.

Most of the analysis in this book is based on interviews with people who had been diagnosed as infertile or who had sought assisted reproduction to become pregnant. In focusing on individuals I mean not to imply that individuals can be understood apart from society but instead to show how individuals can serve as entry points for understanding the emergence of new social collectives.

I identified interview participants much as I located sites: by following connections. I solicited participation continuously throughout the study; I asked participants to refer me to others (a method known as "snowball sampling") and placed ads in publications or put up posters as I learned of a particular forum. I used posters in waiting rooms at infertility clinics (one in the western part of the state, one in the central part of the state, and two in the greater Boston area); posters at low-income clinics; posters at adoption agencies; an ad placed in a newsletter of RESOLVE of the Bay State; an ad placed in a booklet produced by a welfare-rights organization; an ad placed in a newsletter for gay and lesbian parents; Internet newsgroups (including discussion groups for infertility, raising children, and adoption); and an Internet mailing list for lesbian mothers and those considering motherhood. The text that I employed to call for participation varied with each forum. I also posted several calls for participation on the same Internet newsgroup, but each time I asked for something different (for example, to hear from people undergoing treatment, from people who had stopped treatment, or from people who had taken part in the Massachusetts lobbying effort). Except in the ad I placed with the welfare-rights organization (which is specifically oriented toward women), I did not specify the gender of those I was attempting to contact.

I had hoped to reach a diverse group (low-income as well as middle-income individuals, men as well as women, lesbians as well as heterosexual women, people of color as well as whites, and technologically naive as well as technologically sophisticated individuals), and I made conscious efforts to do so. Because ethnography seeks to understand an object of study in its uniqueness, however, I did not aspire to create a subject pool that would accurately represent the infertile population in Massachusetts. I interviewed twenty-six women and one man, including three couples (one heterosexual, two lesbian). All interviewees were white, and all but two had household incomes ranging from $50,000/year to over $100,000/year. At incomes below this level, one woman was pursuing a graduate degree, while the other was a single woman working as an artist.

With one exception, all interviewees had college degrees (the exception had completed one year of college), and eleven had graduate degrees. Two women were in graduate school, two worked as mothers at home, and the majority of the others were engaged in professional occupations. The majority were in their thirties; the youngest interviewed was twenty-nine, while the oldest was forty-four. Some were undergoing medical treatment for infertility at the time of the interview, while others had done so either before passage of the Massachusetts mandate or after its passage but before the time of the interview. Of the women, twenty were single or in heterosexual relationships, and six were in same-sex relationships.

Twenty-four of the women resided in Massachusetts. Of the remaining two, one lived in Ohio, a state that has limited coverage for infertility, and the other lived in Rhode Island but had received some infertility treatment in Massachusetts; I interviewed these two women not to get a comprehensive look at women's experiences in other states but to give myself new perspective on the experiences of the women in Massachusetts. In this book I refer to or quote directly from twenty-three of the interviews (those of twenty-two women and the sole man); brief sketches of these participants appear in Appendix D.

I conducted the interviews at participants' homes or workplaces or over the telephone, depending on where the interviewee felt most comfortable. At their request, I interviewed the heterosexual couple separately and the lesbian couples together. Of the two lesbian couples, one was currently undergoing artificial insemination, while the other had two children through assisted reproduction. Interviews lasted between half an hour and two and a half hours.

The purpose of these interviews was to understand how the interviewees experienced involuntary childlessness. I wanted to learn how they viewed parenthood, medical procedures, infertility, disease, advanced reproductive technologies, and insurance, and I hoped to understand how and why they made certain decisions about their treatment. I began each interview by explaining that the study was focusing on the mandate for infertility treatment. I told them that I wanted to talk to people whose lives had been affected by this legislation. I then explained how the interview would proceed and told them that they could choose not to answer any questions and that they could stop the interview at any time.

I used closed-ended questions at the beginning of each interview to gather demographic data on age, race, ethnicity, and education level. I asked about marital status, household income, number of people in the household, number of children living elsewhere (and whether they were conceived using reproductive technologies), geographic location of residence (rural area, town, suburb, or city), whether the person belonged to any support groups (for lesbian parenting or for infertility, depending on the participant), and to what extent the person used the Internet. I asked about the Internet because I had used it to locate several participants, and I wanted to make sure that I also located a good number of participants who did not use this technology. After completing the demographic questions, I generally began the open-ended part of the interview with a question such as "Can you tell me when you started thinking about having children?" This question usually prompted the participant to narrate her or his experiences.

Because I had no set agenda for the interviews, I typically followed the interviewee wherever she or he took me, unless the interview appeared to be going too far afield. I occasionally asked interviewees to clarify or expand on a point; periodically I developed an idea mentioned by the interviewee in passing. Sometimes, at the end of an interview, I asked questions that occurred to me after I had gotten a sense of the person's experience as a whole. Six months to a year and a half after the first interview, I followed up with ten of the twelve women who were in treatment at the time of the first interview. In these brief telephone interviews, usually lasting no more than fifteen minutes, I attempted to find out whether the woman was still undergoing treatment and, if not, why not.

While I transcribed some of the tapes myself, I hired transcriptionists for most of them. I listened to each of those I did not transcribe myself in its entirety, filling in gaps and correcting errors. This second pass also ensured that the tapes were transcribed fairly consistently.

Data Analysis

Analysis of ethnographic data is never separable from data collection. The process of gathering and understanding data is instead iterative. Rather than conducting all the interviews and gathering all of the other material in one step and sitting down with all the material in a second step, I tacked back and forth between fieldwork and "headwork" as my understanding of the mandate and its cultural context emerged.

The first step in understanding any of the interview material was to subject it to close scrutiny. I adopted a process, outlined by Robert M. Emerson, Rachel I. Fretz, and Linda L. Shaw, that involved two passes: the first pass, called "open coding," was a line-by-line attempt to categorize the data. The purpose behind this close, careful reading was to see what categories emerged from the data rather than imposing preconceived categories onto the data. My role in this procedure was, of course, an active one, and I do not pretend that I discovered categories that existed a priori. As the person who selected the research topic, framed the research questions, solicited and interviewed subjects, coded the data, and made sense of the material, I brought my own assumptions and expectations to the project. Looking at each line of data, however, compelled me to examine the material more closely and to describe it more minutely than I might have otherwise.

After completing the initial coding, I reviewed the data and began to note recurring themes (such as "success" and "lobbying strategies"). I selected a few of these themes and copied text related to each of them into a separate word processing file. My rationale for selecting themes was based not on frequency of occurrence but on whether the theme resonated with my research questions. Because I was interested in the reasons that individuals pursued medical treatment, for example, one of my categories was "success." Similarly, because I was interested in the kinds of knowledge that were reflected in the mandate and how these kinds of knowledge made their way into the debate, another category was "lobbying strategies."

I then reread the text for each theme, making subgroups (such as "limiting debate" and "staying away from the media" within the larger theme of "lobbying strategies"). My goal in making subgroups was to understand the data even more minutely and to hone the analytic categories (Emerson et al. 160). (I used these analytic categories as I combed through my observation notes, transcripts from electronic mailing lists and discussion groups, and printed materials. I searched for items that resonated with

Appendix C / 165

these categories either by supplementation or contradiction.) Figure 1 includes an example of open coding and the identification of themes.

The left-hand column contains the transcript of the interview (I am identified with an "I" and the interviewee with an "R"), and the right-hand column contains the notes I made while coding. Notes appearing in upper and lower case are those that I made during the first pass. During the second pass, I identified themes, indicated in all capitals (for example, RIGHTS, SUPPORT, and LIMBO).

Figure 1. Sample Coded Transcript

[Earlier portion of interview deleted]

R: ...about a year and a half ago we considered moving
I: out of state?
R: out of state. And, we actually did, like five job interviews, and my husband got an offer somewhere else, and we were really tempted to do it because you know, A, we wanted to move, and B, why shouldn't we move, we have every right to move, and C, he, it looked like a good opportunity, but what, what we decided was, we can't. We can't move. We have stay here for the insurance. | Thought about moving out of state, but couldn't because of insurance

"Right" to move; RIGHTS

I: you think if it hadn't been for the insurance you would have moved
R: if there wasn't insurance? If it was all covered everywhere, then that wouldn't have been a factor, if it was not covered anywhere it wouldn't have been a factor, yeah, it definitely influenced us, whether we ultimately would have moved or not you know I can't say with a hundred per cent certainty, but he did have a job offer, we looked at houses, we were, you know, concerned about the kids, and all of this, but, but we were very serious, and we, we may have changed our minds, um, or gotten cold feet or whatever, but we were, we realized that we can't, we can't move because we need this technology to get pregnant. Once we get pregnant, we can't move because we need, because pregnancy is a pre-existing condition, and the insurance company that that hospital had considered, didn't, it wasn't an HMO, so it was an indemnity plan, and it considered, I read the plan to see what our benefits would be, and it said that pregnancy is a pre-existing condition and my delivery wouldn't have been covered, and that got me very very mad, and um, so then we realized that even if we got pregnant in the interim and then could accept an offer, we couldn't move until I | Can't move because they need technology to get pregnant
Can't move if pregnant because pregnancy is pre-existing condition

delivered, so we're talking well over a year later from these interviews, so it screwed everything up in that sense, where if it was covered in that state too, or in all states, just like anything else, and I know there are pre-existing conditions and that's something that I think should be eliminated anyway, but, so it definitely affected a lot of our major decisions, and the other part was that it helped us be in denial what was really going on. I think the shit is hitting the fan emotionally for us now because we didn't deal with it for the last couple of years cause we kept saying, well just next month we'll get pregnant, and nobody will have to know, and it won't, I mean, we'll be pregnant, we won't have to tell anybody what's been going on because it won't matter, it will be behind us, and it'll all have been worth it, and next month it will happen, and next month it will happen, and next month it will happen, and all of a sudden three years have gone by, and next month looks like it's never gonna happen, so, you know, it, it helps kind of fos -- it gave us a false sense of security, I think, though maybe that was just us, it didn't, we chose to be very kind of, okay, you know, so we'll get some shots, and we'll do some medicine, and we were very kind of casual about it, and we wouldn't be the ones, it never, I never was willing to think that we would be the ones who it wouldn't work for, so in that sense, and it was free, it didn't hurt our resources, a few copays for the medicine, you know, it didn't, it gave me a false sense of security, I'd think, yeah, well, money can buy this, and, and, if it hadn't have been covered, I guess it, we talked about this just the other day since I talked to you, because we never would have thought about it like this before, we might have scraped the ten or the fifteen thousand and done, we wouldn't have done IUIs, we would have said, no, we only have	Thinks pre-existing condition clauses should be eliminated Didn't deal with emotions at first because they always thought they'd be pregnant soon No one will have to know; SUPPORT "Next month looks like it is never gonna happen"; LIMBO Insurance gave "false sense of security" Casual attitude toward treatment; POWER OF MEDICINE Never was willing to think it wouldn't work for them Thought money could buy pregnancy; SELF-CRITIQUE OF COMMODIFICATION OF HEALTH

this much money, we want to go right to IVF and see if we're successful, we still might have had the same outcome. It might not have been successful.

I: and then what would you have done if you weren't

R: then we would have tried to save up the money and, and just go to adoption right away, because we don't have ten or fifteen thousand dollars six times over, you know, and, and they'll even do another one for me, if I want, so that would have been seven times over, and I know a cancelled one isn't as expensive, because you don't go so far, but we're talking a lot of money and, and I think that, you know if you don't have it, you don't have it, you'll be mad, we would have been mad and frustrated that we would be denied access to these medical procedures because we didn't have the money, but we would have had to come face to face with that reality a lot sooner, and make our choice based on our resources and we probably would've gone to adoption two years ago, and then we'd have our child now, instead of confusion now, that's, that's a perspective that I'm just realizing.

[interview continues]

If they paid themselves, would have gone straight to IVF

If no insurance and one IVF didn't work, they would have adopted right away

Double-bind: no insurance would have made them mad, but would have made them "face reality"

If no insurance, would have a child now rather than confusion

Appendix D: Interview Participants

The following brief sketches describe the twenty-two women and one man whom I quote in this book. The sketches are arranged in alphabetical order by pseudonym. The age given for each participant is the age at the time of the interview. (If a participant was interviewed more than once, I indicate age at the first interview.) All interviews were conducted between June 1995 and December 1996.

Anne, thirty-five, is an engineer and is in a committed relationship with another woman. She and her partner are both white. Her partner, thirty-seven, is a medical professional. Both have bachelor's degrees; their household income exceeds $100,000. Anne began home-based artificial inseminations at age thirty-two, became pregnant on the fifth attempt, and had a child. Her partner wants to become pregnant with their second child; they plan on using IUI for the second pregnancy because of its higher rate of success.

Betsy, thirty-nine, is white, works as a social worker, and is married to a forty-year-old engineer, who is also white. Both have master's degrees, and their household income falls between $75,000 and $100,000. Betsy and her husband started trying to become pregnant when she was thirty-one. After trying for six or seven months, they consulted physicians, who diagnosed problems with sperm count and motility. Betsy and her husband tried three IUIs and then a GIFT procedure, none of which worked. Their physician advised them to consider ICSI, but Betsy resisted because the procedure was very new and because she felt uncomfortable being treated for her husband's medical condition. They stopped medical treatment and adopted two children.

Cheryl, forty, is white and works as a computer specialist. She is married to a thirty-five-year-old engineer, who is also white. She is working on a doctorate; her husband has a bachelor's degree. Their household income exceeds $100,000. Cheryl started trying to become pregnant at age thirty-eight. After a year, they consulted a physician, who discovered that both of Cheryl's fallopian tubes were blocked. She had a laparoscopy to open up one of the tubes and began taking Clomid and then Pergonal. After several months, she had an IVF procedure and was interviewed when she was waiting to see whether she was pregnant.

Christine, forty-one, is white and works as a realtor. She is married to a forty-two-year-old scientist, who is also white. She has some graduate education; her husband has a master's degree. Their household income falls between $75,000 and $100,000. Christine began trying to become pregnant at age twenty-nine and had four early miscarriages within four years. Over the course of her medical treatment, she was given Clomid, had surgery for a blocked fallopian tube, and was diagnosed and treated for a thyroid condition and a luteal-phase defect. In her fifth pregnancy, her doctor diagnosed her with incompetent cervix and prescribed bed rest for the remaining six months of the pregnancy. She has one child, from the fifth pregnancy.

Diane, thirty-eight, is white and runs a creative business with her husband, who is forty-eight and also white. She has some college education; her husband has a bachelor's degree. Their household income is between $75,000 and $100,000. Diane was diagnosed at twenty-eight with endometriosis; after treating her, the physician advised her to become pregnant if she wanted to avoid a recurrence. After a year of trying, they had an initial fertility workup, which showed a low sperm count. Diane had six IUIs and two IVFs, neither with good fertilization. At the time of the interview, she intended to try ICSI next.

Donna, thirty-four, is married to a thirty-year-old white occupational therapist. Her husband has a bachelor's degree; she has a master's degree and works in education. Their household income falls between $75,000 and $100,000. Donna was diagnosed at twenty with polycystic ovarian disease. She and her husband began trying to become pregnant when she was twenty-eight; her doctor immediately put her on Clomid, which she took for three years. After being placed on another ovulation-regulating hormone, Donna became pregnant and then miscarried. Her doctors recommended IVF; she had a child after the first cycle.

Ellen, forty-two, is a white, single attorney. Her household income falls between $50,000 and $75,000. Ellen had had PID from an IUD; she had become pregnant at twenty-seven and had had an abortion. Deciding at forty that she wanted to have a child, Ellen began medicated inseminations at forty-one. After one home-based insemination and nine medicated IUIs, Ellen ovulated without medication and became pregnant through IUI. She has a child and, at the time of a follow-up interview, is considering having a second child.

Janice, thirty, is white and works as an artisan. She is in a committed relationship with another woman, Theresa, who is forty-two, white, and works as an editor. Janice has some college education; Theresa has a master's degree. Their household income falls between $30,000 and $50,000. Janice and Theresa wanted to have a child that was biologically tied to both of them, so they decided to try to have one of Theresa's eggs fertilized and transferred to Janice. Theresa, who had had a tubal ligation, had a successful egg retrieval, and the eggs were fertilized and frozen, but the doctors refused to transfer them to Janice rather than Theresa. After a long search, they found a clinic willing to do the transfer to Janice, who became pregnant and had a child.

Jennifer, thirty-five, is a white graduate student married to a sixty-seven-year-old white man who is self-employed. He has several children, conceived without assistance, from a previous marriage, and has since had a vasectomy. Their household income falls between $30,000 and $50,000. Jennifer began artificial insemination by a donor when she was about thirty-three. After two years, she was considering using stronger ovulation-regulating hormones.

Judy, thirty-three, is a white homemaker married to a thirty-five-year-old white engineer. Both are enrolled in graduate programs. Their household income falls between $30,000 and $50,000. Judy was diagnosed at twenty-two with endometriosis. At twenty-five, after several surgeries over two years, she conceived and had a child. A year and a half later she and her husband began trying to have another child. They were told that the endometriosis would likely prevent a second pregnancy. Advised to try IUI, Judy became pregnant on the first attempt. Soon after having her second child, she became pregnant with a third and miscarried. She did three more IUIs but decided not to proceed with IVF, both because her insurance wouldn't cover it (her company was self-insured) and because the IVF conflicted with her religious beliefs.

Kim, thirty-three, is white and works as a staff assistant. She is in a committed relationship with another woman, thirty-eight, who is also white and works in education. Both have bachelor's degrees. Their household income falls between $50,000 and $75,000. Both wanted to have a child; her partner tried first, at age thirty, because she was older. After about eleven attempts, they were referred to an infertility specialist, who diagnosed her partner with a luteal-phase defect and prescribed Clomid and IUIs. On the second IUI, she became pregnant and had a child. When their first child was almost two, they decided to have a second child, with Kim carrying the second. She became pregnant on the first IUI and had a child.

Lauren, thirty-four, is white and works as a university administrator. She is in a committed relationship with another woman, also thirty-four and white, who works in finance. Both have master's degrees. Their household income exceeds $100,000. Lauren began trying to become pregnant when she was thirty-two. She became pregnant on the first home-based insemination but had a miscarriage. On the third insemination she became pregnant again and had a child. The couple are thinking about having another child biologically or through adoption.

Leslie, thirty-one, is a white homemaker who is married to a thirty-three-year-old financial analyst. Both have bachelor's degrees. Their household income is between $75,000 and $100,000. She began trying to become pregnant when she was twenty-nine, became pregnant immediately, and had a series of four miscarriages within a year. Her fifth pregnancy resulted in a child. After a year and a half, she became pregnant but miscarried again.

Lisa, forty-one, is white and single, holds a bachelor's degree, and works as an artist. Her household income is between $15,000 and $30,000. Lisa decided to try to become pregnant with her male partner when she was thirty-one. Suspecting she would have a fertility problem because she had never had a regular cycle, she consulted a fertility specialist, who diagnosed and treated a thyroid problem, operated to open blocked fallopian tubes, and advised her to continue trying to become pregnant for another year. After a year, during which time it became clear that her tubes were not open, she tried five attempts at IVF before quitting. Now single, she is going through the adoption process.

Lynn, twenty-nine, is married to a thirty-year-old white engineer. She is employed as a clerical worker; both are working on graduate degrees. Their household income is between $50,000 and $75,000. She began trying to get pregnant when she was twenty-three. After two years, she consulted a physician, who advised her to try for another six months. Initial tests showed no problems, so the physician advised her to continue trying for another six months. She was then diagnosed with an ovulation problem, put on ovulation-regulating hormones, and advised to try IUI. After several IUIs, she stopped trying to become pregnant and began working on a master's degree.

Monica, thirty-eight, and her husband, forty, are both white. Both work in finance and have graduate degrees. Their household income is over $100,000. Monica began trying to get pregnant at thirty-four. After a year, she and her husband consulted physicians, who diagnosed her with endometriosis and diagnosed her husband with a mild motility problem. Over the next year, Monica had eleven medicated IUIs; during one of the cycles she had a hyperstimulation reaction. After being diagnosed with an ovulatory problem, she began IVF and became pregnant.

Paul. See Susan below.

Paula, forty-four, is white and works in finance. Her husband is an Asian-American engineer. Paula has some graduate education; her husband has a bachelor's degree. Their household income exceeds $100,000. Paula started trying to become pregnant when she was thirty-nine. Having had an IUD and believing she might have ovulation problems, she consulted a physician right away, who advised her to chart her cycle. Two years later, she again consulted her doctor; tests showed that her fallopian tubes were blocked. She has had eight IVF cycles, which produced one ectopic pregnancy, and had surgery to remove fibroid tumors. She is ready to stop and adopt, but her husband is not, and her physician is encouraging her to continue.

Sandra, thirty-three, is married to a thirty-six-year-old man. Both are white, have bachelor's degrees, and work as engineers. Their household income falls between $75,000 and $100,000. Sandra started trying to get pregnant at thirty-one. After eight months she and her husband had a fertility workup, which was normal. A later postcoital test showed no live sperm, so she had four medicated IUIs. She became pregnant with twins on a second IVF cycle.

Sarah, thirty-nine, is married to a forty-three-year-old white engineer. Both have master's degrees. Their household income is between $75,000 and $100,000. Sarah became pregnant with her first child at thirty-one, two months after starting to try. Two years after her first child was born, she began trying again. A year later she had an ectopic pregnancy, which damaged one fallopian tube; she began having ovulatory problems immediately afterward and was put on Clomid. She then tried IVF and became pregnant on the second try. She had twins.

Sheri, thirty-five, is white and works as a chef. Her husband is thirty-eight, white, and works in sales. Sheri has a bachelor's degree; her husband has a master's degree. Their household income exceeds $100,000. Sheri started trying to become pregnant at age thirty-one. After three months, her husband had a semen analysis, which was abnormal. Sheri had ten IVF cycles, including many with ICSI, before deciding to adopt.

Stephanie, forty-three, is white and divorced. She works as a writer and designer. Her household income is between $50,000 and $75,000. At thirty-two, she started trying to become pregnant with the man who was then her husband. After two years, she was diagnosed with polycystic ovarian disease and prescribed Clomid and then Pergonal. At this point divorced and with another partner, she began a series of IUIs, becoming pregnant twice and miscarrying. On her first IVF cycle, she became pregnant and miscarried again. On her second IVF cycle, at age thirty-nine, she became pregnant and had twins.

Susan, thirty-seven, is white, has a master's degree and works in finance. She and her husband Paul (also interviewed) have a household income that exceeds $100,000. Paul, who was forty-five at the time of our interview, is white, has a medical degree, and works as a physician. He has three children, conceived without assistance, from a former marriage. Right before her first marriage, Susan had gotten pregnant at twenty-three and had had an abortion. She and Paul started trying to have a child when she was thirty-four. After about seven months, they had preliminary tests, which were normal. After three medicated IUIs, they tried IVF. Susan became pregnant on the first attempt but miscarried. The next two IVF cycles were cancelled before the transfer stage because of poor results. Susan's doctors indicated that she was probably entering early menopause. Susan and Paul adopted a child and are considering trying to have a second child using a donor egg.

Notes

Introduction: Pursuing Normalcy

1. This book is a rhetorical and cultural analysis, rather than a policy analysis, of mandatory insurance coverage for infertility. For policy and legal analyses, see Beh; Gilbert; Ingram; Kerr; Meuller; Millsap; Morgan; O'Rourke; Prager; Rydel; Tischler; and Wandersee. For an analysis of the economic costs of the Massachusetts mandate, see Griffin and Panak, according to whom "0.41% is an upper-limit estimate of the cost of providing infertility-related services" (27).

2. With a few exceptions. As of 1993, businesses owned by Catholic dioceses (which include schools, hospitals, and churches) are exempt under the state regulations, although some provide the benefit. As of 1992, insurers providing policies to small businesses (those with fifty employees or fewer) may apply for exclusion from state-mandated benefits, but almost none does because of the onerous paperwork necessary for exemption. Companies that are self-insured fall under the jurisdiction of the federal Employee Retirement Income Security Act of 1974 (ERISA), which exempts them from state control; federal employees living in the state similarly fall outside the scope of the state regulation. Finally, the mandate does not provide for Medicaid recipients.

By the mid-1990s, only one state (Maryland) mandated any Medicaid coverage for infertility treatment, and that state covered only the reversal of sterilization; in contrast, all states required Medicaid to cover contraceptives (King and Harrington Meyer 16–17). Although Massachusetts originally provided for some infertility treatment through Medicaid, the measure was revoked in 1994 when the administration of then governor William Weld was made aware that about 260 Medicaid recipients had received infertility drugs during the previous year (Wong 1). The administration originally defended the policy, saying that to withhold a treatment that is mandatory for private insurers would be discriminatory (Aucoin 14). Only days later, the administration, withdrawing its support for Medicaid coverage, called the policy "inconsistent" with welfare reform.

Interestingly, when arguing that Medicaid recipients should be excluded from eligibility for fertility drugs, politicians used the argument that they already had at least one child, even though the mandate affecting private insurers did not mention exclusion of "secondary infertility" (the inability to have a child after already successfully bearing at least one child)(Aucoin 1; Wong 18). An administration spokesperson said, "Welfare reform is designed to move people off the caseload, and if women are issuing children, that makes it more difficult to move them off the roles" (quoted in Wong 1). Even U.S. senator Edward M. Kennedy (a Democrat considered one of the most liberal members of Congress) eventually agreed with the decision. Kennedy said, "It's inappropriate for the federal and state government to pay for fertility drugs under Medicaid to encourage persons on welfare to have children" (quoted in Phillips 27). Although these changes were decried by the leadership of RESOLVE of the Bay State, they remain in effect as this book goes to press.

3. Non-Hispanic black women and Hispanic women experience infertility at the rate of 10.5 percent and 7.0 percent, respectively, as compared with non-Hispanic white women (6.4 percent). Women with no high school degree experience infertility at the rate of 8.5 percent, compared with 5.6 for those with college degrees (Abma et al. 70). This phenomenon has been attributed to substandard health care, genetic disorders, substance abuse, nutritional deficiencies, infectious diseases, postsurgical infections, sterilization, workplace and environmental conditions, hysterectomies, medical experimentation, and use of birth control (Nsiah-Jefferson 49–50).

4. Reporting results from a 1986 survey of the membership of two New England chapters of RESOLVE (including RESOLVE of the Bay State), Simons indicates that "in general, members from both states who responded to the questionnaire were married Caucasians with a median household income of between $50,000 and $75,000. . . . Half of the members had received an advanced degree and members were concentrated in professional and white collar occupations" (155).

5. U.S. Census data from 1997 (published in 1998) indicate that 12 percent of non-Hispanic whites are uninsured, compared with 21.5 percent of blacks and 34.2 percent of Hispanics (2). Most insurance is provided by employers. In Massachusetts, the 1994 unemployment rate for whites sixteen and over was 5.6 percent; for blacks sixteen and over, the unemployment rate for the same year was 12.8 percent (U.S. Bureau of Labor).

6. Lennard Davis notes that the premodern meaning of the word "norm" was "'perpendicular': the carpenter's square, called a 'norm,' provided the root meaning" (24).

7. Bateson at al. were not the first to blame women for the problems of their children, and the phenomenon has not escaped feminist critique (see, for example, Chodorow; Chodorow and Contratto; Dinnerstein). For a historical overview of the blaming of mothers for creating schizophrenic children (which predates Bateson et al.), see Hartwell.

1. Defining Infertility

1. Marsh and Ronner note that another British researcher claimed to have had success with IVF but that the births were never verified (236).

2. There is no way of knowing, of course, how many individuals and couples have trouble conceiving and never seek medical or other professional assistance.

3. Because of China's one-child policy and because of the cultural and social preferences for sons, girls fill Chinese orphanages. For a cultural analysis of this policy, see Ann Anagnost.

2. Insuring (In)Fertility

1. This is not to say that fewer lives are taken in an era of biopower. In fact, Foucault argues that attention to entire populations helps to account for an increase in genocide. He writes: "Wars are no longer waged in the name of a sovereign who must be defended; they are waged on behalf of the existence of everyone; entire populations are mobilized for the purpose of wholesale slaughter in the name of life necessity: massacres have become vital. . . . If genocide is indeed the dream of modern powers, this is not because of a recent return of the ancient right to kill; it is because power is situated and exercised at the level of life, the species, the race, and the large-scale phenomena of population" (*Sexuality* 137).

2. See the websites of the American Society for Reproductive Medicine (http://www.asrm.org) and RESOLVE (http://www.resolve.org) for updated information as additional states pass legislation. RESOLVE's website also contains information about pending legislation.

3. While Guernsey's position in the letter to Cardinal Law drew on traditional pro-family arguments, he has recently adopted another stance. When granting permission to reprint from this letter, he wished to amend my analysis as follows (his suggested amendment appears in italics): "In a letter to Cardinal Bernard Law of the Archdiocese of Boston, Sherwood Guernsey, a non-Catholic supporter of the bill, emphasized that IVF is meant to occur within the institution of marriage *or with a caring, loving adult couple.*"

4. Since 1987, when Guernsey wrote the letter, so-called gestational surrogacy has made it possible for surrogacy to join the egg and sperm of a married couple. In gestational surrogacy, an embryo formed from the egg and sperm of one couple are transferred to the uterus of another woman.

4. Order and Discontinuity

1. The Dalkon Shield, an intrauterine device (IUD), was seen as responsible for causing severe infections, many of which led to infertility. The Dalkon Shield was taken off

the market in 1974, but devices already in use were not recalled (Boston Women's Health Book Collective).

2. The U.S. Congress ended a ban on transracial adoption in 1996. The move did not end a controversy, however, over whether allowing white parents to adopt minority children is good policy for individual children or for minority groups as a whole. For various positions on the issue, see McRoy, Oglesby, and Grape; Simon; and Hollingsworth.

3. Within limits. Clinics can set their own age restrictions. One physician even expressed the belief that insurance coverage might be limiting access to reproductive technologies to younger women. With more facilities offering infertility services as a result of the mandate, the competition for patients is growing. Because patients often choose their facility by its success rates, clinics might be more inclined to accept patients with a higher likelihood of success (that is, younger women and those with less severe infertility).

5. Control and Constraint

1. The donor catalog of one sperm bank, for example, is divided by "race" ("Caucasian," "Black/African American," "Asian," and "Two or More Racial Groups/Unique Ancestries"). Within each category, information is given about each donor's ethnic origin, hair color and texture, eye color, height, weight, blood type, skin tone, years of college, and occupation or college major. A descriptive profile (which details medical and genetic history) is available for each donor, and some donors have also prepared audiotapes (California Cryobank).

2. In some cases, pregnancy might be regarded in this way (for example, if the pregnancy is harmful to the health of the woman). Even in this instance, however, the pregnancy itself is less of an abnormality than the conditions (such as severe high blood pressure) under which it is dangerous for a woman to become pregnant.

Glossary

Note: This glossary is meant to help the reader understand the language used in the present book but does not include all terms relating to the medical treatment of infertility.

Advanced reproductive technologies: The distinction between what is *advanced* and what is not is, of course, relatively arbitrary. I use the term to include forms of assisted reproduction that require manipulation of reproductive material (other than sperm alone) outside the body. I do not include in this category artificial insemination, intrauterine insemination, hormonal therapy, or diagnostic surgeries.

Anovulation: Absence of ovulation. Women who do not ovulate are typically prescribed an ovulation-inducing hormone, such as clomiphene citrate or gonadotropins.

Artificial insemination: A procedure in which sperm is inserted into the woman's vagina by means other than intercourse. In artificial insemination by donor, the sperm is donated by a man other than the woman's partner. While intrauterine insemination is sometimes classified as artificial insemination, I have defined them separately because of the level of intervention required. Artificial insemination can be conducted at home with low-tech equipment (this home-based insemination is sometimes called the "turkey baster method"), but IUI must be performed in a doctor's office with equipment for moving the sperm past the cervix into the uterus.

Assisted reproduction: I use this term to include all forms of reproduction except that attempted through heterosexual intercourse without intervention.

Clomid: A brand name of clomiphene citrate.

Clomiphene citrate: A drug, taken orally, that is commonly used to induce ovulation. Clomid is a brand name.

DES: See Diethylstilbestrol.

Diethylstilbestrol (DES): A drug commonly given to women in the 1950s and the 1960s to prevent miscarriage. Adults (both male and female) whose mothers had taken DES while they were in utero may exhibit deformities of the reproductive organs and are at greater risk for cancer. Because of malformations in the fallopian tubes or uterus, daughters of women who took DES may be unable to become pregnant or to carry a pregnancy to term.

Donor egg: The use of an egg from a woman other than the one undergoing treatment for infertility. Eggs from donors may be recommended for women who have entered menopause or have premature ovarian failure. Donor eggs may be used in any of the advanced reproductive technologies such as in vitro fertilization, gamete intrafallopian transfer, or zygote intrafallopian transfer.

Donor sperm: For heterosexual couples, the use of sperm from a man other than the male partner. For single women and women in same-sex couples, all artificial insemination involves donor sperm.

Endometrial biopsy: A diagnostic procedure in which a piece of the endometrium (the lining of the uterus) is examined to evaluate the woman's hormonal levels. Endometrial biopsies can be used to determine whether a woman has an inadequate luteal phase.

Endometriosis: A condition in which material like the lining of the uterus develops outside the uterus, in the abdominal cavity, sometimes binding the reproductive organs and impairing fertility.

Fibroid tumors: Benign growths, attached to the inside or outside of the uterus, that sometimes cause infertility or miscarriage.

Follicle: A part of the ovaries that produces eggs during ovulation. Follicles can be imaged on ultrasound.

Gamete intrafallopian transfer (GIFT): A procedure in which eggs and sperm are mixed together outside the body and then introduced into the woman's fallopian tube(s) in the hope that fertilization will occur.

GIFT: See Gamete intrafallopian transfer.

Gonadotropins: Hormones that stimulate ovulation, often used when a woman does not respond to clomiphene citrate. These hormones, taken by injection, create a higher risk than clomiphene citrate of hyperstimulation and multiple births (Berger, Goldstein, and Fuerst 135–136).

Hyperstimulation: A condition that sometimes occurs after a woman has been given a hormone designed to trigger ovulation. Reactions range from mild to severe, with mild reactions causing discomfort and severe reactions requiring hospitalization. Severe hyperstimulation can be serious and has been known (in rare cases) to result in death.

Hysterosalpingogram: A procedure in which dye is inserted past the cervix into the uterus and fallopian tubes so that any abnormalities or blockages will appear on x-rays.

ICSI: See Intracytoplasmic sperm injection.

Inadequate luteal phase: A condition in which the body does not produce enough progesterone to prepare the lining of the uterus for embryo implantation.

Incompetent cervix: A condition in which the cervix dilates before a fetus is full-term, often resulting in miscarriage.

Intracytoplasmic sperm injection (ICSI): A procedure, conducted as part of in vitro fertilization or zygote intrafallopian transfer, in which sperm is injected into an egg. This procedure is often used to overcome male factor infertility.

Intrauterine device (IUD): A birth control device associated with tubal infertility and pelvic inflammatory disease.

Intrauterine insemination (IUI): A procedure in which sperm is injected past the cervix into the uterus. IUIs can be medicated (accompanied by hormones, such as Clomid or Pergonal, which are designed to regulate the menstrual cycle or stimulate egg production), or unmedicated. IUI is a favored method for treating unexplained infertility.

In vitro fertilization (IVF): A procedure in which eggs are removed from the ovaries, mixed with sperm in the laboratory, and allowed to incubate. One or more embryos may then be transferred to the uterus.

IUD: See Intrauterine device.

IUI: See Intrauterine insemination.

IVF: See In vitro fertilization.

Laparoscopy: The insertion into the abdomen of a thin instrument that allows a physician to examine the reproductive organs. This procedure may be performed to diagnose problems (such as determining whether the fallopian tubes are blocked) or to correct problems (such as removing pelvic adhesions or fibroid tumors).

Laparotomy: Abdominal surgery used to diagnose or treat conditions such as endometriosis, pelvic adhesions, or fibroid tumors. Developments in microsurgery allow most of these conditions to be treated less invasively through laparoscopy.

Ovarian cysts: See Polycystic ovarian disease.

Pelvic adhesions: Scar tissue, usually the result of infections or surgery, inside the abdominal cavity. This tissue can bind together the reproductive organs, impairing fertility.

Pelvic inflammatory disease (PID): An infection, causing scarring, of the uterus, fallopian tubes, and/or ovaries. PID is associated with sexually transmitted diseases and is more common among women with multiple partners and with those who douche regularly (Abma et al., 18). PID is considered the leading cause of blocked fallopian tubes.

Pergonal: A brand name for one of several gonadotropins.

PID: See Pelvic inflammatory disease.

Polycystic ovarian disease: According to Tan, Jacobs, and Seibel, "polycystic ovary disease is a misnomer; . . . the condition we are talking about is a syndrome, not a disease" (90). In this condition, a woman has ovaries that are "usually larger than normal, with a smooth outer covering that is thicker than normal," along with a "menstrual disturbance," "the symptoms of too much testosterone," and "obesity" (90). Not all women with polycystic ovaries have trouble conceiving.

Postcoital test: A procedure in which a sperm sample is taken from the cervix the morning after (or the morning of) intercourse to determine how many sperm are present and moving. Poor results might indicate that sperm are not reaching the cervix, that the man has a low sperm count, or that the mucus is "hostile" to the man's sperm.

Premature ovarian failure: A condition in which a woman enters menopause before age forty.

Surrogacy: In traditional surrogacy, a woman is inseminated with the sperm of a man who plans to parent that child alone or with someone other than the woman who carries the child. In gestational surrogacy, a woman carries the embryo of another couple; she is not genetically related to the child she carries.

Tubal ligation: A procedure for sterilization involving cutting or tying the fallopian tubes.

Ultrasound: A nonsurgical method of imaging the internal organs using sound waves, used to evaluate the condition of the abdominal cavity and to determine when ovulation is occurring.

Undescended testicle: A condition, possibly signifying decreased fertility, in which a testicle does not descend from the abdominal cavity.

Unexplained infertility: A diagnosis given to an individual or couple after all known tests have been administered and have failed to account for the inability to conceive. Those diagnosed with unexplained infertility might be encouraged to try medicated or unmedicated intrauterine insemination. Those who do not become pregnant through this method might be advised to undergo in vitro fertilization, both to see whether fertilization is occurring and to try to create a pregnancy.

Varicocele: A varicose vein in the testicle, which may impair male fertility.

Vasectomy: A method of male sterilization involving the surgical removal of a portion of the tube that carries sperm.

ZIFT: See Zygote intrafallopian transfer.

Zygote intrafallopian transfer (ZIFT): A procedure similar to in vitro fertilization. As in IVF, fertilization occurs outside the body. ZIFT differs from traditional IVF, however, in that the material is introduced into the woman's fallopian tubes *before* cell division occurs rather than afterward.

Works Cited

Cases

Bradgon v. Abbott, 118 S. Ct. 2196 (U.S. 1998)
Egert v. Connecticut General Life Insurance Company, 900 F.2d 1032 (7th Cir. 1990)
Kinzie v. Physician's Liability Ins. Co., 750 P.2d 1140 (Okl. App. 1987)
Krauel v. Iowa Methodist Medical Center, 95 F.3d 674 (8th Cir. 1998)
Marsh v. Reserve Life Ins. Co., 516 So. 2d 1311 (La. App. 2nd Cir. 1987)
Murphy v. United Parcel Service, Inc., 66 U.S.L.W. 3800 (U.S. Jan 8, 1999)
Pacourek v. Inland Steel Co., 64 U.S.L.W. 2550 (N.D. Ill. Feb. 16, 1996)
Regnier v. Industrial Commission of Arizona, 707 P.2d 333 (Ariz. App. 1985)
Reuss v. Time Insurance Company, 340 S.E.2d 625 (Ga. App. 1986)
Sutton et al. v. United Air Lines, Inc., 119 S. Ct. 790 (U.S. Jan. 8, 1999)
Witcraft v. Sundstrand Health & Disability Group Benefit Plan, 420 N.W.2d 785 (Iowa 1988)
Zatarain v. WDSU-Television, Inc., 881 F. Supp. 240 (E.D. La. 1995)

Statutes and Regulations

Ark. Stat. Ann. §§ 23-85-137, 23-86-118 (1999)
Cal. Health & Safety Code § 1374.55 (West 1990)
Cal. Ins. Code § 10119.6 (West 1993)
Conn. Gen. Stat. Ann. § 38a-536 (West Supp. 2000)
Haw. Rev. Stat. §§ 431: 10A-116.5, 432: 1-604 (1993)
215 ILCS 5/356m, 125/5-3 (Smith-Hurd Supp. 2000)
Mass. Gen. Laws Ann. ch. 175, § 47H (West 1998)
Mass. Gen. Laws Ann. ch. 176A, § 8K (West 1998)
Mass. Gen. Laws Ann. ch. 176B § 4J (West 1998)

Mass. Gen. Laws Ann. ch. 176G § 4 (West 1998)
211 Code Mass. Regs. 37.00 (1987)
Md. Ins. Code Ann. § 15-810 (1997)
Mont. Code Ann., §§ 33-22-1521, 33-31-102 (1999)
N.Y. Ins. Law §§ 3216, 3221, 4303 (McKinney Supp. 2000)
Ohio Rev. Code Ann. § 1751.01(7) (Anderson Supp. 1999)
R.I. Gen. Laws §§ 27-18-30, 27-19-23, 27-20-20, 27-41-33 (1998)
Tex. Ins. Code Ann. Art. 3.51-6 3A (West Supp. 2000)
42 U.S.C. § 12102(2) (1995)
W. Va. Code § 33-25A-2 (Supp. 1999)

Other Sources

Abma, J., A. Chandra, W. Mosher, L. Peterson, & L. Piccinino. 1997. *Fertility, Family Planning, and Women's Health: New Data from the 1995 National Survey of Family Growth.* National Center for Health Statistics. *Vital Health Stat* 23(19).

Anagnost, A. 1995. "A Surfeit of Bodies: Population and the Rationality of the State in Post-Mao China." In F. Ginsburg & R. Rapp, eds., *Conceiving the New World Order: The Global Politics of Reproduction,* 22–41. Berkeley: University of California Press.

Aucoin, D. 1994. "State Defends Medicaid Coverage for Fertility Drugs." *Boston Globe,* March 2, p. 14.

Bartholet, E. 1993a. *Family Bonds: Adoption and the Politics of Parenting.* New York: Houghton Mifflin.

Bartholet, E. 1993b. "Why is Adoption the Last Resort?" *RESOLVE National Newsletter* (Fall): 5–6.

Bateson, G., D. D. Jackson, J. Haley, & J. Weakland. 1956. "Toward a Theory of Schizophrenia." *Behavioral Science* 1: 251–264.

Beck, P. 1990. "Periods of My Infertility." *RESOLVE of the Bay State Newsletter* (Summer): 6.

Beck, P. 1994. "It's a Family Affair: Grandparents in Waiting." *RESOLVE of the Bay State Newsletter* (Fall): 6–7.

Becker, G. 1994. "Metaphors in Disrupted Lives: Infertility and Cultural Constructions of Continuity." *Medical Anthropology Quarterly* 8: 383–410.

Becker, G., & R. D. Nachtigall. 1992. "Eager for Medicalisation: The Social Production of Infertility as a Disease." *Sociology of Health and Illness* 14: 456–471.

Becker, G., & R. D. Nachtigall. 1994. "'Born to Be a Mother': The Cultural

Construction of Risk in Infertility Treatment in the United States." *Social Science and Medicine* 39: 507–518.

Beh, H. G. 1998. "Sex, Sexual Pleasure, and Reproduction: Health Insurers Don't Want You to Do Those Nasty Things." *Wisconsin Women's Law Journal* 13: 119–177.

Bellah, R. N., R. Madsen, W. M. Sullivan, A. Swidler, & S. M. Tipton. 1986. *Habits of the Heart: Individualism and Commitment in American Life.* New York: Perennial.

Berger, G. S., M. Goldstein, & M. Fuerst. 1995. *The Couple's Guide to Fertility.* Rev. ed. New York: Doubleday.

Berson, A. R. 1993. "President's Message: The Importance of Continuity." *RESOLVE of the Bay State Newsletter* (Summer): 1.

Bombardieri, M. 1985. "Clean Sweep for Spring: Clearing the Path to Family and Friends." *RESOLVE of the Bay State Newsletter* (May): 2–4.

Bonchek, R. 1987. "Grief and Loss Associated with Infertility." *RESOLVE of the Bay State Newsletter* (Summer): 6.

Boston Women's Health Book Collective. 1992. *The New Our Bodies, Ourselves.* New York: Touchstone.

Burke, E. L. 1987. Burke to Cardinal Archbishop Bernard Law. March 11. Papers of E. L. Burke, Framingham, Mass.

Burke, K. 1945. *A Grammar of Motives.* Berkeley: University of California Press.

Butler, J. 1983. *Bodies That Matter: On the Discursive Limits of "Sex."* New York: Routledge.

California Cryobank. 1995. *Donor Catalog.* Los Angeles: California Cryobank.

Canguilhem, G. *The Normal and the Pathological.* 1991. Trans. C. R. Fawcett & R. S. Cohen. New York: Zone.

Carson, S. A., P. R. Casson, & D. J. Schuman. 1999. *The American Society for Reproductive Medicine Complete Guide to Fertility.* Lincolnwood, Ill.: Contemporary.

Carter, J. W., & M. Carter. 1989. *Sweet Grapes: How to Stop Being Infertile and Start Living Again.* Indianapolis: Perspectives.

Chodorow, N. 1978. *The Reproduction of Mothering.* Berkeley: University of California Press.

Chodorow, N., & S. Contratto. 1992. "The Fantasy of the Perfect Mother." In B. Thorne & M. Yalom, eds., *Rethinking the Family: Some Feminist Questions,* 191–214. Boston: Northeastern University Press.

Ciganovic, K. 1988. Letter. *RESOLVE of the Bay State Newsletter* (Spring): 2–3.

Cintron, R. 1997. *Angels' Town: Chero Ways, Gange Life, and Rhetorics of the Everyday*. Boston: Beacon.

Cole, W. C. 1990. "Infertility: A Survey of the Law and Analysis of the Need for Legislation Mandating Insurance Coverage." *San Diego Law Review* 27: 715–743.

Collier, J., M. Z. Rosaldo, & S. Yanagisako. 1992. "Is There a Family? New Anthropological Views." In B. Thorne & M. Yalom, eds., *Rethinking the Family: Some Feminist Questions*, 31–48. Boston: Northeastern University Press.

Collins, M. S., & J. A. Bleyl. 1990. "Seventy-one Quadruplet Pregnancies: Management and Outcome." *American Journal of Obstetrics and Gynecology* 162: 1384–92.

Collins, P. H. 1991. *Black Feminist Thought: Knowledge, Consciousness, and the Politics of Empowerment*. New York: Routledge.

Coltrane, S., & N. Hickman. 1992. "The Rhetoric of Rights and Needs: Moral Discourse in the Reform of Child Custody and Child Support Laws." *Social Problems* 39: 400–420.

Condit, C. M. 1990. *Decoding Abortion Rhetoric: Communicating Social Change*. Urbana: University of Illinois Press.

Conrad, P., & R. Kern. 1990. *The Sociology of Health and Illness: Critical Perspectives*. 3d ed. New York: St. Martin's.

Cooper, S., & E. S. Glazer. 1994. *Beyond Infertility: New Paths to Parenthood*. New York: Lexington.

Corea, G. 1985. *The Mother Machine: Reproductive Technologies from Artificial Insemination to Artificial Wombs*. New York: Harper & Row.

Corea, G. 1987. "The Reproductive Brothel." In *Man-Made Women: How New Reproductive Technologies Affect Women*, 38–51. Bloomington: Indiana University Press.

Covington, S. 1986. "Childfree: The 'Closet' Choice." *RESOLVE of the Bay State Newsletter* (Fall): 8–9.

Crockin, S. 1990. "Insurance Coverage of Infertility: Current Problems." *RESOLVE of the Bay State Newsletter* (Summer): 9.

Crockin, S. 1991. "President's Message." *RESOLVE of the Bay State Newsletter* (Summer): 1.

Cullen, K. 1987. "Law Orders Coverage for Infertility." *Boston Globe*, October 9, p. 1+.

Davis, A. 1983. *Women, Race, and Class*. New York: Vintage.

Davis, L. J. 1995. *Enforcing Normalcy: Disability, Deafness, and the Body.* London: Verso.

DeCherney, A. H., & G. S. Berkowitz. 1982. "Female Fecundity and Age." Editorial. *New England Journal of Medicine* 306: 424–426.

Dinnerstein, D. 1977. *The Mermaid and the Minotaur: Sexual Arrangements and Human Malaise.* New York: Harper Colophon.

Domar, A. D., D. Clapp, E. A. Slawsby, J. Dusek, B. Kessel, & M. Freizinger. 2000. "Impact of Group Psychological Interventions on Pregnancy Rates in Infertile Women." *Fertility and Sterility* 73: 805–811.

Dreyfus, H. L., & P. Rabinow. 1983. *Michel Foucault: Beyond Structuralism and Hermeneutics.* 2d ed. Chicago: University of Chicago Press.

Emerson, R. M., R. I. Fretz, & L. L. Shaw. 1995. *Writing Ethnographic Fieldnotes.* Chicago: University of Chicago Press.

Ewald, F. 1991. "Norms, Risks, and the Law." In R. Post, ed., *Law and the Order of Culture,* 138–161. Berkeley: University of California Press.

Faludi, S. 1991. *Backlash: The Undeclared War Against American Women.* New York: Anchor.

Fédération CECOS, D. Schwartz, & M. J. Mayaux. 1982. "Female Fecundity as a Function of Age." *New England Journal of Medicine* 306: 404–406.

Fleming, A. T. 1994. *Motherhood Deferred: A Woman's Journey.* New York: Fawcett Columbine.

Fortun, K. 1998. "The Bhopal Disaster: Advocacy and Expertise." *Science as Culture* 7: 193–216.

Fortun, M. 1998. "Institutionalizing Indirection: Science at the Crossroads of Scholarship and Politics." *Science as Culture* 7: 173–192.

Foucault, M. 1979. *Discipline and Punish: The Birth of the Prison.* Trans. Alan Sheridan. New York: Vintage.

Foucault, M. 1990. *The History of Sexuality, Vol. 1: An Introduction.* Trans. Robert Hurley. New York: Vintage.

Foucault, M. 1994. *The Order of Things: An Archaeology of the Human Sciences.* New York: Vintage.

Fragola, L. 1985. "Support Group: A Personal Experience." *RESOLVE of the Bay State Newsletter* (November): 8.

Frazer, E., & N. Lacey. 1993. *The Politics of Community: A Feminist Critique of the Liberal-Communitarian Debate.* Toronto: University of Toronto Press.

Friedan, B. 1963. *The Feminine Mystique.* New York: Dell.

Friedman, L. M. 1990. *The Republic of Choice: Law, Authority, Culture.* Cambridge, Mass.: Harvard University Press.

Gilbert, B. 1996. "Infertility and the ADA: Health Insurance Coverage for Infertility Treatment." *Defense Counsel Journal* (January): 42–57.

Ginsburg, F., & R. Rapp, eds. 1995. *Conceiving the New World Order: The Global Politics of Reproduction.* Berkeley: University of California Press.

Goffman, E. 1986. *Stigma: Notes on the Management of Spoiled Identity.* New York: Touchstone.

Good, B. J. 1994. *Medicine, Rationality, and Experience: An Anthropological Perspective.* Cambridge, Mass.: Cambridge University Press.

Greil, A. 1991. *Not Yet Pregnant: Infertile Couples in Contemporary America.* New Brunswick: Rutgers UP.

Griffin, M. 1985a. Untitled. *RESOLVE of the Bay State Newsletter* (January): 1.

Griffin, M. 1985b. "President's Message." *RESOLVE of the Bay State Newsletter* (May): 1.

Griffin, M. 1986. "President's Message." *RESOLVE of the Bay State Newsletter* (Fall): 1.

Griffin, M., & W. F. Panak. 1998. "The Economic Cost of Infertility-Related Services: An Examination of the Massachusetts Infertility Insurance Mandate." *Fertility and Sterility* 70: 22–29.

Guernsey, S. 1987. Guernsey to Cardinal Archbishop Bernard Law. March 13. Papers of S. Guernsey, Williamstown, Mass.

Haley, J. 1976. "Development of a Theory: A History of a Research Project." In C. E. Sluzki & D. C. Ransom, eds., *Double Bind: The Foundation of the Communicational Approach to the Family,* 59–104. New York: Grune & Stratton.

Haraway, D. J. 1991. *Simians, Cyborgs, and Women: The Reinvention of Nature.* New York: Routledge.

Haraway, D. J. 1997. *Modest_Witness@Second_Millennium.FemaleMan©_Meets_OncoMouse^{TM}: Feminism and Technoscience.* New York: Routledge.

Hartwell, C. E. 1996. "The Schizophrenogenic Mother Concept in American Psychiatry." *Psychiatry* 59: 274–297.

Heitman, E. 1995. "Infertility as a Public Health Problem: Why Assisted Reproductive Technologies are Not the Answer." *Stanford Law and Policy Review* 6: 89–102.

Hershlag, A. 1999. "Multifetal Prophylaxis—A Reality?" *Fertility and Sterility* 72: 973–974.

Hollingsworth, L. D. 1998. "Promoting Same-Race Adoption for Children of Color." *Social Work* 43: 104–116.

Ingram, J. D. 1993. "Should in Vitro Fertilization Be Covered by Medical Expense Reimbursement Plans?" *American Journal of Family Law* 7: 103–108.

Inhorn, M. C. 1994. "Kabsa (a.k.a Mushahara) and Threatened Fertility in Egypt." *Social Science and Medicine* 39: 487–505.

Jamieson, K. H. 1995. *Beyond the Double Bind: Women and Leadership*. New York: Oxford University Press.

Jette, S. 1988. "President's Message." *RESOLVE of the Bay State Newsletter* (Spring): 1–2.

Kerr, L. M. 1999. "Can Money Buy Happiness? An Examination of the Coverage of Infertility Services Under HMO Contracts. *Case Western Reserve Law Review* 49: 599–643.

King, L., & M. H. Meyer. 1997. "The Politics of Reproductive Benefits: U.S. Insurance Coverage of Contraceptive and Infertility Benefits." *Gender & Society* 11: 8–30.

Kornhauser, L. A. 1998. "Interest, Commitment, and Obligation: How Law Influences Behavior." In B. G. Garth & A. Sarat, eds., *Justice and Power in Sociolegal Studies*, 208–232. Chicago: Northwestern University Press.

Lewin, E. 1995. "On the Outside Looking In: The Politics of Lesbian Motherhood." In F. Ginsburg & R. Rapp, eds., *Conceiving the New World Order: The Global Politics of Reproduction*, 103–121. Berkeley: University of California Press.

Lipitz, S., Y. Frenkel, C. Watts, Z. Ben-Rafael, G. Barkai, & B. Reichman. 1990. "High-Order Multifetal Gestation—Gestation and Outcome." *Obstetrics and Gynecology* 76: 215–218.

Lyotard, J.-F. 1993. *The Postmodern Explained: Correspondence 1982–1985*. Trans. D. Barry, B. Maher, J. Pefanis, V. Spate, & M. Thomas. Minneapolis: University of Minnesota Press.

Maman, E., E. Lunenfeld, A. Levy, H. Vardi, & G. Potashnik. 1998. "Obstetric Outcome of Singleton Pregnancies Conceived By In Vitro Fertilization and Ovulation Induction Compared with Those Conceived Spontaneously." *Fertility and Sterility* 70: 240–245.

Marcus, G. E. 1995. "Ethnography In/Of the World System: The Emergence of Multi-sited Ethnography." *Annual Review of Anthropology* 24: 95–117.

Marsh, M., & W. Ronner. 1996. *The Empty Cradle: Infertility in America from Colonial Times to the Present*. Baltimore: Johns Hopkins University Press.

Martin, E. 1992. *The Woman in the Body: A Cultural Analysis of Reproduction.* Boston: Beacon.

Massachusetts General Assembly. Joint Health Committee. 1987. Statement of B. Woo & J. Cunningham. Hearing on S. 457, *An Act Providing a Medical Definition of Infertility.* March 2. Boston.

May, E. T. 1995. *Barren in the Promised Land: Childless Americans and the Pursuit of Happiness.* New York: HarperCollins.

McNaught, M. 1987. "Dream Baby." *RESOLVE of the Bay State Newsletter* (Summer): 9.

McRoy, R. G., Z. Oglesby, & H. Grape. 1997. "Achieving Same-Race Adoptive Placements for African American Children: Culturally Sensitive Approaches." *Child Welfare* 76: 85–104.

Melnick, H. D., & N. Intrator. 1998. *The Pregnancy Prescription: The Success-Oriented Approach to Overcoming Infertility.* Mount Kisco, N.Y.: Josara.

Meuller, M. W. 1995. "Financing High-Tech Reproductive Medical Expenditures." *Stanford Law and Policy Review* 6: 113–120.

Milki, A. A., J. D. Fisch, & B. Behr. 1999. "Two-Blastocyst Transfer Has Similar Pregnancy Rates and a Decreased Multiple Gestation Rate Compared With Three-Blastocyst Transfer." *Fertility and Sterility* 72: 225–28.

Millsap, D. 1996. "Sex, Lies, and Health Insurance: Employer-Provided Health Insurance Coverage of Abortion and Infertility Services and the ADA." *American Journal of Law and Medicine* 23: 51–84.

Morgan, K. C. 1997. "Should Infertility Be a Covered Disability Under the ADA?: A Question for Congress, Not the Courts." *University of Cincinnati Law Review* 65: 963–990.

Neff, D. L. 1994. "The Social Construction of Infertility: The Case of the Matrilineal Nayars in South India." *Social Science and Medicine* 39: 475–485.

Nsiah-Jefferson, L. 1989. "Reproductive Laws, Women of Color, and Low-Income Women." In S. Cohen & N. Taub, eds., *Reproductive Laws for the 1990s,* 23–55. Clifton, N.J.: Humana.

O'Rourke, M. R. 1992. "The Status of Infertility Treatments and Insurance Coverage: Some Hopes and Frustrations." *South Dakota Law Review* 37: 343–87.

Phillips, F. 1994. "Kennedy Hits Medicaid for Fertility Coverage." *Boston Globe,* March 16, p. 27.

Plato. 1914. *Phaedrus.* Trans. H. N. Fowler. Cambridge, Mass.: Harvard University Press.

Potashnik, G., L. Lerner-Geva, L. Genkin, A. Chetrit, E. Lunenfeld, & A. Porath. 1999. "Fertility Drugs and the Risk of Breast and Ovarian Cancers: Results of a Long-Term Follow-up Study." *Fertility and Sterility* 71: 853–59.

Prager, P. J. 1989–1990. "Infertility: The Unrecognized Illness in the Health Insurance Industry." *Drake Law Review* 39: 617–44.

Reichman, N. 1998. "Power and Justice in Sociolegal Studies of Regulation." In B. G. Garth & A. Sarat, eds., *Justice and Power in Sociolegal Studies,* pp. 233–271. Chicago: Northwestern University Press.

RESOLVE. 1994. *Infertility Insurance Advisor: An Insurance Counseling Program for Infertile Couples.* Somerville, Mass.: RESOLVE.

Robin, P. 1993. *How to Be a Successful Fertility Patient.* New York: W. Morrow.

Rossing, M. A., J. R. Daling, N. S. Weiss, D. E. Moore, & S. G. Self. 1994. "Ovarian Tumors in a Cohort of Infertile Women." *New England Journal of Medicine* 331: 771–776.

Rothman, B. K. 1989a. *Recreating Motherhood: Ideology and Technology in a Patriarchal Society.* New York: Norton.

Rothman, B. K. 1989b. "Women as Fathers: Motherhood and Child Care Under a Modified Matriarchy." *Gender and Society* 3: 89–104.

Rowland, R. 1987. "Of Woman Born, But for How Long? The Relationship of Women to the New Reproductive Technologies and the Issue of Choice." In P. Spallone & D. L. Steinberg, eds., *Made to Order: The Myth of Reproductive and Genetic Progress,* 67–83. Oxford: Pergamon.

Rowland, R. 1992. *Living Laboratories: Women and Reproductive Technologies.* Bloomington: Indiana University Press.

Ruddick, S. 1992. "Thinking about Fathers." In B. Thorne & M. Yalom, eds., *Rethinking the Family: Some Feminist Questions,* 176–190. Rev. ed. Boston: Northeastern University Press.

Rugen, L. 1998. "Waiting Room . . ." *RESOLVE of the Bay State Newsletter* (Fall): 3+.

Rydel, P. K. 1999. "Redefining The Right to Reproduce: Asserting Infertility as a Disability Under the Americans with Disabilities Act." *Albany Law Review* 63: 593–636.

Sandelowski, M. 1990. "Failures of Volition: Female Agency and Infertility in Historical Perspective." *Signs* 15: 475–99.

Sandelowski, M. 1991. "Compelled to Try: The Never-Enough Quality of Conceptive Technology." *Medical Anthropology Quarterly* 5: 29–47.

Santiesteban, M. 1987. Santiesteban to Governor Michael Dukakis. Telegram in Governor's File on H. 3721. 30 September 1987. Massachusetts State Archives, Boston.

Schenker, J. G., & Y. Ezra. 1994. "Complications of Assisted Reproductive Techniques." *Fertility and Sterility* 61: 411–422.

Schneider, D. M., & R. T. Smith. 1973. *Class Differences and Sex Roles in American Kinship and Family Structure.* Englewood Cliffs: Prentice-Hall.

Sedgwick, E. K. 1990. *Epistemology of the Closet.* Berkeley: University of California Press.

Serono Symposia, USA. 1992. *Pathways to Parenthood.* Norwell, Mass.: Serono Laboratories.

Silverstein, D. 1990. "President's Message: The Hero Within." *RESOLVE of the Bay State Newsletter* (Spring): 1.

Silverstein, D. 1991. "President's Message." *RESOLVE of the Bay State Newsletter* Winter: 1.

Simon, R. J. 1998. "Adoption and the Race Factor: How Important is It?" *Sociological Inquiry* 68: 274–279.

Simons, H. 1988. "RESOLVE, Inc.: Advocacy Within a Mutual Support Organization." Ph.D. dissertation, Brandeis University, Waltham, Mass. No. 8819281. Ann Arbor, Mich.: University Microfilms International.

Smart, C. 1989. *Feminism and the Power of Law.* Sociology of Law and Crime. London: Routledge.

Sontag, S. 1978. *"Illness as Metaphor.* New York: Farrar, Straus and Giroux.

Spallone, P., & D. L. Steinberg. 1987. *Made to Order: The Myth of Reproductive and Genetic Progress.* Oxford: Pergamon.

Stein, H. F. 1990. *American Medicine as Culture.* Boulder: Westview.

Stone, D. 1999–2000. "Beyond Moral Hazard: Insurance as Moral Opportunity." *Connecticut Insurance Law Journal* 6: 12–46.

Talmadge, S. 1986. Talmadge to Patricia McGovern. Women's Bar Association of Massachusetts, Boston. July 28.

Tan, S. L., H. S. Jacobs, & M. M. Seibel. 1995. *Infertility: Your Questions Answered.* New York: Birch Lane.

Thorne, B. 1992. "Feminism and the Family: Two Decades of Thought." In B. Thorne & M. Yalom, eds., *Rethinking the Family: Some Feminist Questions,* 3–30. Rev. ed. Boston: Northeastern University Press.

Time Life Medical. 1996. *Infertility at Time of Diagnosis.* Videocassette. New York: Time Life Medical, Patient Education Media.

Tischler, R. S. 1994. "Infertility: A Forgotten Disability." *Wayne Law Review* 41: 249–271.

U.S. Bureau of the Census. 1998. Current Population Reports. *Health Insurance Coverage: 1997.* P60-202. Washington, D.C.: U.S. Government Printing Office.

U.S. Bureau of Labor. 1996. "Local Area Unemployment Statistics: Massachusetts." *Current Population Survey.* January 26. Available at http://stats.bls.gov:80/top20.html

U.S. Centers for Disease Control, American Society for Reproductive Medicine, & RESOLVE. 1999. *1997 Assisted Reproductive Technology Success Rates: National Summary and Fertility Clinic Reports.* Atlanta: Centers for Disease Control.

U.S. Congress. 1988. Office of Technology Assessment. *Infertility: Medical and Social Choices.* OTA-BA-358. Washington, D.C.: U.S. Government Printing Office.

U.S. Congress. 1989. House of Representatives. *Infertility in America: Why is the Federal Government Ignoring a Major Health Problem?* 101st Cong., 1st sess. Report 101-389. Washington, D.C.: U.S. Government Printing Office.

U.S. Congress. 1999a. House of Representatives. HR 2706. *Family Building Act of 1999.* 106th Cong., 1st sess. Washington, D.C.: U.S. Government Printing Office.

U.S. Congress. 1999b. House of Representatives. HR 2774. *To Amend Chapter 89 of Title 5, United States Code, to Provide That Any Health Benefits Plan Which Provides Obstetrical Benefits Shall Be Required Also to Provide Coverage for the Diagnosis and Treatment of Infertility.* 106th Cong., 1st sess. Washington, D.C.: U.S. Government Printing Office.

U.S. Congress. 2000. Senate. S. 2160. *Fair Access to Infertility Treatment and Hope Act of 2000.* 106th Cong., 2d sess. Washington, D.C.: U.S. Government Printing Office.

Wagner, M. G., & P. Stephenson. 1993. "Infertility and In Vitro Fertilization: Is the Tail Wagging the Dog?" In P. Stephenson & M. G. Wagner, eds. *Tough Choices: In Vitro Fertilization and the Reproductive Technologies,* 1–22. Philadelphia: Temple University Press.

Wandersee, M. S. 1999. "The Far-Reaching Effects of Reproduction as a 'Major

Life Activity' Under the ADA: What Will This Expansion Mean to Employers and Their Insured?" *Journal of Small and Emerging Business Law* 3: 429–449.

Wattenberg, B. J. 1987. *The Birth Dearth*. New York: Pharos.

Whiteford, L. M., & L. Gonzalez. 1995. "Stigma: The Hidden Burden of Infertility." *Social Science and Medicine* 40: 27–36.

Whittemore, A. S., R. Harris, J. Itnyre, & the Collaborative Ovarian Cancer Group. 1992. "Characteristics Relating to Ovarian Cancer Risk: Collaborative Analysis of Twelve U.S. Case Studies: Part II, Invasive Epithelial Ovarian Cancers in White Women." *American Journal of Epidemiology* 136: 1184–203.

Wolfson, L. 1993. "Accepting the Unacceptable: An Outcome of No Children." *RESOLVE of the Bay State Newsletter* (Spring): 3+.

Wong, D. S. 1994. "State, in About-Face, Bars Medicaid From Funding Fertility Treatments." *Boston Globe*, March 5, pp. 1+.

Index

abortion: and insurance coverage for infertility, 61, 64; and middle-class white women, 22, 24; feminist stance on, vs. reproductive technologies, 136

adoption: and race, 180 (n. 1); and RESOLVE, 46; anxieties about, 42–44; as end of the medical journey, 112–16; biases against, 44; in colonial America, 20; in twentieth-century America, 25, 26; international, 42; introduction of laws governing, 21; ranking system, 114–15

advanced reproductive technologies, 181. *See also* medical treatment for infertility

age and infertility, 99–100, 180 (n. 3)

American Medical Association, 28

Americans with Disabilities Act, 52, 56–57

An Act Providing a Medical Definition of Infertility. *See* Massachusetts infertility insurance statute

anovulation, 181

artificial insemination, 23, 26, 181

assisted reproduction, 181. *See also* reproductive technologies

averages, role in normalization, 55

baby boom, 25

Bartholet, Elizabeth, 46, 114–15

Bateson, Gregory, 12, 147

Becker, Gay, 90, 91

bell curve, 9

Bellah, Robert N., 70

biopower, 2, 8, 50–51; and definition, 57–58; and double binds, 7, 147

birth control. *See* contraception

birthrates: government intervention into, 25, 50; in late twentieth century, 27; reports of declining, 49

Bradgon v. Abbott, 57

Brown, Louise, 28

Burke, Edward L., 60, 65

Burke, Kenneth: on irony, 12; on metonymy, 6

cancer, risks linked to fertility drugs, 35

careers: and childbearing, 100–101, 105–6; and endometriosis, 101

Carter, Jean W., 41, 64, 107, 116, 135, 136–37, 143

Carter, Michael, 64, 107, 116, 135, 136–37, 143

categorization, function in normalization, 69

Catholic opposition to insurance coverage for infertility, 61, 65
cesarean section, 35
childfree: as a choice, 135; as an aberration, 116; as end of the medical journey, 112–16; movement, 27; vs. childless, 115–16, 136
childlessness: as selfish, 108; historical meanings of, 19–29
children: perception of only, 45; timing of, 98, 100–101; value of, 20, 21, 25, 27
choice and infertility, 135–38
Cintron, Ralph, 6
class: and access to infertility treatment, 3, 24; and encouragement to reproduce, 50; and interpretations of investment in medical treatment, 86; and motivations to persist in medical treatment, 91
Clinton, William Jefferson, 59
Clomid. *See* clomiphene citrate
clomiphene citrate (Clomid), 26, 34, 181, 182
commonplaces: and double binds, 149; desires as, 6
Condit, Celeste M., 119
contraception: and controlling fertility, 119; and middle-class white women, 22, 24; and treatment for infertility, 24; blamed for infertility, 101–3
control, desire for, 119–41
Crockin, Susan, 60
cultural work: of definitions, 17–19, 57–58; of double binds, 142–50; of mandatory insurance coverage for infertility, 6

Dalkon Shield, 102, 179 (ch. 4, n. 1)
Davis, Lennard J., 8
definition of infertility: as social construction, 18; cultural work of, 17–19, 57–58; importance to law's normative role, 52; ontological implications, 17; role in biopower, 57–58; role in normalization, 18; stabilization of, 60; stasis of, 57
diethylstilbestrol (DES), 28, 32, 182
disability, infertility as, 52, 56–57
disease: as an explanatory model, 5; infertility as, 52–56
domesticity, ideology of, 21
donor: egg, 182; sperm, 182. *See also* artificial insemination
double binds, 11–14: and commonplaces, 149; and irony, 12, 14; and schizophrenia, 12; as ironic imperatives, 12; as unstable, 149; cultural work of, 142–50; disrupting, 147; role in normalization, 2, 7, 145–50
Dukakis, Michael, 63

Egert v. Connecticut General Life Insurance Company, 52–53
Emerson, Robert M., 164
endometrial biopsy, 33, 182
endometriosis, 101, 182
estrogen, discovery of, 23
ethnography, 159
eugenics, 24
experimental medical treatment, insurance coverage for, 52

failure: infertility as, 75; metaphors of, in medical treatment for infertility,

72; to become normal, 94; of medical treatment for infertility, 90
fallopian tubes, treating blocked, 23
Faludi, Susan, 49, 101
family: definitions of, 66; ideology of, 19
fecundity vs. infertility, 99
female infertility. *See* infertility, female
feminism blamed for infertility, 101
feminist criticism: of blaming mothers, 178 (n. 7); of ideology of the family, 19; of public/private dichotomy, 120; of reproductive technologies, 5, 136
fertility: as a cultural category, 3; as a natural right, 68; assumption of, 123; government intervention into, 1, 25, 50–52; normal, 10; vs. fecundity, 99
fibroid tumors, 182
follicle, 182
Fortun, Kim, 13
Fortun, Michael, 13
Foucault, Michel: on biopower, 2, 50–51; on observation, 129; on order, 96; on power, 121, 146; on rehabilitation in normalization, 10
Frazer, Elizabeth, 120
Fretz, Rachel I., 164
Friedan, Betty, 25
Friedman, Lawrence M., 76, 80, 92, 121

gamete intrafallopian transfer (GIFT), 34, 182
Ginsburg, Faye, 3
Goffman, Erving, 46
gonadotropins, 34, 182

gonorrhea and infertility, 22
Good, Byron, 5
government intervention into fertility, 1, 25, 50–52
grandchildren, duty to provide, 108
Greil, Arthur, 64
Griffin, Martha, 47, 60, 62, 67, 107
Guernsey, Sherwood, 65, 67, 179 (ch. 2, n. 3)

Haraway, Donna J.: on irony, 14; on statistics, 29; on technology, 2
health care debates, 59
Health Security Act, 59
Heitman, Elizabeth, 140
HIV status and reproduction, 57
hormones, 23, 26, 85, 132
hyperstimulation, 183
hysteria, 22
hysterosalpingogram, 23, 34, 183

identity and infertility, 42
in vitro fertilization (IVF): defined, 283; diagnostic uses of, 34; first successful, 27, 28
inadequate luteal phase, 183
incompetent cervix, 183
individualism: and order, 96; and success, 70
industrialization: and normalization, 8; role of language in, 11
infertility: and age, 99–100; and birth control, 101–3; as a couple's condition, 23, 58; as a cultural category, 3, 143–44; as a disease of choice, 139; as disability, 56–57; as disease, 52–56; as disruption, 104–10; as failure, 75; as injustice, 75–76, 92;

as loss of control, 122–25; as socially constructed, 5, 64; as spoiled identity, 42; causes, male vs. female, 5, 29; definitions of, 10; 17–19, 30, 63; female, 22–23, 26–27, 32–33, 138; history of, in America 19–29; government intervention, 1, 25, 50–52; implications for social collectives, 3, 7, 144; male, 22, 26, 31; medical vs. social, 4, 66; medicalization of, 2, 142; rates, 55, 178 (n. 3); research methods, 159–68; social, 4, 30, 66, 84, 127, 131; stigma of, 40–45; unexplained, 34, 37, 185; vs. involuntary childlessness, 6; vs. reproductive impairment, 64; vs. sterility, 24. *See also* childlessness; medical treatment for infertility

injustice, infertility viewed as, 75–76, 92

insurance: and class, 3; and race, 3, 178 (n. 5); as justice, 68–69. *See also* insurance coverage for infertility

insurance coverage for infertility: and marital status, 3, 59; and number of embryos transferred, 34, 36; and RESOLVE, 47–48, 59–69; as a technology of normalization, 2, 7, 67–69, 143–44; Catholic opposition to, 61, 65; case law, 52–57; mandates to offer and cover, 58, 153–57; state laws, 58–59, 153–57. *See also* Massachusetts infertility insurance statute

interview participants: biographies, 169–75; locating, 161

intracytoplasmic sperm injection (ICSI), 35, 183

intrauterine device (IUD), 102, 183

intrauterine insemination (IUI), 34, 183

investment in medical treatment for infertility, 81–87

involuntary childlessness: medicalization of, 2; vs. infertility, 6

irony, 12, 14

Jamieson, Kathleen Hall, 145, 147

justice, insurance as, 68–69

Kennedy, Edward M., 178 (n. 2)

King, Leslie, 3

Kinzie v. Physician's Liability Insurance Co., 53–54

knowledge: as key to success, 78; role in control, 128

Kornhauser, Lewis A., 70

Krauel v. Iowa Methodist Medical Center, 57

Lacey, Nicola, 120

laparoscopy, 34, 183

laparotomy, 26, 184

law: and equity, 68; and technology, 140; as a resource for changing cultural attitudes, 60; as a resource for enforcing individual rights, 60; as a resource for removing barriers, 2; as a resource for restoring order, 117; cases considering infertility, 52–57; locations of power, 51; role as appraiser of difference, 69; role as normative, 52; statutes affecting infertility, 58–59

Law, Cardinal Bernard, 65

lesbian parenthood, 28, 108. *See also* infertility, social

Lyotard, Jean-François, 96

male infertility. *See* infertility, male
Malinowski, Bronislaw, 19
mandates: to cover infertility treatment, 58; to offer insurance coverage for infertility, 58
marital status and insurance coverage for infertility, 3, 59
Marsh, Margaret, 19–29
Marsh v. Reserve Life Ins. Co., 55
Massachusetts infertility insurance statute: as a technology of normalization, 2, 7, 67–69, 143–44; as authorization of a preferred path, 116–18; cultural work of, 6, 142–50; definition of infertility in, 17; economic costs of, 177 (n. 1); exemptions, 177 (n. 2); policy positions on, 177 (n. 1); role in encouraging persistence, 90–92; scope, 1, 3; text of, 151–52. *See also* insurance coverage for infertility
May, Elaine Tyler, 19–29, 140
media: reports on infertility, 25, 27, 49, 101; role in advocating for insurance coverage for infertility, 60
medical experimentation within poor and minority communities, 4
medical necessity and insurance coverage, 53, 63
medical treatment for infertility: and age, 180 (n. 3); as a process of continual improvement, 110–12; as a right, 1, 70; as an obligation, 71; as constraining, 129–34; as investment, 81–87; as mandatory, 139–40; compelling nature of, 40, 73–74, 111–12; contemporary approaches, 29–36; definitions of success in, 74–75; history of, in America, 19–29; risks, 35–36, 82; stopping, 87–90, 112–16; vs. correction, 31, 38, 53, 57; vs. prevention, 4; women's bodies as sites for, 4, 31; work ethic in, 76–81; uncertainty of, 126–29. *See also* reproductive technologies
Menning, Barbara Eck, 45
menopause, early, 35
menstrual cycle: charting, as a technology of normalization, 32; regulating, 34
methods, research, 159–68
Meyer, Madonna Harrington, 3
middle class: as audience for insurance coverage for infertility, 3; desire for success, 71; expectations of control, 119–20, 140; fear of regret as motivating factor in medical treatment for infertility, 91; work ethic, 76
motherhood, portrayals of, 23, 25
multiple births, 35
Murphy v. United Parcel Service, Inc., 57

Nachtigall, Robert, 90, 91
National Infertility Awareness Week, 1, 59
New England Journal of Medicine, 99, 101
normal distribution, 9
normalization, 7–11; and discipline, 9; and industrialization, 8; and irony, 14; and rhetoric, 11; and statistics, 8; and writing, 33; failure as necessary, 10; insurance coverage for infertility as a technology of, 2, 7, 67–69, 143–44; of fertility, 7; of infertility, 7; rehabilitation, 10; role of averages, 55; role of categoriza-

tion, 69; role of definition, 18; role of double binds, 2, 145–50; role of law as appraiser of difference, 69; role of models, 144; tension necessary to sustain, 2, 7, 144
normative orders, 70
norms: emergence of, 8; vs. ideals, 8
nymphomania, 22

obligations vs. rights, 70–71
only children, 45
Open Door Society of Massachusetts, 45, 114
order: as metaphorical, 95; desire for, 95–118
ovariotomy, 22
ovulation, charting, 23

Pacourek v. Inland Steel Co., 56
pelvic adhesions, 184
pelvic inflammatory disease (PID), 32, 184
Perganol, 26, 184
polycystic ovarian disease, 184
populations: and biopower, 8, 50, 146; infertility in, 10; growth of, 49–50
postcoital test, 33, 184
power, 121, 146
pregnancy complications, as a result of medical treatment for infertility, 35
premature births, as a result of medical treatment for infertility, 35
premature ovarian failure, 35, 184
private sphere, 120–22
procedure, stasis of, 58
progress, principle of, 96
public sphere, 120–22

race: and adoption, 180 (n. 1); and insurance, 178 (n. 5); and rates of childlessness or infertility, 24, 178 (n. 3); and sperm donation, 180 (n. 1); white interest in black fertility during slavery, 4
Rapp, Rayna, 3
rates of infertility, 55, 178 (n. 3)
Regnier v. Industrial Commission of Arizona, 55
religion: exemptions from insurance coverage for infertility, 59; explanations for infertility, 20
reproduction: as a major life activity under the ADA, 56; stratified by race, class, and sexual orientation, 3
reproductive endocrinology, beginnings of, 23
reproductive technologies: feminist criticism of, 5, 136; success rates, 23, 26, 93. *See also* medical treatment for infertility
research methods, 159–68
RESOLVE: and adoption, 46; formation of, 45–47; role in mandatory insurance coverage for infertility, 1, 47–48, 59–69
Reuss v. Time Ins. Co., 56
rhetoric: commonplaces and double binds, 149; cultural work of double binds, 142–50; desires as commonplaces, 6; double binds as ironic imperatives, 12; double binds as rhetorical mechanisms of normalization, 2, 145, 147; normalization as a rhetorical process, 11; rhetorical strategies of RESOLVE, 59–67; stases of definition and procedure, 57–58;